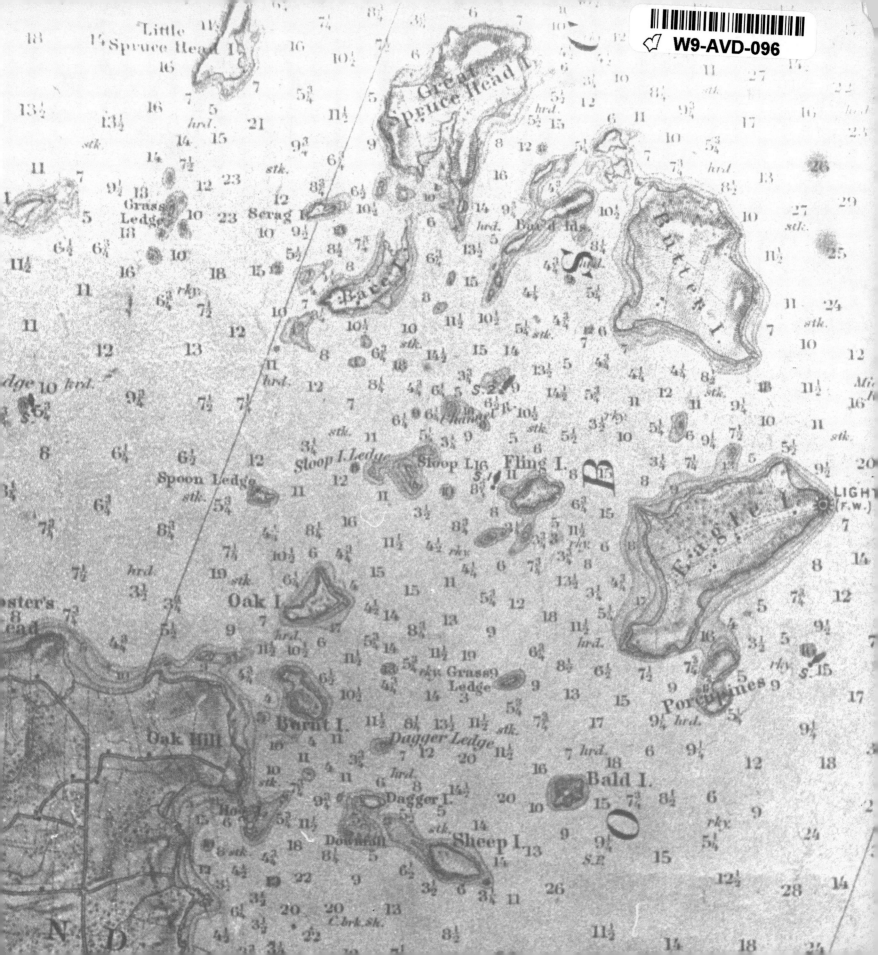

❖ ❖ ❖

PENOBSCOT

THE
FOREST,
RIVER
AND BAY

❖ ❖ ❖

David D. Platt, Editor

ISLAND INSTITUTE, 1996

©1996 by the Island Institute, 410 Main Street, Rockland, Maine 04841

This book was set in Adobe Garamond by the Island Institute and was printed and bound by the J. S. McCarthy Company, Augusta, Maine, U. S. A.

Library of Congress Cataloging-in-Publication Data

Penobscot: the forest, river and bay/edited by David D. Platt

204 pages

ISBN 0-942719-16-6 (paper)

The Island Institute is a non-profit, membership-based organization founded in 1983 to serve the islands of Maine.

The Island Institute serves as a voice for the balanced future of Maine islands. We are guided by an island ethic which recognizes that the resources of the Maine islands and the waters of the Gulf of Maine are fragile and finite.

Along the Maine coast, the Island Institute plays a pivotal role in the dialogue about wise use of resources by positioning itself at the boundaries between competing interests; by developing solutions that balance the needs of the coast's cultural and natural communities; by supporting the islands' year-round communities; by conserving Maine's undeveloped islands in their natural state, and by monitoring and helping to protect the Gulf of Maine's natural systems, on which we all depend.

We carry out this mission through publications, education, community services, marine resources, and science and stewardship programs.

Front cover: The data in this Landsat TM satellite image was collected in the summer of 1995. The water area is depicted using Band 6, which records the thermal infrared energy emitted by the surface layer of the ocean. The water temperature is colder in the darker blue areas, which outline the nutrient-rich waters that flow along the eastern coast of Maine and circulate into the Gulf of Maine outside of Penobscot Bay. The land area is depicted using the natural color bands—red, green, and blue. The full image is 115 miles by 115 miles, centered on the Penobscot Bay region. Image processing by the Island Institute.

Back cover: This aerial photograph, taken at low tide in October of 1992, shows the rich zonation of intertidal and subtidal vegetation in Gilkeys Harbor, Islesboro. The darkest bands at the mouths of the coves are eelgrass beds, which remain submerged even at low tide. The rocky peninsula heads are covered with rockweed species, showing as yellow-brown. The gray-brown areas above the low-tide line are intertidal mudflats. Aerial photography by James W. Sewall Company, courtesy of Maine Department of Transportation.

Endpapers: Various detail sections are shown of U.S. Coast & Geodetic Survey chart No. 104, 1880.

Table of Contents

Part Three: ***What Does the Future Hold?***

Appendix: ***Bibliography of Penobscot Bay Scientific Research***

Preface

This book is offered as a report on the vital signs of the Penobscot region. It was developed with the knowledge that this vast area looks very different today than it did a century ago and that the condition of the Penobscot watershed 100 years from now will depend, to some extent, on decisions we make today. The historical frame of reference for viewing our present situation, however, is an essential part of this work, for without understanding where we have been, it is impossible to say where we ought to be going.

We have therefore made use of statistics, historical data, scientific research and the observations of people who live and work here, organized by themes which run through the fabric of our economic history. We consider the prospects for the region's transportation and energy systems, and we examine how the people in the region live and earn their livelihoods. We explore the often poorly understood connections between natural systems and the people who depend on them. We consider the region's long relationship with seasonal visitors in order to address what it means to become one of the country's major tourist destinations. We catalogue evidence of a growing interest in stewardship in efforts to clean up and monitor bodies of water, to conserve land, and to ensure that important regional resources of fish and shellfish are available for use.

This book catalogues the risks this region faces. We bring scientific focus to pollution from industrial, municipal, domestic and "non-point" sources. For although the Penobscot River and Penobscot Bay are cleaner today than they were a generation ago, persistent pollutants and toxins remain in the environment, posing real problems that will continue to haunt us until they are dealt with — particularly those that pose a risk to the region's rich marine resources. In addition to these environmental threats, there are risks associated with the economy as "downsizing" and other shifts in employment patterns make it harder for the youngest and oldest members of the workforce to find jobs. The region's growing "mailbox economy," based on retirees living here who receive pensions or government transfer payments, must face the risk that these payments might dwindle or prove inadequate in the future.

Information enables citizens to make better decisions. *Penobscot* was designed to provide information about a region whose unique qualities have endowed it with national and even global significance for three centuries, in hopes that the choices its people make will be made on the best available information. If this book imparts new knowledge or deepens our existing understanding of the factors that have made the Penobscot region what it is today, as well as the trends that are likely to shape it in the years to come, it will have achieved its purpose.

Introduction

On a satellite image or a nautical chart, Penobscot Bay is a huge wedge of water that splits the coast of Maine in half. It extends nearly 60 miles north from the edge of the Gulf of Maine to the mouth of the Penobscot River, and its upland drainage runs inland for another 200 miles, taking in more than a quarter of the state of Maine. Twenty percent of the river water entering the Gulf of Maine passes through the Penobscot watershed, which is the state's largest; the bay is the largest in Maine and the second largest embayment on the Atlantic Coast of the United States.

For centuries, the area's physical beauty and generous natural resources made it a candidate for permanent settlement and development. The 16th-century Florentine navigator Giovanni da Verrazano, the first visitor to leave a record, was captivated by the sight of channels and islands which he described as, "all near the continent; small and pleasant in appearance, but high, following the curve of the land; some beautiful ports and channels are formed between them, such as those in the Adriatic Gulf in Illyria and Dalmatia ...." These sheltered waters led all the way upriver to the site of modern Bangor, extending the reach of ocean-going vessels far inland and creating a natural transportation system. Ample rainfall, elevation and good dam sites made the upper Penobscot River ideal for hydropower development as well, and today its West Branch is home to the largest privately owned hydroelectric system in the world.

Together the river, the bay, the coastline and the islands form a distinct region of Maine. It is a region populated today by a quarter of a million people scattered over a landscape that was first settled by Europeans more than two centuries ago, and that was inhabited by Native Americans for more than ten thousand years before that. It is a vast rural area with scattered seaports, manufacturing centers, farms and rocky headlands, all bound together by geography, history, transportation, demographic patterns, shared values and problems.

Fisheries — their discovery, exploitation and, in some cases, their virtual destruction — form a large portion of our story, because they loom so large in this region's history. In a sense the fisheries speak for the Penobscot region's entire heritage of natural resources. Fisheries brought people here in the first place; they sustained them over the generations and the centuries. The success or failure of a fishery can affect the economic health of the entire region, changing even the lives of people who live far from salt water and don't think of themselves as "coastal" residents.

We really don't know when the first fishermen arrived in Penobscot Bay, but it was almost certainly before the explorers of the early 17th century such as Champlain, Waymouth and Pring, who left early accounts and maps of the coast, including interesting and readable descriptions of the islands and waters of Penobscot Bay. Fishermen from France and Britain had been making successful annual voyages to the fishing grounds on Newfoundland's Grand Banks since the 1450s, and it is highly likely that some of them, by storm, chance or design, found their way into the Gulf of Maine. There is evidence of a primitive fishing station on Matinicus at the outer edge of Penobscot Bay, where a snug harbor would have made an ideal spring and summer berth.

During the first hundred years of settlement of Penobscot Bay towns, from about 1760 to

1860, a fisherman in a small vessel could row to certain fishing "grounds" and make a day's catch of several hundred pounds of cod.

By the latter part of the 19th century, however, things had begun to change. The first comprehensive study of American fisheries published by the U.S. Fisheries Commission in 1888 contains the following reference to the decline of codfish: "Formerly the waters abounded in this fish to such an extent that a large supply could be taken throughout almost the entire year, especially in the vicinity of the mouths of the larger rivers. It is well known to the old residents of Eastport that from thirty to fifty years ago cod could be taken in abundance in Passamaquoddy Bay, where only stragglers are now to be caught. The same is the case at the mouth of the Penobscot River and at other points along the coast, where fish once came close in to the shore, and were readily captured with the hook throughout the greater part of the year."

Today Penobscot Bay is the economic domain of a thousand or more working boats of every size and description, built to harvest everything from the delicate northern shrimp to scallops, lobsters, green urchins, red rock crabs, periwinkles, dulse, cod, haddock, hake, flounder, smelt, herring, alewives, mackerel, pollock, pogies, skates, dogfish, salmon, tuna, eelpout and wolf fish, to mention only some of the species that end up in fish markets throughout New England and, increasingly, the rest of the world. Penobscot Bay is the center of Maine's lobster industry, as measured by the volume and value of lobster landings, and is believed to be the most productive piece of lobster habitat in the world.

The timber that has flowed out of the forests of the Penobscot watershed is as vital to the towns of the region as the marine resources that drive the economy of the coast. Satellite images show some of the deeply integrated connections between the aquatic system of the Penobscot River watershed and the rich, island-studded marine system at the mouth and edge of Penobscot Bay. Scientists can't say with certainty where one part of the system ends and the other begins. Ecologically speaking, there are no separate entities here, but pieces of ecological and economic systems that merge into each other through both space and time. Bangor couldn't have developed into the lumber capital of the world 130 years ago without its deep-water connection to the sea; Penobscot Bay's lobster resource today couldn't have become a valuable regional export without the proximity of the Bangor International Airport.

Ecological interconnectedness is easier to understand when viewed from space. During the spring freshet, satellite images show the Penobscot River as a huge outfall, emptying into the most productive part of the marine ecosystem. It becomes obvious that the people who control the discharge of sewage and paper mill effluent into the Penobscot River affect the livelihoods of fishermen hundreds of miles downstream — out of sight, perhaps, but we hope not out of mind.

By linking scales of time with views from space, we hope this book will deepen our understanding of the way a major region of Maine "works." It is our intention to celebrate the flowering of an ecologically based stewardship ethic; to identify important trends affecting the whole region; and, finally, to establish some measurable criteria by which to evaluate our progress toward restoring and enhancing the natural resource treasures with which we have been endowed.

David D. Platt, Philip W. Conkling, Annette Naegel, Scott Dickerson, Ted Ames, Charles Oldham

Island Institute
Rockland, Maine
June, 1996

Acknowledgments

Penobscot is an outgrowth of the Penobscot Bay Conferences held in Searsport in 1992 and 1993, which led to the formation of the Penobscot Bay Network. Members of the Network include the Hancock County and Knox-Lincoln Cooperative Extension offices, the Maine Coastal Program of the State Planning Office, the Maine Department of Marine Resources, the Eastern Maine Development Corporation, the Maine Aquaculture Innovation Center, Maine/New Hampshire Sea Grant, the Penobscot Land Trust Alliance, the Penobscot Marine Museum, Penobscot Riverkeepers and the Island Institute. The Alliance and its member groups have encouraged this project from the start and lent their expertise where appropriate.

The Penobscot Bay Council, a group of business, industry and community leaders, was convened to advise the Island Institute on this project. Representing business and industry were Jim Chandler of the Maine Marine Trades Association; David Cousens of the Maine Lobstermen's Association; Chip Davisson of the Maine Aquaculture Association; John Foss of the North End Schooner Association; David Gelinas of the Penobscot Bay pilots; Austin Goodyear, president of EBS; Mike Hastings of the Maine Aquaculture Innovation Center; Polly Saltonstall of Courier Publications; Jim Thompson of the Maine Publicity Bureau; and Bob Turner of Champion International. Representing community interests were Franklin Eggert, Pat Jennings, Nigel MacEwan, Cheri Mason, Roger Moody, Chellie Pingree, Ken Rich and Esperanza Stancioff.

The book is a group effort. Major credit is due to Bob Moore of Freeport, an environmental consultant and freelance writer who produced the four sets of town profiles, plus all or part of the chapters on the region's economy and demographics, the river and watershed, risk factors and stewardship. After presenting a draft of his work to the Penobscot Bay Network steering committee last year, he incorporated many recommendations into the text. His contribution to this project was immense and is greatly appreciated.

Others who made major contributions are Lloyd Irland, who wrote the chapter on transportation and energy, and Michael Herz, who co-authored the chapter on environmental risks. Steve Miller collected the material for the scientific bibliography, which was also published separately earlier this year.

Renny Stackpole of the Penobscot Marine Museum and John F. Battick of the Department of History at the University Maine graciously permitted the use of their previously published material in Chapter 1. Charles McLane's assistance with Chapter 1 is acknowledged and appreciated as well.

Several staff members at the Island Institute made important contributions. Leslie Fuller of the Institute's Science and Stewardship Department compiled the list of non-government organizations and other information for the Appendix. Wendy Norden, an intern in the Science and Stewardship Department for a four-month period, conducted a search of the fisheries data that exists for the region and assembled it for analysis. Scott Dickerson produced all of the satellite images that appear in the book. Sandra Smith kept the Publications Department functioning smoothly during the editing process.

Most of the contemporary pictures in the book are from the files of Christopher Ayres, a photographer with 25 years' experience on the Maine coast, particularly in Penobscot Bay, while the historic images are from the collection of Frank E. Claes of Bucksport. The color aerial photograph of Gilkey Harbor, Islesboro, was taken by the James W. Sewall Company and is reproduced courtesy of the Maine Department of Transportation.

Copy editor for the project was Anne Leslie, whose sharp eye spotted many errors, small and large, which might otherwise have gone unnoticed.

Graphically, **Penobscot** is the work of Charles G. Oldham of the Publications Department at the Island Institute, whose hard work and many suggestions are greatly appreciated.

Funding for this project is gratefully acknowledged from the following sources: the Dillon Dunwalke Trust, Chichester duPont Foundation and Branta Foundation. Funding to edit and design the book was received from the Association of U. S. Delegates to the Gulf of Maine Council on the Marine Environment.

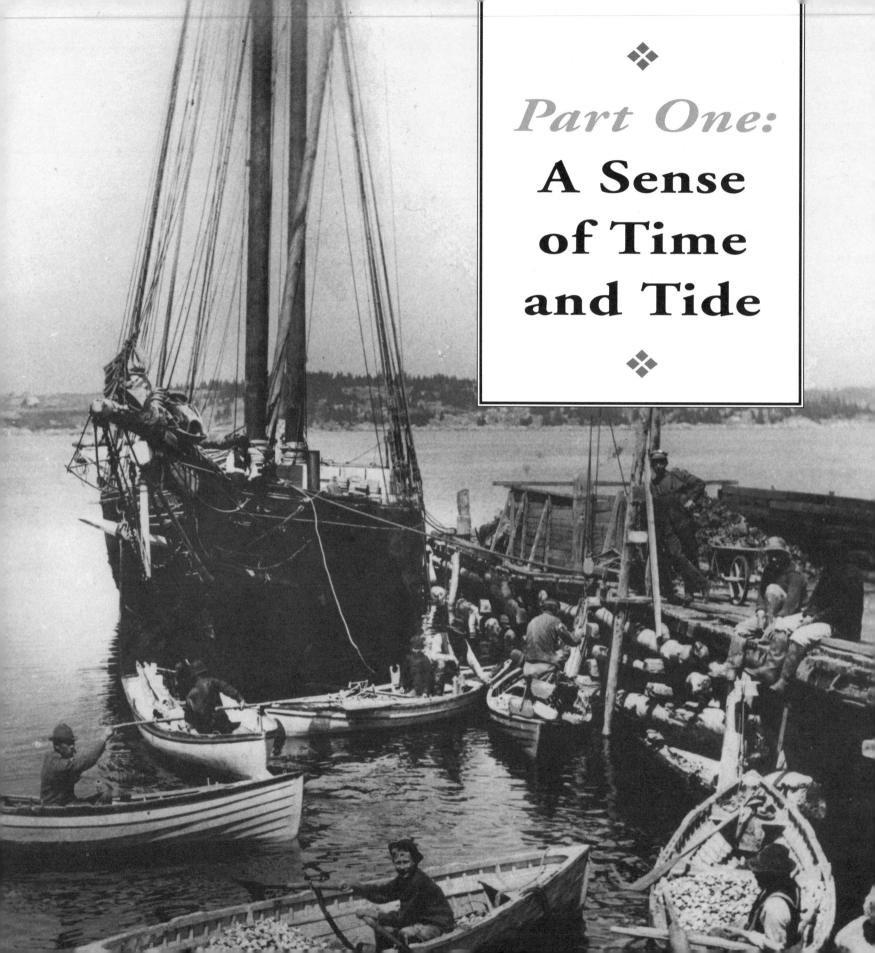

Chapter 1: The Penobscot Region, 1880 – 1996

By David D. Platt, Renny Stackpole and John F. Battick

"Looking down Penobscot Bay on a fine summer day," wrote historian George S. Wasson in 1931, "there was often to be seen a marine picture which, taken as a whole, was not to be equaled on the entire coast." The scene Wasson then described was what one might have encountered on Penobscot Bay in the 1880s: sailing vessels in two lines, one proceeding up the bay toward the Penobscot River and its major port, Bangor; the other moving south, loaded with cargoes for Boston, New York and Philadelphia. "Up the Bay they sped in almost endless procession," Wasson wrote, referring to the northbound fleet, "the last barely to be distinguished in the distance."

Penobscot Bay in 1880 was indeed a busy place. Bangor's lumber trade, which boomed with the Civil War, had slackened somewhat as white pine was depleted, but the shipborne trade in spruce lumber, brick, granite, firewood, lime, salted and canned seafood and other products destined for manufacturers and consumers in the growing cities of the eastern seaboard was still brisk. Wooden shipbuilding had begun to feel the competition of iron and steam, but it would persist for another 35 years. Railroads had spanned the continent and reached into Maine, but moving goods by water was still competitive.

In 1880, the Penobscot region — the Penobscot River, Penobscot Bay and the communities that touched them — was a center of commerce and manufacturing, a place on the main highway to other thriving places in the United States and around the world.

"The westering sun lighted up with warm glow each swelling sail," Wasson wrote. "The flashing wings of gulls added touches to a vision of marine activity never to be forgotten and of which the present generation can have but the slightest conception."

Wasson's nostalgic view may obscure much of the economic activity that continued in the Penobscot region after shipping by sail had declined. Midcoast Maine by Wasson's day (1931) no longer sent much granite to Boston, New York or anywhere, but it had begun sending out considerable amounts of paper from mills on the Penobscot River. Banks, newspaper publishers, small manufacturers, boat builders, fishermen, department stores, dairy farmers, canneries and hotels were very much in business; railroads provided Bangor and Rockland with freight and passenger service to the rest of the nation; the region's roads and bridges weren't much worse than those in other rural regions of the United States. Even the building of wooden ships had been briefly revived by World War I.

By 1931, the Great Depression was settling over Maine as elsewhere; the pain and subsequent prosperity associated with World War II were still a decade away. The Penobscot region could indeed look back, as Wasson did, to more prosperous times, but its people also knew that their fortunes would rise and fall, as they always had, with those of the rest of the country.

Opposite: Clam diggers and schooner E.A. WHITMORE at the Oceanville, Maine, clam factory dock (Frank Claes collection)

Early history

Penobscot Bay did not develop significantly until the end of the American Revolution, as the British and French imperial designs placed this strategic area in the center of conflict from the late 17th to the late 18th century. Of signal importance to the commercial and maritime development of Penobscot Bay was the arrival of Major General Henry Knox in Thomaston in July, 1785. The recently retired Secretary of War under President George Washington, Knox had inherited through his marriage to General Samuel Waldo's granddaughter, Lucy Fluker Knox, a huge piece of real estate: the Waldo Patent, which extended from the Medomak River across midcoast Maine up the west shores of the Penobscot Bay out to Islesboro.

General Knox and his agents granted quit rents to settlers, dug canals, established lime quarries, cleared timberland for ship building and invited trained artisans to migrate from Cape Ann, southern New Hampshire and the southern Maine coast to join the effort of developing new enterprise and industry. During this Federalist period, in fact, eastern Maine was the new nation's most important frontier.

The death of General Knox in 1808 was a setback for his adopted town of Thomaston, but it provided opportunities for investors to buy out shares of interest in the Waldo Patent from the destitute Knox family. Montpelier, Knox's large, Federal-style mansion and the most elegant home of its kind in midcoast Maine, remained for 75 years a symbol of the general and his efforts to develop the area of the state that now bears his name.

By the end of the hated Embargo (1807-09) and the War of 1812, Mainers in the region, bereft from hard times and war, turned to the sea with a will, as whole villages awoke to the rhythm of the broad ax and adze, the song of the caulker's maul and the sight of vessels being launched into rivers and harbors, from South Thomaston and Owls Head in the southwest to Belfast and Frankfort (Searsport) in the north and Castine and Deer Isle in the east bay.

The period 1809-1861 was one of vigorous growth and enterprise, amid the hardscrabble existence of local townsfolk and farmers, who in many ways "followed" the sea for their livelihood. Between 1783 and 1820, Maine's population grew by 450 percent. The founding of the region's towns, including many on islands, reflected this rapid expansion.

Bangor, the Penobscot region's principal city, developed from a settlement called "Kenduskeag" by the Indians and was given its present name by the Reverend Seth Noble. Incorporated in 1791, Bangor was chartered as a city in 1834. Situated at the head of navigation on the Penobscot River, 60 miles from the open sea, it grew steadily as a shipbuilding and lumber center, until it became the lumber capital of the world immediately after the Civil War. Bangor owed its success to the engineering feats that dammed, sluiced and altered the hydrology of much of the North Maine Woods to bring timber to her riverside mills. The development of steam tugs and passenger ferry service on the river enabled a town far inland to be easily connected to the maritime trade routes of the Atlantic Rim.

Rockland, at Penobscot Bay's southwestern entrance, developed at a spot the Indians called "Catawamteak," which translates as "great landing place." Eight families located in the area in 1769 under Dodge Mountain near the "meadows." Shipbuilding began here in earnest in 1795 in connection with the lime trade, which linked the Shore Village (later Rockland) with cities along the east coast of the United States. By 1854, the numbers had become impressive: in that year alone, builders produced 11 ships, three barks, six brigs and four schooners: a total of 17,365 tons.

Belfast launched its first schooner in 1795, its first full-rigged ship in 1805. In 1818, Belfast was named a Customs Port of Entry, along with Bath, Portland and Eastport, suggesting the region's pre-dominance in international trade.

Similarly, Searsport, initially settled in the 1760s, evolved from a small farming community into one of the most prominent shipbuilding centers on the Maine coast. Incorporated in 1845, Searsport supported eight shipyards by the 1870s. Between 1792 and 1891, 244 vessels ranging from sloops to steamers were fashioned from native woods in Searsport

Logging booms, Bangor, 1880 (Bangor Historical Society)

yards and launched into Penobscot Bay. By the 1870s, approximately one-tenth of all deep water shipmasters in the American merchant marine hailed from Searsport.

Castine, known initially as "Pentagoet," was settled as early as 1630 by the traders from the Plymouth Colony. Recognized by the French and Dutch as a vital key to the rich Penobscot hinterland, Castine boasted a deep, spacious and securely protected harbor for whole fleets of ships; it became a mercantile settlement of international significance to the fishing and coastal trading industries along much of the Maine coast, and held that position for half a century.

The Penobscot River

The singular natural feature defining this region is the Penobscot River. Dams on this river were first built for log driving and hydropower in the early 19th century, and they altered the course and the manner in which the river flows through its watershed. The energy created by harnessing its water have spawned industries and communities along the river, from Chesuncook's sparsely settled shores to the intensely developed waterfronts of Bangor, Brewer and Bucksport. This development, not surprisingly, has affected water quality in the river, its estuary and Penobscot Bay.

The Penobscot River begins far above Bangor at the headwaters of its East and West branches. The West Branch starts near the Quebec border, 1,350 feet above the point where the Penobscot River's two branches join to form its main stem in a broad delta and wetlands area at Medway.

Even if it is no longer "wilderness" in any accepted sense, the river supports impressive populations of wildlife, including both landlocked and migratory salmon, otter, mink and moose to mention but a few high profile species. The river's entire length is bald eagle territory, and golden eagles are known to nest in the vicinity of Chesuncook Lake. Harbor seals frequent the lower river. Pilot whales have appeared in Bangor. By tradition, the first sea-run salmon caught at the Bangor Salmon Pool each spring goes to the White House. Rich cod and haddock spawning grounds once existed at the river's mouth.

The bay

Penobscot Bay, with its vast treasuries of fish, timber and wildlife, has spawned dreams of empire ever since the first European sail whitened the horizon. Islands were among the earliest places settled by Europeans in the Penobscot region, writes historian Charles McLane, noting that the bay's islands were accessible to shipping, better located for offshore fishing, and frequently more secure from Indian attack than most mainland locations. Islesboro, Deer Isle and North Haven possessed considerable amounts of prime farmland, according to McLane, while others had good timber for shipbuilding or convenient access to mainland supplies. With the opening of granite quarries in the mid 19th century, several islands (most notably Vinalhaven, Hurricane and Dix Islands) enjoyed a period of intense growth and prosperity fueled by growing cities' demand for this prized construction material.

"Island prosperity proved to be vulnerable," McLane writes in the revised Volume 1 of his *Islands of the Mid-Maine Coast*. "Construction methods changed, ending the demand for island granite. Transportation routes shifted to railroads and mainland highways, lessening the transportation advantage islands once enjoyed. The marine engine meant that fishermen no longer needed to live offshore to reach the fishing grounds. Refrigeration brought Midwestern and Western produce to markets in the East early in the 20th century, leaving island farms with a shrinking share of the market."

Schooners at anchor, late 1800s (Frank Claes collection)

Vinalhaven and North Haven

The two Fox Islands developed differently in the 19th century, as divergent occupations increasingly drove their communities apart. Throughout the first half of the century, McLane reports, Vinalhaven grew rapidly as a fishing port so that by mid century, a hundred vessels were owned by Vinalhaven fishermen, more than three times as many as were owned on North Haven. Meanwhile, farming on North Haven, which was made possible by its comparatively richer soils, attracted other settlers with a different outlook. (During a brief, 20-year period, North Haven fishermen who specialized in fishing under sail became the highliners of the region, surpassing even Vinalhaven in the tonnage and value of their fishing fleet.)

"Quarrying began on Vinalhaven as early as the 1820s, but erratically," McLane writes. "It was not until after mid century that the large granite companies were organized. Moses Webster came to Vinalhaven from New Hampshire in 1851 and soon joined Joseph R. Bodwell (a future Maine governor) in a firm named Bodwell and Webster.

"The Bodwell Granite Company was organized in 1871 and for more than forty years played the dominant role in Vinalhaven quarries. It absorbed most of the quarries of the earlier firms. At times the company employed more than 1,500 quarrymen, inevitably taking many from the fisheries. For many years Bodwell Granite handled lucrative government and private contracts across the nation."

"Rusticators" arrived on North Haven within two decades of the Civil War. Some of them might have seen the Fox Islands as they passed through the Thorofare on their way from Rockland to Bar Harbor on the early steam ferry MOUNT DESERT. By the 1880s, Bostonians such as William and Charles Weld and J. Murray Howe had begun building cottages on the shore of the island.

McLane uses North Haven's tax records to show how much of the "North Island" was taken over by the summer vacationers: in 1890, the ratio of non-resident real estate valuations to resident was about 1 to 4; in 1900, it was 1 to 2; and in 1916, it was 1.5 to 1. The land, in short, was being gradually taken over by outsiders and this process continued as the great estates of Cabots, Lamonts and Gastons were shaped.

"Inevitably the influx affected the lives of indigenous residents," he reports. "North Islanders became boatmen, builders, groundsmen and caretakers. The number of farms declined; fishermen became an endangered species. Meanwhile, the differences between "north" and "south" islanders, already more defined because of quarrying on Vinalhaven, became even more so because of gentrification on North Haven. It was a difference based on changing values and occupations — a difference discernible in many neighboring island communities that waxes and wanes over time."

Islesboro

The residents of Islesboro were predominantly farmers and fishermen in the early days, although the island's population of sea captains rivalled that of Searsport across the bay. The elongated shape of the island encouraged settlers to be both, McLane writes: "All lots in the original town plan in the 1790s included both shore front and interior land. A historian writing in the 1820s reported a saying that 'Islesborough has neither a rich man nor a poor man in it.'"

McLane makes use of the mail-delivery pattern on Islesboro over the years to profile the island's growth and relationship to neighboring mainland communities. The earliest regular mail route was via Lincolnville once a week by packet, evidently straight across the western bay to Grindle Point — the route of the modern ferry. "Some years later the mainland terminal shifted to Northport and mail delivery, said to have been by rowboat, was apparently to one of the coves on the northwest shore."

The North Islesborough Post Office was formally opened in 1880 at Ryders Cove, McLane notes, suggesting that the heaviest concentration of population had by mid century shifted to the north end of the island. "The first post office for Islesborough proper, located in the Guinea sector, was opened in 1889; the next year the spelling of the township was changed to Islesboro." Finally, the decision in 1933 to allow motor vehicles on the island changed many patterns of life on Islesboro, including the delivery of mail, and the new car ferries from Lincolnville to Grindle Point henceforth brought mail directly to mid island, "as the packets had a century before."

Deer Isle

Most of the smaller islands surrounding Deer Isle were inhabited within 50 years of the American Revolution. North Deer Isle, the part of the island settled first (in the 1760s), was predominantly a farming community at the outset. Lots were laid out in parallel strips from the northwest shore and some fields cultivated in that era were still under cultivation at the end of the 20th century, McLane reports. Several 18th-century homesteads (or parts of them) still stand. The village of Deer Isle, with its saw and grist mills, harness and blacksmith shops, as well as the first meeting house and church, came into existence to meet the needs of the north Deer Isle settlers. Many of the early settlers on the mid-Penobscot islands came from the western shore of Deer Isle.

During the early part of the 19th century, maritime activity was concentrated in the deep water coves on the opposite side of the island, not along the Deer Isle Thorofare but rather at Southeast Harbor. The settlement of Oceanville on Babbidge's or Whitmore Neck, which makes Southeast Harbor, became a thriving center by the mid 19th century. According to McLane, the large number of fishermen and mariners on Deer Isle in 1850 lived principally in this sector of the island.

The rocky southern shore of the Deer Island Thoroughfare was the one sector of Deer Isle that

Sardine fishery, cannery and steamer, Green's Landing, Maine (Frank Claes collection)

was not significantly settled during the first three-quarters of the 19th century. Though Crotch Island had had a thriving community in the early 1800s, the only settlement on the Thorofare itself was Green's Landing, where a few fishermen lived to be closer to the seaward fisheries. By the end of the 1870s, quarrying, already established for some years on Vinalhaven and in the Muscle Ridge Islands, had spread to Green's Landing, and soon huge new wharves began to be built along the Thorofare. Job Goss and his son John L. were the pioneers of an industry that outlasted most similar enterprises in Maine and survived well into the 20th century.

"The peak of this era," McLane writes, "came in the last two decades of the 19th century, when Green's Landing became a bustling settlement of stonecutters, blacksmiths, teamsters, and other indispensable players in the industry; rough dwellings sprang up among the granite boulders for married quarrymen, boardinghouses accommodated single workers, and two rival music halls (Green's 'Eureka' and Eaton's 'Olympic') vied for customers."

Green's Landing became a regular stop for steam ferries carrying passengers from Rockland to distant corners of Penobscot and Frenchman Bays, McLane writes. "By 1895, the noisy community on the southern shore of Deer Isle had so outgrown its casual association with Deer Isle proper that by mutual consent it was incorporated separately as Stonington. Stonington embraced, in addition to Green's Landing (which adopted its name), the communities of Oceanville, south Deer Isle, and all of the islands between the Thorofare and Merchant Row."

These small islands, as well as Isle au Haut and its satellite islands, were influenced in the 19th century more by activities in southern Deer Isle than by those in the northern sector of the parent island. The dichotomy, McLane concludes, "was as old as the earliest settlement in New England: the frontier versus settled centers; the swagger of exploration versus the smugness of consolidation; the leaky homesteads among the boulders versus the white clapboard farms of north Deer Isle."

Quarrymen, early 1900s

Maine in the 19th century: a different tempo

The differences between Maine of the 19th century and Maine in the 1990s are both quantitative and qualitative. Then, as now, the Maine economy depended upon its fields and hills, its forests and its adjacent waters. But, at that time, most of the central and southern parts of the state of Maine were given over to agriculture. The majority of Maine residents lived in small farming communities, and the state's population was more evenly distributed within the coastal counties than it is today. The tempo of life was different, the variety of occupations was much greater, the kinds and quantities of products were both greater and more varied than today.

Much of the land, for 50 miles or so back from the sea, was stripped of trees. Market and subsistence farming prospered. Each community was largely self-sufficient, with blacksmith shops, sawmills and gristmills common to each city, town and village. The larger towns might also have had tool-making shops, shoemaking shops, tanneries, tinware and textile factories, brickyards, foundries, machine shops and canneries. The general store and the one-room schoolhouse were ubiquitous, and only the smallest communities had fewer than two churches.

There does not appear to have been a distinct "town hall" building in most coastal Maine towns until late in the century. Local government was in the hands of the citizenry. Elected selectmen and assessors carried out the wishes of the citizens as determined at the annual town meetings. As there were few state (and no federal) requirements to comply with, their chief responsibilities were to raise and supervise the spending of funds for schools, the "poor farm" and town roads.

The broken nature of the coastline meant that the best, and sometimes the only, way from one community to the next was by water. Even today, the distance by highway from Belfast to Castine, on the other side of Penobscot Bay, is about 35 circuitous miles by asphalt paved roads. It is slightly over 10 miles by water. A century ago, it would have taken an entire day to make the trip by land, one way, if the state of the roads was ideal and barring delays at the Penobscot River ferry crossing at Bucksport. The preferred journey was by boat, directly across the bay. Given a steady breeze from north or south, an hour or two would get you there.

Beginning in the 1830s, a few steamer lines connected the major ports along the coast with Boston and Portland. Small feeder lines tied the lesser coastal communities into the network of commerce, while river steamers continued the voyages to the heads of navigation.

Before the advent of steam tugs, beginning in the 1840s, the voyage of a vessel from bay to head of navigation might take days or even weeks. Were the wind or river to take an unfavorable direction, or when the tide turned, a captain had to drop anchor and wait it out.

The steam tug changed all that. Though at added expense of towing charges, a schooner could make the same voyage in half a day that once took a week. The sight of a steam tug with a squadron of schooners tied up two-by-two on the towing warp behind her meant that river cities could prosper as never before. Any community with access to the sea and the hinterland could flourish, and flourish many did.

The well-being of Penobscot Bay's shipbuilding communities mirrored the fortunes of America's merchant marine. As European iron and steel vessels and ocean-going steamers absorbed more and more business, the demand for wooden ships slowed, and by 1900 had practically ceased. The last sizable vessel built in Searsport, the ship WILLIAM H. CONNOR, was completed in 1877. By 1880, shipbuilding in town was virtually moribund. From a population of 3,000 in 1870, Searsport witnessed a migration that cut its population in half by 1900. The same hemorrhaging effect reduced the populations of neighboring communities as Penobscot Bay's shipbuilding and ship management professions followed the downward spiral of America's merchant marine. The appurtenances of a maritime past remained, but largely as artifacts, and the area's economy by 1900 relied on agriculture and some manufacturing, not ships, for employment.

George Wasson's description of the Penobscot and its fleet of sailing ships in the 1880s was a snapshot of a particular time in the past. This book attempts to characterize the same region at a different time — the mid 1990s. Like *Sailing Days in the Penobscot* (half of which is devoted to detailed listings of the ships built in the region's many towns), it looks back through the eyes of historians, through statistics and through sources such as an 1882 *Maine Gazetteer* that describes all Maine towns of that day in considerable detail.

Unlike Wasson's classic account, however, we take the present into account as well, profiling the 39 towns that surround Penobscot Bay and line the lower Penobscot River, in hopes that future generations will come to appreciate yet another snapshot of an important Maine region and its people, as they continue to live in a steadily changing world.

Opposite page: The data in this Landsat TM satellite image was collected in the summer of 1995. The water area is depicted using Band 6, which records the thermal infrared energy emitted by the surface layer of the ocean. The water temperature is colder in the darker blue areas, which outline the nutrient-rich waters that flow along the eastern coast of Maine and circulate into the Gulf of Maine outside of Penobscot Bay. The land area is depicted using the natural color bands—red, green and blue. The full image is 115 miles by 115 miles, centered on the Penobscot Bay region. (Image processing by the Island Institute)

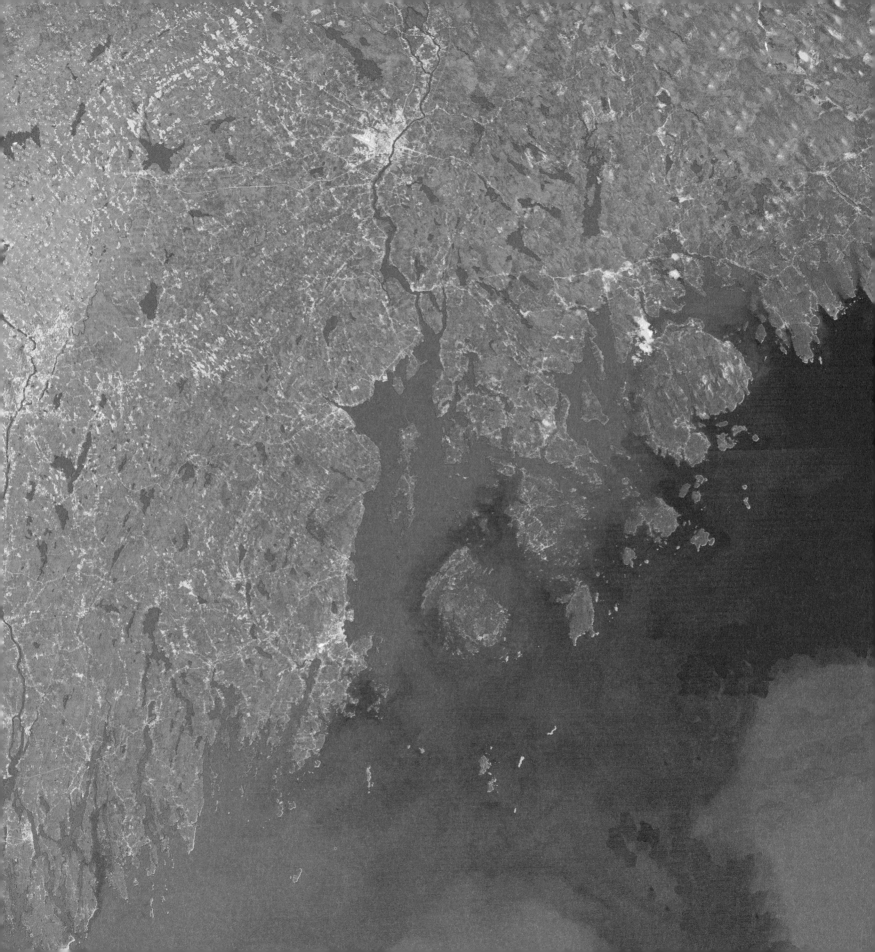

Chapter 2: The River and Its Watershed

By Bob Moore and David D. Platt

The Penobscot River watershed is a vast landscape covering approximately 8,592 square miles, riven by drainages extending all the way to the Canadian border. It comprises more than a quarter of the state of Maine.

The river has enormous influence on the physical and chemical makeup of Penobscot Bay. That influence varies from season to season, depending on the volume of water in the river.

Variations in flow cause major changes in temperature and the load of nutrients in the river. In the river below Hampden, these variations affect salinity. At different times of the year, depending on flows, the river transports varying amounts of pollutants to the bay.

This infusion of fresh water and nutrients from upland watersheds into coastal waters is what defines an estuary: a place where tides and currents mix fresh and salt water and flow through marshes and over mudflats. Estuaries support a rich diversity of marine life. They act as nursery grounds for scores of different species of finfish and shellfish that spend their adult lives in the sea, and teem with the broad spectrum of marine life that forms the foundation of the food chain.

A classic estuary in form and function, the Penobscot's is nonetheless different from the mouths of other Maine rivers and the bays those rivers feed. Penobscot Bay receives far greater amounts of fresh water than Casco Bay, for example. The Kennebec River drains a large upland watershed, but injects fresh water directly into the open ocean.

The further up the estuary, the larger the range of salinity and temperature. Fewer species can tolerate such extremes, and the number of different species that can live there is small. The ones that can survive are abundant, however: in one area in the upper bay, researcher Peter Larsen found 12,000 amphipods in a square meter of mud. During times of low flow in the river, salt water extends as far upstream as Hampden.

Dams have changed the manner in which water flows through a large portion of the Penobscot watershed, and the energy and mobility created by harnessing this water have spawned industries and communities along the river, from the sparsely settled shores of Chesuncook Lake up the river's West Branch to the intensely developed waterfronts of Bangor and Bucksport — development that, not surprisingly, has affected water quality in the river and its estuary.

Year-round river flows have bestowed still more advantages on Millinocket, Medway, Lincoln, Old Town, Orono, Veazie and Bangor — all of which are able to dilute and export their wastewater in the river. Dilution even helps modern sewage treatment systems, by making it possible to discharge higher volumes of treated waste water (plus storm water in some cases) than would be possible if flows were low at certain times of the year.

Opposite: Bald eagle (Christopher Ayres)

*Veazie Dam
(Christopher Ayres)*

When Chesuncook Lake is full it contains 45 billion cubic feet of water, making it the largest single piece of a system that holds, in all, 58 billion cubic feet. The 19 dams, 31 electrical generating turbines and two paper mills on the West Branch of the Penobscot are all under the control of Bowater/Great Northern, which built or rebuilt them in the early years of the 20th century as part of an engineering effort of staggering proportions. Today the West Branch system is the largest privately owned hydroelectric development in the United States, and, some believe, the largest in the world.

Even a hundred years ago, the upper Penobscot was by no means pristine. Logging operations began on the West Branch in 1828, necessitating the construction of dozens of small dams to control the energy and flow of water so the logs could be floated downriver to mills near Bangor. A total of 137 different dams have been built on the West Branch and its tributaries — and still more on the East Branch and the river's main stem — since then.

The coming of groundwood paper technology at the end of the 19th century, with its need for year-round water to generate electricity and its reliance on a steady supply of four-foot "pulpwood" rather than long logs, transformed the region. The river that once rushed and rose as the snow melted in the spring, then gradually dropped and formed quiet pools in summer, became a series of ponds and lakes controlled by dams and filled to the brim each spring, and then drained down slowly in summer to maintain the river's steady flow. By autumn and certainly by early winter under this regime, the lakes are again low enough to accommodate another spring melt. What still looks like "wilderness" to some people is, in fact, a highly regulated system, carefully engineered for the paper industry's purposes.

In terms of elevation, the West Branch system starts at Penobscot Lake in Prentiss Township on the Maine-Quebec border, 1,350 feet above the point where the Penobscot River's two branches join to form its main stem at Medway.

What the river might have looked like before log drivers and engineers controlled the spring freshet and raised the summer flow is anyone's guess. Overall, the pre-industrial Penobscot above Bangor probably resembled today's Saint John River in northern Maine. In late May, the north-flowing Saint John provides some of New England's finest whitewater canoeing; by July, as the saying goes, it is "a mile wide and an inch deep."

Supplying the vessels that came upriver to Bangor during its lumber-sawing heyday were dozens of water- and steam-powered sawmills, whose effects on the river are still evident today: a large part of the river bottom between Hampden and Bucksport is still covered with bark and saw-

Opposite page: This Landsat TM satellite image from summer 1995 shows the 39 towns, outlined by red boundaries, that are the subject of this book. (Image processing by the Island Institute, town boundary data from Maine Office of GIS)

dust. This carpet of organic material is believed to be several feet thick in places and doesn't leave the river, explains University of Maine oceanographer Jim McCleave, because it is trapped at the point where outgoing fresh water meets incoming salt water from Penobscot Bay.

An interesting question is whether the dams upstream, by evening out the annual flow somewhat (the river's height can still fluctuate by as much as 21 feet), have altered the salinity of the lower Penobscot or Penobscot Bay. The point where salt water actually meets fresh depends on the interaction of incoming tide and out-flowing fresh water — and the location of that point changes as the balance between fresh and salt water shifts. Where the fresh-salt interface was in the days before dams is anyone's guess. (McCleave suspects the regime wasn't greatly different, pointing out that the bay's watershed is vast and that only part of the runoff reaching the bay comes down the river.)

When an Atlantic salmon swims upstream to spawn, it can jump about 10 feet into the air. Thus a salmon heading up the Penobscot in pre-dam days could get as far as Ripogenus Falls, reasons Ed Baum of the Atlantic Sea-Run Salmon Commission, the agency responsible for salmon restoration in Maine. Spawning runs of that length probably ended with the construction of an early dam at Old Town between 1830 and 1835. The Bangor Dam, built at the head of river navigation in 1875, didn't stop fish migrations, says Baum, because it wasn't high enough to stop the fish at high tide. Still, today's active salmon fishery on the river between Bangor and Veazie dates from the breaching of the Bangor Dam about 30 years ago, and when a developer proposed closing the breach and redeveloping the dam to generate electricity in the early 1980s, salmon fishermen opposed the project and were largely responsible for killing it.

Mercury contamination is associated with reservoirs, including several along the West Branch downstream of Chesuncook, and should be included in the list of environmental changes associated with the development of the river.

Overall, water quality in the Penobscot is less of an issue today than it was 30 years ago, when impoundments and untreated waste water combined to lower the amount of dissolved oxygen in the entire river. As far as salmon are concerned, says Ed Baum, water quality is "now excellent in most areas." Low oxygen above the Mattaceunk Dam at Medway, near the juncture of the West Branch and the main stem of the river, is a problem locally, says Baum, but doesn't seem to affect salmon in the river downstream.

From river to bay

Over 180,000 people live in the Penobscot watershed, and cities, mills, forestry, agriculture and other human activities combine to degrade

the water quality of the Penobscot River long before it reaches the bay. A look at pollution sources in the Penobscot watershed reveals a mixed picture of formidable challenges and encouraging improvements.

In small but significant ways, individual people contribute to the daily pollutant load carried downstream to the bay. Pollution sources — those that enter the river from sources as diffuse as farm fields, parking lots, septic systems and fertilized lawns, referred to as "non-point" sources — collectively account for as much as 50 percent of the organic pollution in the river.

Non-point sources become diluted in the main stem of the river, but they tend to overpower pollution from other sources in the river's tributaries, and in the near-shore areas of the bay itself. Half of the pollutant "loading" that affects dissolved oxygen and bacteria in the river may be from non-point sources, according to the state Department of Environmental Protection (DEP), but those sources are spread over the entire watershed.

Very little is understood about the impact upstream pollutants have on the marine environment. What is known is that chemicals and heavy metals that were discharged at much higher rates in the recent past have accumulated in the flesh of aquatic life in the river and bay.

Pollutants that entered the system years ago still persist at the mouth of the river. Residual sawdust and mercury have already been mentioned. Ann Hayden and Peter Larsen surveyed the area in the early 1980s for hydrocarbons (from petroleum products and combustion), and trace heavy metals. They also surveyed the number and kinds of living organisms they found. Their study points to a gradient of pollutants in the sediments gradually dispersing towards the outer bay. They also found relationships between the contaminant gradient and the benthic (bottom dwelling) community structure. When pollutants that are dissolved or suspended in the relatively acidic river water mix with the relatively alkaline ocean waters, they "floc," or fall out of suspension. The movement of currents at the interface of fresh and salt water keeps the contaminants in the upper reaches of the estuary.

Penobscot Bay's high flushing rate may act to remove fresh water, and therefore its load of riverborne pollution, at a rapid rate. Joceline Boucher, a marine chemist at Maine Maritime Academy, estimates that the residence time of fresh water in the bay is two weeks, a high flushing rate for a bay the size of Penobscot Bay. (For comparison, Boucher notes that the flushing rate in Narragansett Bay averages one month.) The estuary, it would seem, is relatively well-flushed and not prone to pollution problems associated with stagnation and stratification. Understanding how water quality affects marine life in the bay, however, requires more careful study and observation.

The Penobscot River once supported runs of American shad, alewife, salmon, blue-back herring, sturgeon, striped bass and rainbow smelt. Historical records describe annual shad runs of two million adult fish, extending 170 miles upriver. Such fish migrations are a good indicator of the health of the river because they require clean water and adequate spawning habitat.

Species of special interest

A rare species of sedge or a little known and unassuming beetle are equally significant in their contribution to the diversity of an ecological community. However, humans tend to prioritize which animal species are more "important," and in Penobscot Bay, Atlantic salmon, seals and birds have generated keen interest from researchers and resource managers.

Salmon

Penobscot Bay is good salmon habitat. It receives cold, nutrient-rich water from the Gulf of Maine, and the water quality in the estuary is favorable. But salmon runs have been down in recent years, and biologists working on salmon restoration say returns from the oceans are disappointing. One critical factor in the restoration effort is the quality of habitat in the rivers. "We can control the fresh-water environment, making sure habitat and stocks are the best possible," said Jerry Marancik, a biologist at the Craig Brook Fish Hatchery in East Orland, "but the biggest challenge to restoration is dams blocking fish passage, inundating habitat, and changing water flow and temperatures." Because of its industrial heritage, the Penobscot River contains toxic residues in its water and sediments. What effect these contaminants have on salmon health and reproduction is not known.

There is much about salmon biology that is poorly understood. While biologists are not entirely sure where they go once they leave the river in April and May, salmon have been considered as indicators for ecosystem health because their life cycle includes rivers, estuaries and the ocean. They disappeared from the Penobscot and nearly went extinct in the 1940s because of pollution, overfishing and the construction of dams without fish passage.

As water quality has improved, so have the runs of Atlantic salmon. "There is still some way to go before we can be confident" of restoring a population, says Marancik. "They are sensitive to warm water and pollution. If we didn't have a hatchery program on the Penobscot, there wouldn't be salmon there."

Marancik now sees runs of only 2,000 to 4,000 fish. He considers 6,000 naturally produced fish his goal for a good run. Biologists avoid taking pen raised fish from the aquaculture industry and dumping them in rivers as a stocking method. Pen-raised fish would cross with native wild fish and dilute the genetic pool of fish that evolved to survive the rigors of anadromous migration. According to Marancik, introduced stocks wouldn't survive as well since they have been artificially selected. Biologists can tell whether a fish was raised in a hatchery or the wild by comparing the annual growth patterns on fish scales.

Seals

Seals are another key wildlife component in Penobscot Bay. Seals are mostly year-round residents in Maine, and harbor seals are the most abundant species. Three other Arctic species migrate into Maine in winter: harp, and occasionally ring and hooded seals. Maine has always had gray

Seals (Christopher Ayres)

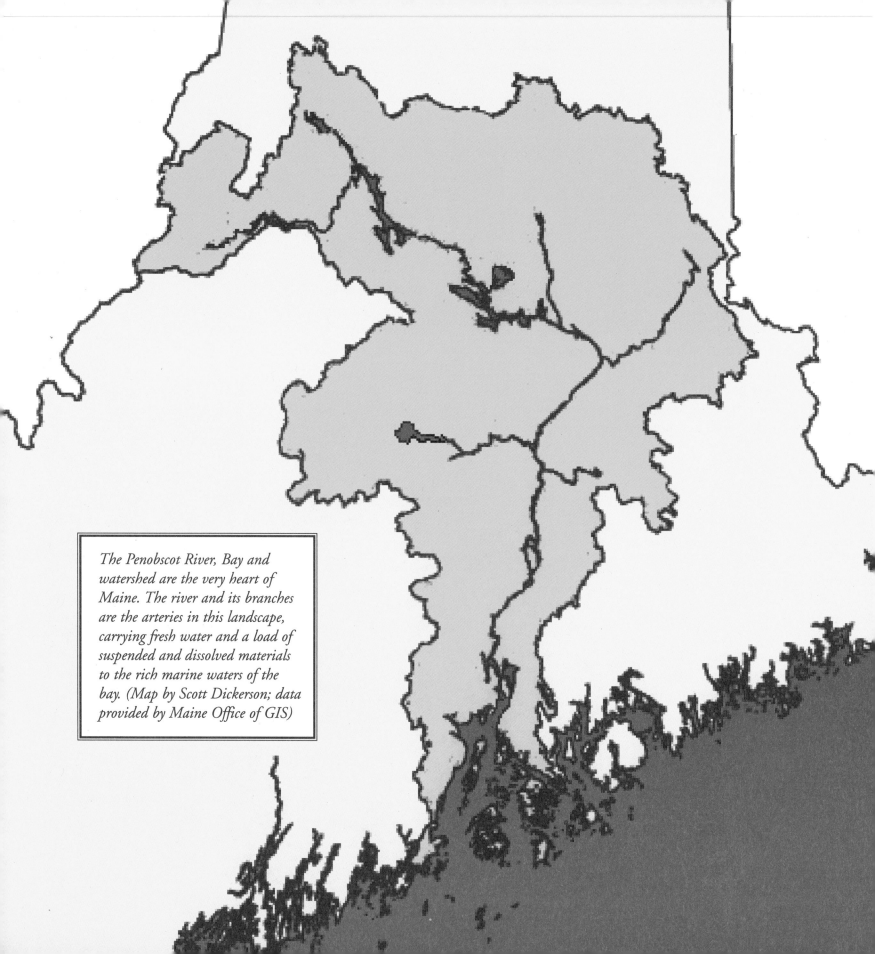

The Penobscot River, Bay and watershed are the very heart of Maine. The river and its branches are the arteries in this landscape, carrying fresh water and a load of suspended and dissolved materials to the rich marine waters of the bay. (Map by Scott Dickerson; data provided by Maine Office of GIS)

eals as summer visitors, but they have become a recent winter addition as well. In a recent winter, a olony of gray seal pups was observed in Penobscot Bay.

The Maine harbor seal population increased from 7,000 in the mid 1970s to 28,800 in 1993, nd the population numbers keep going up with every survey. "Penobscot Bay is a good stronghold or them," says Jim Gilbert, a researcher at the University of Maine. "There are a lot of haul-outs, nd they tend to 'pup' [rear their young] inside the bay more than on outer islands." Penobscot ay, like all of the Maine coast, is ideal because of the abundance of pupping habitat and haul-out hoices. According to Gilbert, the entire coast of the Oregon has about 30 seal haul-outs, where here are approximately 100 haul-outs in Penobscot Bay.

Birds

Birds dependent on coastal habitats re at the core of the Maine Department f Inland Fish and Wildlife's interest in enobscot Bay. Department biologists monitor a broad range of waterfowl, vading birds, seabirds, shorebirds and ndangered and threatened species (primarily bald eagles) in an effort to protect heir critical habitat for breeding and urvival. In the case of migratory topover species like shorebirds, the critial habitat is comprised of feeding and oosting areas.

Many areas in Penobscot Bay are sed by wildlife year-round, but by different species in different seasons. Bill Krohn of the Maine Cooperative Fish nd Wildlife Research Unit of the National Biological Survey said that it is

Eiders (Christopher Ayres)

not known what characteristics are driving the concentration of wildlife to specific coastal areas.

One of the most significant wildlife habitats in Penobscot Bay, according to Alan Hutchinson of the Maine Department of Inland Fisheries and Wildlife, is the black duck wintering area between Cape Rosier and Deer Isle. A globally significant harlequin duck wintering area for between 500 and 700 ducks, about half the population in eastern North America, is located off the western and southern shores of Isle au Haut.

According to the U.S. Fish and Wildlife Service, there are approximately 93 seabird nesting islands in Penobscot Bay. Of these, approximately 63 are considered nationally significant — islands where at least one percent of a species' population nests. About a quarter of the 265 islands in Maine that are considered nationally significant by the Fish and Wildlife Service are located in Penobscot Bay.

The largest and most important seabird nesting islands in Maine are owned by The Nature Conservancy, National Audubon Society, Maine Audubon Society, the U.S. Fish and Wildlife

Service, the State of Maine and private individuals. "These owners know they have a precious resource," says Hutchinson of Inland Fisheries and Wildlife. "Some private owners may be better stewards than government agencies, and we like to give them the positive reinforcement they deserve for their stewardship."

A biophysical region

Penobscot Bay's variety of land forms and widespread marine and island systems, the rich mixing of its large tidal estuary, and abundant flora and fauna give the region a unique biological character. Its combination of abundant and diverse plant and animal species is not found in other areas of the state.

The sheer size of the Penobscot estuary, with its significant influx of fresh water and nutrients from the river, high tidal amplitude, the number of islands and diverse shoreline habitats, makes Penobscot Bay a suitable habitat for a wide range of species. There are mudflats to provide food, and undeveloped shoreline where shorebirds can feed and roost undisturbed. Islands and headlands provide prime nesting habitat in close proximity to abundant feeding areas.

Penobscot Bay is the meeting of the Acadian (northern) and Virginian (southern) habitat zone for many species. It is the northern range limit for horseshoe crabs and quahogs, and has natural oyster beds (though it is believed they are relics from a warmer era, trapped here when the climate grew cooler). At least 22 woody plant species reach their northern range limits in Penobscot Bay, including familiar species like white oak, hickory and Atlantic white cedar. Plants like crowberry and roseroot stonecrop survive at the southern limit of their ranges on Penobscot Bay's outer islands, where the growing conditions are more akin to their preferred northern habitats. Bird species at both northern and southern extremes of their ranges nest on the same islands in Penobscot Bay: petrels, razorbills, guillemots, laughing gulls and Arctic and roseate terns.

Chapter 3: Marine Ecology of Penobscot Bay

By Philip W. Conkling

Penobscot Bay's diverse marine habitats provide either important spawning, nursery or feeding grounds for virtually all of the 70 commercially harvested species of fish and shellfish landed around the rim of the Gulf of Maine. Lobsters are the bay's most high-profile species, and rightly so, since the highest density of lobsters recorded anywhere in the world are found in Penobscot Bay, and their economic value exceeds all other species. But Penobscot Bay waters also produce a virtual treasure chest of other valuable sea life. The diversity of Penobscot Bay's commercially valuable marine resources includes large herring spawning sites off Seal Island, cod and haddock spawning grounds on the deep sand and gravel bottoms of east and west Penobscot bays, more than 23,000 acres of clam flats, countless mussel bars and sea scallop beds and the legendary runs of Atlantic salmon that once thrashed their way far up into the headwaters of the Penobscot and Ducktrap rivers. The diversity and abundance of these rich marine resources have sustained human life around the bay's edges for millennia, and their abundance sustains large concentrations of wading birds, waterfowl, seabirds and seals that rear their young in Penobscot Bay.

Matinicus Rock to the 50 fathom line

Any attempt to catalog the diverse marine environments of Penobscot Bay confronts the question of where the embayment's boundaries might be drawn. This is a more straightforward exercise at the head and flanks of the bay than on its seaward margin, where the bay merges imperceptibly with the waters of the Gulf of Maine.

From the hills of the mainland looking far out to sea, if the wind is west, you can see the dark shapes of Matinicus and Criehaven Islands, and at night catch the loom of the first order light at Matinicus Rock Light Station. The name Matinicus, according to Fanny Hardy Eckstrom, Maine's respected Indian ethnographer, is derived from the Micmac language, which combines the Indian word for "island" with a word meaning "cut off" or "at the edge." One of the earliest fishing stations in America, Matinicus is still cut off from the shore and for most of us remains at the edge of the known world. Protected by the immense fortress of the sea around its rocky shores, and close to large fishing grounds for cod a dozen more miles further offshore on Matinicus South Southwest Ground, the island still provides a perfect spot from which fishermen can put out to sea and fish the margins of the 50 fathom line.

To mark the line offshore where the bay ends and the Gulf of Maine begins is to make a somewhat arbitrary distinction. However, the 50 fathom line just outboard of Matinicus Rock represents a physical oceanographic boundary of sorts. Sunlight penetration to such depths begins to

Looking south over Vinalhaven to the Gulf of Maine (Christopher Ayres)

diminish to near darkness, and especially in the summertime, the 50 fathom line is where the stratification between these deeper waters and the warmer surface becomes evident. Deep-water channels and currents bring cold, nutrient-rich waters far up into the embayment, to be sure, but most of the bay's biological processes are concentrated in the shallower waters inshore of the 50 fathom line.

East bay, West bay, head of the bay

At the head of the bay, where the Penobscot River spills into the tidal basins of east and west Penobscot bays, Verona Island splits Maine's largest river into two channels. The main flow of the river's fresh water surges through a narrow deep gorge that has long been guarded by a military fortification, while the lesser part of its flow is shunted around Verona to form a quiet-flowing backwater lined with mud flats.

To the extent that it is useful to draw lines on charts, the bay's western boundary might be said to run along the shore of the Muscle Ridge Channel (often spelled "Mussel" on older charts referring to this area's abundant mussel bars) to Mosquito Island, where it begins to merge with Muscongus Bay. A line drawn from Mosquito through the deep water to the west of Roaring Bull Ledge is as close as one might want to define this western edge. The bay's eastern boundary is even harder to define; the line between Penobscot and Jericho bays might be arbitrarily drawn from the midpoint of Eggemoggin Reach in a southerly direction between Isle au Haut and Marshall Island.

County political boundaries do not much matter out on the water, although town boundaries certainly do. But county lines are important in terms of the way landings of commercially valuable species are reported by state and federal authorities. Much of this watery realm is considered to be part of Knox County, although Waldo County takes in all of Islesboro and its associated chain of islands down to Lime Island. The shores of Deer Isle and Stonington front on east Penobscot Bay, but they have been considered part of Hancock County for over a century.

The seasonal bloom and bust

Ultimately, the marine productivity of Penobscot Bay depends on the annual bloom of a vast pasture of plants too small to see with the naked eye. During the past two decades marine ecologists have increasingly turned to satellites in space to try to understand how, when and where the annual bloom of tiny marine plants — called phytoplankton — appear and how this bloom affects waters such as those in Penobscot Bay. Because satellites are designed to sample entire oceans, however, their ability to delineate temperature and color in a local body of water such as Penobscot Bay is limited. Nevertheless a preliminary picture has begun to emerge that suggests how the bay's phytoplankton "pasture" appears season after season.

In winter, the surface waters of most parts of the bay hover around the freezing mark during late January and throughout February when the bay's biological activity is restricted to deeper areas where, contrary to what you might think, warmer water is found. However, this is an inherently unstable water condition, and results in the replacement of cold surface waters by warmer bottom waters. This seasonal "turnover" helps jump-start the ecology of near-shore waters because nutrients that have sifted out of surface waters and been stored in deeper waters are in effect recycled back to the surface.

Each March, long before shoots of grass have begun to show any green on the mainland coast, the first phytoplankton begin to reproduce. It appears that the annual phytoplankton bloom begins at different "hot spots" in eastern and western areas of the Gulf of Maine; for Penobscot Bay, the bloom is sustained by the nutrient-rich water that wells up off the eastern coast of Maine and is carried southwestward on the coastal current's gyre. By early May, when spring is just getting going in the terrestrial environment, the phytoplankton bloom in the Gulf of Maine is dense and well established along most of the coast and it has helped stimulate local blooms in bodies such as Penobscot Bay. Satellite imagery shows a strong and early local bloom that appears in east Penobscot Bay between Vinalhaven and Deer Isle and which may result from an upwelling of nutrient-rich water flowing up the deep channel between these two islands.

By June, the cycles of production of phytoplankton, followed by explosions of zooplankton (tiny marine animals that feed on phytoplankton) that are in turn fed upon by filter-feeding fish, become self-sustaining. They keep churning in the water column, nourished both by inputs of offshore water and the nutrients carried off the land in streams and rivers. Even in the fall, when the land begins to cool off and terrestrial productivity begins to slacken, Penobscot Bay waters are at their warmest — and so biological activity continues until early December. Thus the bay's vast pasture and all its marine life operate for nine months of the year, much longer than the growing season on the mainland. This long season of planktonic production helps explain why the marine productivity of Penobscot Bay is of world-class dimensions.

Currents, eddies and tides

The annual phytoplankton bloom is cycled and refreshed throughout Penobscot Bay by the complex interaction of tides, wind and currents. Penobscot Bay is referred to as a "macrotidal estuary," where a large tidal range interacts with river runoff to create vigorous tidal mixing. Tidal ranges measured in the bay range from eight feet on neap tides to over 13 feet on spring tides, when the moon and sun line up to exert greater gravitational pull. Although every lobsterman, sailor and small boat handler knows only too well that the rising tide floods northward between two and three knots at full flood up west Penobscot Bay, less is known about the bay's currents than one might expect. We do know that a well-defined westward-trending current, referred to as the "Gulf of Maine Gyre," develops off eastern Maine and circulates southwestward along the outer edge of the bays of Maine. Recent studies by University of Maine oceanographer Neil Pettigrew show that when this current encounters the submerged peaks and plateaus below Penobscot Bay (South Southwest Ground and Jefferies Bank), it is deflected towards the Northeast Peak of Georges to form the western edge of a smaller gyre encompassing the eastern Gulf of Maine.

Where the coastal gyre meets a rising tide near the mouth of a north–south-trending embayment such as Penobscot Bay, the Coriolis effect (caused by the spinning earth) deflects this current to the left-hand (western) side of the bay. Thus tide and current combine to produce a strong drift

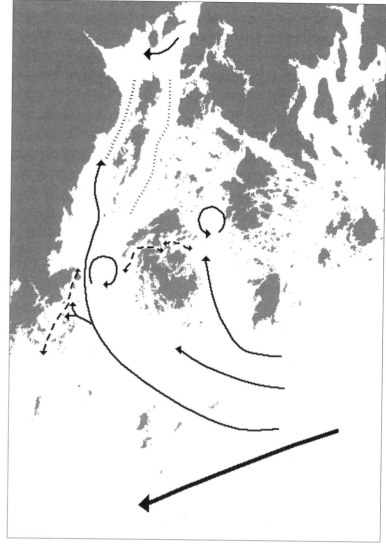

The circulation pattern throughout the Penobscot Bay varies with time of the tide, wind direction and velocity, barometric pressure and season of the year. It changes at different depths in the water column. No single graphic could incorporate all these factors into a representation of circulation of the bay as a general pattern. Nonetheless, important, persistent circulation features exist in east and west Penobscot Bay which are likely to influence productivity. (Coastline data from Maine Office of GIS; graphic by the Island Institute)

up west Penobscot Bay. The long, narrow island of Islesboro, which runs north and south for almost four miles, splits the upper bay into eastern and western channels. Studies of the currents around Islesboro suggest that a persistent circular flow may be maintained around Islesboro (called "residual current flow" by hydrographers), independent of the state of the tide. This residual current flow appears to move northwards along the western edge of the bay and southerly along the eastern shore of Islesboro. Eddies (vortices) develop and keep redeveloping where the tides and residual current flow interact. The long, narrow lines of "spindrift" that form in west Penobscot Bay are the most visible evidence of the vortices created where tide and current flows run past each other. These preliminary data suggest a basic clockwise circulation around Islesboro near the head of the bay.

At the lower end of the bay, the current picture is complicated by the presence of the large islands of Vinalhaven, North Haven and Isle au Haut, which create complex anomalies in tidal direction. In the Fox Island Thorofare, which runs between Vinalhaven and North Haven, the tide splits near Iron Point, flooding from both the east and west to meet at the narrows between Iron and Crockett Points. Then, after high slack, the tide falls back away in opposite directions to east and west. Some studies suggest large vortices persistently develop in west Penobscot Bay in the region off Crabtree Point, North Haven, off the southern tip of Islesboro and in the waters between North Haven and Deer Isle (Burgund 1995). If confirmed, these are areas where we would expect increased biological activity from the enhanced mixing that keeps nutrients stirred in the water column and enables phytoplankton blooms to keep regenerating themselves.

River outflow

Because salt water is heavier than fresh water (or more "dense," as oceanographers describe it), the mixing of waters at the head of the bay sets up unique ecological conditions. Here the river's fresh water rides up over and "floats" out over the bay's marine water. When the tide is rising, a "wedge" of salt water is forced under the river's fresh water flow, far upstream of Bucksport. With the falling tide, the salt water recedes. Although fresh and salt water mix in this productive estuarine zone of the Bay, it is important to understand that masses of fresh and salt water move up and down the river channel, depending on the state of the tide.

This feature of the Penobscot estuary explains why lobsters that cannot tolerate even small amounts of fresh water are nevertheless trapped well upstream of Bucksport. When the tide ebbs, the flow of the river and tide combine to increase the currents and mixing in a large area south of Verona Island, down as far as Cape Jellison, Sears Island and across to Castine.

The volume of river outflow from the Penobscot varies from month to month, season to season. Flow increases in April and May when snow melt from the vast interior of the Penobscot watershed combines with spring rains. November is another peak month, on average. A distinct pattern of river outflow emerges, with spring and fall peaks followed by low to moderate flows during summer and winter months.

Although dams along the Penobscot have altered the hydrographic input of the Penobscot River and hence the degree of mixing in the upper embayment, we would expect the general pattern of spring and fall peak outflow to have ecological significance: the higher the flows, the greater the load of sediments that are carried suspended in the river water, and to such sediments adhere nutrients that help fertilize plankton blooms. To the extent that spawning activity of fish and shellfish species has "co-evolved" with this pattern of river flow and nutrient availability, we might expect to find higher survival among those populations that have timed spawning with peak river flow. At the same time, to the extent that river outflows also carry toxic wastes that adhere to the same sediments, impacts to finfish and shellfish larvae that spawn in the spring and fall might also be greater.

Islands as substrates

Maine, with 4,617 islands listed by the state's Coastal Island Registry, has more islands than any other state or province in the region; more islands, in fact than anywhere else on the Atlantic coast. This high density of islands sets up conditions for enhanced near-shore productivity all along the Maine coast, but nowhere more so than in Penobscot Bay. The number of islands between Marshall Point in Port Clyde and Naskeag Point in Brooklin is 1,809 – or almost a quarter of those found along the entire coast. Over three quarters of the Bay's islands are smaller than an acre, meaning most of those surface area and hence their ecological value is subtidal. The remaining 400 islands larger than an acre have additional great significance as wildlife habitat and prime recreation sites.

As Penobscot Bay's water circulates among the islands, each island helps to mix, oxygenate and enrich the water. The islands also cause local upwelling of deeper, colder, nutrient-rich water. Tide-induced vertical water currents around islands bring an astonishing abundance of nutrients and marine life up from the sea floor. Tide-driven currents also surge through passages between islands, creating a funnel effect that increases the volume of feed available to filter feeders, as well as those species that prey on the filter feeders. Individually, islands support many wetlands, the runoff from which helps enrich the surrounding waters. These factors help explain the inshore movement of lobsters, crabs and fish during the spring and summer, as well as the high density of lobster traps around island margins.

Marine ecologists measure productivity by estimating the yearly amount of carbon fixed by plants through photosynthesis. Ecologists at the Bedford Institute of Oceanography in Nova Scotia have been measuring the primary production of seaweeds in the shallows of Gulf of Maine for more than two decades. Data on nearshore productivity is crucial to understanding how islands scattered along the shore lead to enriched coastal food chains. Studies in St. Margaret's Bay, Nova Scotia, show that as much as 1,000 gC/m2/yr (grams of carbon per square meter per year) is captured by the seaweeds along the shores there. This compares with estimates of only 125 gC/m2/yr for the open ocean adjacent to the gulf, and translates to 370 kilograms (815 pounds) of carbon per year for every meter of shoreline.

The coast of Penobscot Bay is over 1,000 miles (approximately 1,613 kilometers) in length; perhaps as much as a billion pounds of carbon are produced annually merely by seaweeds along its intricate coastline. These values are among the highest for coastal productivity recorded anywhere. In part, they are due to the large and intricate topography of the shallows around the many islands in Penobscot Bay. Without these islands, the near-shore zone would be a much simpler place, without the biological richness we currently observe.

A stupendous bounty of lobsters

Perhaps nowhere is the inherent productivity of Penobscot Bay more apparent than in its lobster fishery. Research by University of Maine lobster biologist Robert Steneck, a leading authority

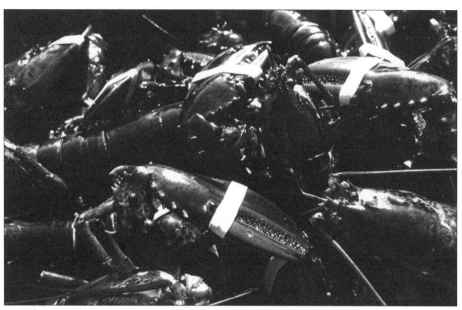

(*Christopher Ayres*)

on the ecology of Maine lobster, indicates that the highest density of lobsters recorded anywhere in the western North Atlantic, and perhaps in the world, occurs in the waters of the Muscle Ridge Channel that flank west Penobscot Bay. Juvenile lobster densities throughout Penobscot Bay in summer may average one lobster per square meter, suggesting that on the order of 10 to 20 million young lobsters are utilizing the bay's feeding and shedding grounds each summer.

In the spring of the year, mature lobsters that have overwintered in deeper warmer waters begin crawling toward shore as shallow waters begin to warm. There they seek cover during the time that they shed their old shells and grow new ones. During this period in their annual cycle, they do not scavenge for food, but transform themselves into filter feeders. While their new shells are hardening they are uniquely susceptible to predation and require areas that provide adequate protection. The extensive underwater seaweed and kelp forests surrounding islands in Penobscot Bay provide necessary cover, and together with the rich broth of food which is produced by the self sustaining plankton bloom, create the necessary combination of ecological factors lobsters require.

Rockland, at the edge of Penobscot Bay, has long proclaimed itself the "Lobster Capital of Maine," and it is no accident that Maine's largest lobster harvests are found along this section of the coast, with its large number of islands, its relative abundance of cobble habitats and abundant submerged aquatic vegetation.

Edges of the bay: intertidal habitats

Before slipping beneath the surface of the water to consider subtidal habitats where most of Penobscot Bay's life is sequestered, we will survey the more familiar intertidal habitats to get a mental picture of habitats that few of us have seen.

The rocky intertidal

A great deal has been written about the rocky intertidal zone ever since Rachel Carson's elegant descriptions were first published over 35 years ago. And no wonder: this zone is one of the most diverse and productive habitats found anywhere at the oceanic-continental edge. In Penobscot Bay, hundreds of species of plants and animals are commonly found here.

The dominant species of the rocky intertidal are the brown seaweeds that attach themselves directly to the rocky shore areas of the bay. Two species, sea wrack and knotted wrack (*Fucus* and *Ascophyllum*), together comprise an immense community around the edge of Penobscot Bay. Their long, thin fronds with conspicuous float bladders hang limply over rocks when the tide is out, sequestering large numbers of marine snails, crabs and brine shrimp; these float upwards as the tide rises to form dense rockweed "pastures" that provide critical shelter and feeding areas for juvenile fish.

Beneath the rockweed zone lies the Irish moss zone, named for its dominant species, the red-lish, short, tufted algae that coats the rock like a carpet. Irish moss is collected worldwide for its carrageenan, an important emulsifying agent and food additive used in toothpaste, gels, ice cream, puddings and a host of other products. The largest carrageenan plant in the United States, Marine Colloids, maintains a large plant on the Rockland waterfront, although it now imports all its raw materials from other regions of the world.

Cobble, gravel and boulder beaches

Here and there along the shores of Penobscot Bay where wave energy is too intense for sand or mud to settle out of the water column, we find beaches composed of rock-sized particles, ranging in size from gravel to cobble to boulders. The average size of the particles found at any beach or subtidal area is a rough index of the force of waves affecting that part of the shore: the larger the size, the more intense the wave climate.

Sand beaches

Penobscot Bay, like most of the Maine coast, has few stretches of long sandy beach, but there are hundreds of little sandy "pocket" beaches in protected coves where storm waves do not carry the sand offshore. Larger sand beaches are found near the head of Penobscot Bay, where sand accumulated in delta-like formations during glacial melting. The beaches of Pond and Butter islands in the upper bay were formed in this way and are replenished by annual infusions of sediments transported by the spring runoff of the Penobscot River. Although sandy beaches are a relatively rare intertidal habitat, deposits of sand cover hundreds of square miles of the bottom of the bay.

The sandy intertidal zone is colonized only by those animals that are able to deal with the difficult environmental conditions presented by grinding sand particles. Species like the surf clam, found at the extreme low water mark of the sandy intertidal, have exceptionally thick shells that enable them to withstand the harsh conditions of sandy habitats. Sand hoppers (sometimes referred to as "beach fleas") and other small crustaceans are also found in the sandy intertidal zone where they become food for shorebirds patrolling the surf line.

Mud flats

Mud flats are distributed throughout Penobscot Bay, wherever quiet waters permit silt and clay-sized particles to drop out of the water column, and are potentially the most economically valuable intertidal habitat of Penobscot Bay region, because they are colonized by soft-shelled clams. However, approximately half of the bay's 23,000 acres of clam-producing mud flats are closed due to pollution from sewage treatment plants and overboard discharge pipes; yet many of these areas could be reclaimed simply by improving efforts to monitor water quality. Most of the formerly productive flats are found at the head of the bay nearer to where the annual load of sediment from the Penobscot River empties into the bay, but large and important mud flats also are

Cobble beach
(Christopher Ayres)

*Digging clams, Little
Deer Island, late 1800s
(Frank Claes collection)*

found surrounding the larger islands, including Islesboro, North Haven and Vinalhaven.

Salt marshes

Salt marshes are specialized mud flat habitats that have been colonized by sea grasses that have adapted to the specialized conditions found there: changing salinity, fluctuating tides and seasonal temperature variations. During colonial times, salt marshes were an important adjunct to coastal "salt water farms," because they provided fresh pasture during the growing season and fodder during the winter months.

Today we know that salt marshes serve as valuable nurseries for most commercially significant species of fish and shellfish. Clams, mussels, oysters and crabs inhabit salt marshes throughout their adult lives. Other species such as shad, alewives and striped bass pass through salt marshes on their way upriver to spawn in fresh water. Waterfowl feed and nest in such marshes and deer feed along their edges.

Acre for acre, undisturbed salt marshes are among the most productive parts of an estuary or embayment as a result of their ability to trap and store nutrients during the growing season. Taken up by salt marsh grasses, these nutrients form the intricate food web that sustains nursery areas for marine life. The periodic storms and floods that rush through salt marshes release part of the annual store of nutrients to a wider area.

In the Penobscot embayment, most of the salt marsh acreage is concentrated near the head of the bay, up into the Bagaduce River near Castine and lining the Penobscot River north to Winterport. The largest single salt marsh in the Penobscot embayment is found within the town of Frankfort in Marsh Cove, whose 100 acres release nutrients to a far larger area.

The bottom of the bay

The "benthic" or bottom environments of Penobscot Bay, like the communities of the edge of the bay, are largely the result of geological events associated with glaciation. A short 16,000 years ago, a vast continental ice shelf covered the entire northeast region of North America, extending southward over a rocky plateau that would become Georges Bank. In the process of advancing and retreating, the ice sheet also scraped and scoured the rolling coastal lowlands that would become the bottom of the Gulf of Maine.

At glacial maximum, approximately a third of the continent's entire supply of fresh water was tied up as ice, compared with 3 percent today. Then in a relatively short period of time, all of this ice melted, resulting in floods of what must have been Biblical magnitude. The water pouring forth from the melting ice fields caused sea level to rise by hundreds of feet along the coast of Maine. As the sea rose, it surrounded thousands of hilltops, ridge lines and mountains, creating Penobscot Bay's distinctive endowment of islands and ledges. But just beneath the surface the ice age created an equally distinctive and intricate constellation of ledges, shoals, pinnacles, deltas, sand plains and gravel ridges that figure significantly in the bay's marine biodiversity.

Today, the Penobscot River drains nearly 9,000 square miles of the interior of northern Maine, lowing at an average rate of 35,000 cubic feet per second. But for several thousand years, as the continental glacier melted, the Penobscot must have flowed at rates several orders of magnitude greater. If a small stream has enough force to roll a grain of sand along its bottom, the force of the raging Penobscot during glacial melting could not only roll large boulders and cobbles along its bottom, but could also carry immense volumes of sand, silt and clay suspended in its milky, muddy waters. Where these waters spilled into Penobscot Bay, their loads began settling out, the heaviest first, then the next heavier and so on to create a mixture of underwater substrates from cobble and sandy deltas strewn with boulders to extensive plains of mud. The torrents of glacial meltwaters were thus the primary agents that gave structure to the marine environments of Penobscot Bay.

Fishermen's knowledge

Marine scientists have only begun to map the underwater environments of Penobscot Bay. Until recently such mapping was accomplished by use of a sediment "grab," a bucket with attached scoop sent over the side of a research vessel to bring up a sample of the bottom. Considering that this method samples the bottom a square foot at a time and that Penobscot Bay's benthic area exceeds 600 square miles, it is perhaps understandable that our knowledge of important marine communities is limited.

Nevertheless, fishermen have been "sampling" these same bottom environments while fishing for most of this century and are thus an important source of information for piecing together the physical and biological structure of the bay. Every time an otter trawl net goes over the side of a fishing boat,

(Christopher Ayres)

it is critical for the captain to know not only the habits of the fish he hopes to catch, but also the nature of the bottom over which his net will be towed. Over his career, a fisherman spends much of his time "learning the bottom" where he fishes. At the same time, he has been identifying benthic communities among which the fish and shellfish live. Because many species are associated with particular types of substrate at certain times of year, a good fisherman must catalogue bottom types in the area he fishes.

To interpret what fishermen say about bottom sediments, however, it is helpful to remember that these deposits are constantly undergoing change. The swiftness of local currents, the movement of tides and the turbulence of waves control the size of the particles deposited in sediment. Currents sweep away smaller particles and leave behind those too large to be carried. By identifying sediment type and depth, a knowledgeable fisherman can deduce both the relative velocity of currents close to the bottom and what marine species may be present.

A fisherman may be targeting sandy bottom, a gravel ridge or a muddy plain. Because rocky ledges or boulder-strewn areas are where an otter trawl gets hung up and damaged, resulting in lost fishing time, such areas are remembered and handed down from one fisherman to another.

Unique bottom environments

Belfast Bay's pockmark field

In recent years a new tool, the side-scanning sonar, has been developed that can add greatly to our understanding of benthic communities in places like Penobscot Bay. Side-scanning sonar is simply a sound pulse that is emitted from a sending unit mounted on the underside of a research vessel. The sound wave bounces off the sea bottom and creates different patterns depending on the nature of the bottom. It is therefore useful for identifying areas of mud, sand, gravel and rock. Combined with navigational equipment such as a GPS (Global Positioning System), side-scanning sonar can be used to create detailed maps of the sea floor.

Recently Joseph Kelley, a geologist for the State of Maine and the University of Maine, used side-scanning sonar to describe a unique marine environment near the head of Penobscot Bay: a field of 2,000 giant pockmarks in soft sediments on the bottom of Belfast Bay that has not been described at any other location in the Gulf of Maine. Using an unmanned submersible, Kelley collected side-scanned sonar images of the pockmark field, showing circular depressions in the muddy bottom, some as large as a football field. In 1992, a local fisherman, Russell Coombs, from Islesboro, reported seeing "enormous numbers of gas bubbles" erupting from this part of the bay.

Kelley hypothesizes that this field may have resulted from muddy sediments that covered a large peat bog that formed at the edge of an earlier incarnation of the Penobscot River when sea level was lower. Such a bog is characteristic of parts of the Penobscot River today in areas east of Old Town and Orono, where old meanders in the river have been cut off from the main channel to form extensive wetlands. Kelley hypothesizes that large volumes of methane gas are trapped beneath the sediments as organic material from the bog decomposes. When the pressure builds up sufficiently, an eruption occurs, producing the odd-looking craters in the overlying muddy sediments.

Although their significance to the bay and its associated marine life is unknown, these giant pockmarks are among the largest yet described in the world. At the very least, they suggest how much more there is to learn about the bottom of the bay.

Eelgrass

The National Marine Fisheries Service has characterized the marine habitats of upper Penobscot Bay as among the most highly productive along the Maine coast, especially in areas where there is a confluence of large bodies of fresh water wetlands and shallow eelgrass beds. These eelgrass beds, in turn, serve as important nursery areas for virtually every commercially important marine groundfish and inshore shellfish species found in the Gulf of Maine. A concentration of eelgrass beds exists in the vicinity of Sears Island, which was intensively studied during the review of the Maine Department of Transportation's proposal to build a cargo port there. The largest and most prolific eelgrass beds in the Penobscot embayment are found along the upper reaches of the Bagaduce River.

It is estimated that approximately 1,797 acres of eelgrass beds are located in Penobscot Bay, making it a relatively rare subtidal habitat. Over a third of these beds are found in the area of the Bagaduce River, while the rest are mostly distributed around the shores at the head of the bay, usually near areas where fresh water wetlands empty into quiet waters.

Marine biologists recognize that these eelgrass beds are more than just isolated pieces of marine wetlands; they once provided a vital ecological link in protecting the productivity of commercial fishing in Penobscot Bay and will be important as the state and federal governments work to restore the depleted groundfisheries. The beds closest to the bay's historic inshore cod-spawning grounds are located along the eastern and western shores of Sears Island, at the periphery of Long Cove, in the northeastern portion of Stockton Harbor and off Sandy Point. Collectively these beds have high resource value for fisheries, since they once provided vital nursery habitat for spawning populations of commercially valuable fish.

Subtidal cobble habitat

University of Maine marine biologist Robert Steneck and his colleague Rick Wahle at Bigelow Laboratory have recently published findings of their underwater work that suggest that subtidal cobble habitats represent critical habitat for juvenile lobsters. Steneck and Wahle have shown that the annual supply of lobsters in Penobscot Bay depends upon a healthy broodstock to produce a supply of larval lobsters that passively float on coastal currents for the first few months of their lives. Steneck believes that the propensity of larval lobsters to settle out of the water column and sink to the bottom is keyed to surface water temperatures. Larval settlement along midcoast Maine generally occurs in late July or early August, when the prevailing southerly winds are pushing larval lobsters up into the bays of Maine. However, recruitment is dependent upon the availability of cover for the tiny lobsters that otherwise suffer extraordinarily high rates of predation — the median time to the first attack from small predatory finfish (which are nearly ubiquitous) is approximately 15 minutes. Cobble bottoms in less than 50 feet of water that have a good deal of space between the rocks into which the young lobsters can crawl provide crucial protection. Steneck hypothesizes that lobster populations in Penobscot Bay are high due to the relative abundance of this habitat around the islands near the edge of the bay.

Kelp forests

Only the very top of kelp forests is exposed at the very lowest tides of the month, and it is only then that most of us can begin to appreciate the forests' importance to the ecology of Penobscot Bay. This zone extends subtidally down the edges of rocky areas to the limit of light penetration, 90 to 150 feet beneath the surface of the sea. Depending on local conditions, kelps in Penobscot Bay (technically known as "laminarians") are capable of reaching 20 to 30 feet in length, the height of small trees. Commercially important species find food and refuge within these underwater "forests." Rocky islands add an important dimension to the bay's marine productivity simply by creating a huge underwater surface area where kelps and other algae colonize, forming the base of important food webs for lobster, urchins, herring and cod, to mention but a few of the species that depend on this habitat.

Deep canyons

A careful look at a Penobscot Bay chart reveals soundings of deep water, where Gulf of Maine waters are able to enter the Bay and extend their reach northward. One such area in West

Penobscot Bay may represent an ancient channel carved by the Penobscot River when the Gulf of Maine was still a rolling coastal plain. On the walls of these canyons live unique communities of encrusting algaes, bryozoans and other deep-water marine invertebrates, unlike any other inshore marine communities.

Seeing the system of the bay

Within Penobscot Bay's vast underwater regions lives an abundance of marine resources of immense importance — a diversity hinted at by the complexity and richness of intertidal habitats that line the bay's shores. More than 1,000 species of invertebrates have been recorded here, representing some of the highest levels of marine biodiversity in any coastal ocean area on earth.

Standing at the edge of Penobscot Bay, we are still like the proverbial blind men describing an elephant; some parts are beginning to be understood, but making sense of the whole is an undertaking that has just started. It is important to continue the effort to see the bay as a whole and to monitor how changes — biological changes such as the removal spawning cod, physical changes caused by trawling and dragging or chemical alterations from the "inputs" of industry along the Penobscot River — influence the system of this magnificent, valuable whole.

Chapter 4: Penobscot *Fisheries in the 20th Century*

By Philip Conkling and Ted Ames

By 1887, when the United States Fisheries Commission published the results of its decade-long research into the biology and economics of the nation's commercially important fisheries, the United States had become a world fishing power. The American fleet, heavily concentrated in Maine and Massachusetts, was able to compete successfully throughout the Northwest Atlantic with the more established and better capitalized fleets of Great Britain, France and Spain.

In 1894, Maine established its own Department of Sea and Shore Fisheries, with the dual mission of both conserving and developing the state's marine resources.

Maine's new department published detailed fisheries statistics by county, by species and by fisheries product for the first decade and a half of the 20th century, providing a comprehensive picture of the diversity and regional structure of Maine's coastal fisheries. From these statistics, a picture of Penobscot Bay landings can be reconstructed. Between 1916 and 1929, however, no state records of any fisheries landings were published; and it appears, unaccountably, that none were collected. Some records collected by the federal government during this period survive, though they are difficult to find and contain gaps in information. After 1929, detailed records again became available.

By compiling statistics from Knox and Waldo counties and estimating what portion of Hancock County's landings can be attributed to Penobscot Bay, it is possible to extrapolate approximate landings data for the towns surrounding Penobscot Bay for most of this century.

What fish landings can tell us

Landings data for the Penobscot Bay region reveal how the patterns of landings of different commercially valuable species varied over long periods of time, possibly telling us whether certain fishing practices or levels of fishing effort were (or were not) sustainable. Are there clues in the historic record, in other words, that suggest ways to manage some of our stocks sustainably, or are the familiar boom-and-bust patterns inherent in the nature of these fisheries?

Viewing landings data over a long period of time provides insight into the economic effects of changes in markets and technology on the livelihoods of fishing families from communities that surround Penobscot Bay. If Penobscot Bay's depleted marine resources are to be restored to their former prominence, it is essential to have an accurate historical context.

We tend to think of Maine fisheries as inherently resistant to change, but fisheries history in the 20th century is replete with examples of fishermen and managers trying to cope with innova-

Opposite: In 1993, Penobscot Bay lobster landings exceeded 12 million pounds for the first time since records had been collected. Lobster landings have continued to rise, despite predictions that they would fall. Only an ecosystem-based approach can lead to a true understanding of this region's marine systems. (Christopher Ayres)

tions. In 1900, wooden vessels were already being eclipsed by steel. The development of mechanized fishing from steam-powered vessels decreased the labor needed to supply the market with fish. At the turn of the century on Vinalhaven, for example, it took 200 fishermen in boats to supply 100 persons processing salt fish on shore; within a few years, new technology and economics had reversed these ratios.

The introduction of the otter trawl, which is a large net towed over the bottom and attached by cables to winches aboard a steam-powered fishing boat, played a key role in the industrialization of New England fishing. The otter trawl was first developed in England for North Sea fishing in 1905; by 1912 or 1913, virtually no new fishing boat in Maine was launched without one.

Small gasoline-powered engines were in general use by the Vinalhaven lobster fleet by 1910, according to local historian Sidney Winslow, although the "fishermen were wont to fool themselves with the remark, 'We'll use the engine only when there is no wind.' But it was only a short period of time before we saw them going to and from their work when there was a good breeze, with all sails set and the engine running wide open."

Engines dramatically increased the catch of individual lobstermen by increasing their effective fishing range, but lobsters were still trapped in the same pots that had existed prior to the development of gas engines. The mechanization of groundfishing, however, not only increased vessel size and range but also encouraged rigging with efficient otter trawls — with the result that whole populations of groundfish would be eliminated from many fishing grounds. Improvements in refrigeration and cold storage around 1900 doomed the salt fish trade. Consumers preferred fresh fish over salt fish if given the choice. Better transportation gave impetus to the fresh fish market as well.

Together, these technological changes were a radical departure from the first 200 years of fishing in the Gulf of Maine, bringing with them a whole new environment.

Clams

During the early decades of the 20th century, an astounding number of clams were harvested from Penobscot Bay flats. In April, 1902, the Deer Isle *Messenger* reported on "the magnitude of the clam business in Maine," and noted that Eaton and Company of Stonington had shipped "more than 800 barrels, one shipment of 400 bbls. going to Portugal."

In 1903, there were 19 clam canning factories along the coast of Maine, eight of which were in Knox and Hancock counties. In 1904, two more clam factories opened up in Knox County and from these canneries some 53,000 cases of clams were packed. An additional 4,000 to 5,000 barrels of clams were sold for bait and still more were sold fresh in the shell. All told, an average of roughly two million pounds of clams were produced annually from Penobscot Bay flats between 1900 and 1906, employing upwards of 1,000 residents of both sexes in the harvesting and the packing plants.

Between 1928 and 1930, clam landings from the bay fell from over eight million pounds to less than two million, spurring interest in what we today call aquaculture, but which was referred to at the time as clam "propagation."

Early state efforts to propagate clams never took hold, however. By 1934, the Sea and Shore Fisheries commissioner's report to the Legislature was a voice crying in the wilderness: "We have literally hundreds of thousands of acres of clam flats. These great fields are especially suitable for clams and yet they are seriously depleted due to excessive digging without measures for conservation and propagation. Sections where clams were abundant are now practically barren. The marine arming of clams is a proven and practical operation. At a comparatively small cost per acre vast beds could be cultivated and planted to yield from $450 to $750 an acre each year. We have an opportunity to build up an industry that would rival the Aroostook County potato crop or Washington County blueberry fields. Work would be given to hundreds of persons and the natural wealth of the state greatly increased."

In 1935, the shortage of clams from over-digging and the harvesting of small clams led the Legislature to prohibit the sale of clams smaller than two inches. In November, 1937, the Deer Isle *Messenger* reported that the local clam shortage was so serious that factories were only able to work a few hours per week.

By 1948, the closure of clam flats due to pollution was sufficiently widespread to convince the Legislature to appropriate $25,000 for a "clam cleansing" plant, but it was never built because a suitable location could not be found. In 1959, clam harvests in Penobscot Bay, as well as along the entire coast of Maine, reached an all-time low. Department biologists blamed green crabs, which feed on young seed clams, for the near-collapse of clam populations along the coast. In 1963, the Legislature turned over the management of clam flats to towns with approved clam conservation programs. Landings in Penobscot Bay increased during the 1970s and early 1980s, but by the early 1990s they had declined again.

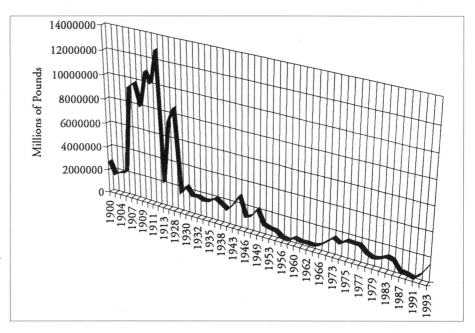

Figure 1: Clams landed in Penobscot Bay from 1900 to 1993 (Chart by Wendy Norden)

An article from the Stonington *Island Ad-Vantages* in 1972 suggests some of the difficulties of local clam management. A survey of clam flats in Deer Isle revealed "an alarming absence of seed and small clams," the newspaper reported. Selectmen and members of the town's clam commission held a public meeting to inform citizens of the seriousness of the situation with the idea of passing a clam ordinance. According to the newspaper, "Other than the selectmen and commission members, a total of eight community members appeared. A representative of the Department of Marine Resources was invited but did not appear. The selectmen accepted defeat and no ordinance was enacted."

Today over half of Penobscot Bay's clam flats are closed due to pollution or because there isn't verifiable water quality data showing they are free of bacterial contamination. Recently volunteer groups have begun collecting data to reopen closed flats, and a clam hatchery in eastern Maine has begun to supply seed clams and expertise. Nevertheless, the history of the clam fishery in Penobscot Bay represents a serious and prolonged marine resource management failure.

Lobstering

The accompanying graph of a century's worth of lobster landings from Penobscot Bay frames a number of important periods. During the five years between 1908 and 1912, Penobscot Bay landings hovered between seven and nine million pounds, followed by a nearly catastrophic decline in 1913 for unknown reasons.

Apart from the 1913 harvest, these figures do not show any dramatic effects caused by the 1907

Lobstering under sail, late 1800s (Frank Claes collection)

increase in the minimum size of lobsters that could be taken. (The original minimum had been established in 1874.) According to many contemporary reports, the 1907 law was ignored by Penobscot Bay lobstermen for several years after its passage. In his biennial report to the Legislature for 1913-14, the commissioner of Sea and Shore Fisheries complained about the difficulties of enforcing the law: "One of the most detrimental practices known to the industry is the housing of short lobsters in blinds or sunken hides, to be sold to smacks coming from nearby States, where the law allows a shorter measure than in our State. It is also impossible to check this practice as the fishermen who have these lobsters in hides carry on this traffic with smacks when anchored beyond State jurisdiction, in face of all opposition."

The collapse of lobster landings in 1913, when fewer than two million pounds were harvested from the bay, is mirrored by a similar disastrous decline in the local herring fishery. Bait was scarce and expensive, which may have exacerbated the decline in lobster landings.

For most of the 1930s, lobster landings were lower than at any other time before or since. The low landings occurred during the Depression, and it is worth asking if this was the result of lack of customers for a luxury seafood, but such an explanation can't account for the fact that the low landings began as early as 1928 and lasted through the early 1940s. In the year between July 1, 1934 and June 30, 1935, less than 1.7 million pounds were landed from Penobscot Bay, less than a third of the annual harvests of earlier decades. For families already stressed by the collapse of the national economy, this must have represented a severe hardship.

From the mid 1940s until the 1980s, lobster landings in Penobscot Bay varied less than 10 percent from the eight-million-pound level. During the same period there was a substantial increase in fishing effort — a testament to the effectiveness of the various conservation measures that lobstermen had imposed on themselves, such as marking ("V-notching") females with eggs and adding escape vents to lobster traps.

In 1993, the most recent year for which we have complete data, Penobscot Bay landings exceeded 12 million pounds for the first time since records had been collected. Landings increased to over 13 million pounds in 1994 (not shown) and exceeded 12 million pounds again in 1995, representing approximately $32.4 million. Landings have increased all along the coast of Maine, but Penobscot Bay has been especially fortunate; today almost 40 percent of the lobsters landed in Maine are caught here.

According to biologist Bob Steneck, the steady increase in lobster landings over the past five to seven years represents "a real expansion of the population." Furthermore, "the vital signs look

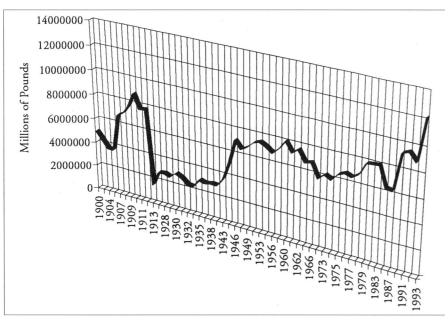

Figure 2: Lobster landed in Penobscot Bay from 1900 to 1993 (Chart by Wendy Norden)

ood," Steneck says. "There are lots of small lobsters in the water and the broodstock appears to be ealthy."

Scallops

Of all the species of shellfish harvested from Penobscot Bay, less is known about the basic life ycle and biology of the sea scallop populations than any other commercially valuable species. This gnorance is particularly unfortunate: in the past two decades, sea scallops have become, on a per-ound basis, the most valuable wild species harvested in the bay. In recent years, local fishermen ave been able to sell their catches for between $6 and $7 per pound for shucked meats. (See hart.)

The scallop fishery in Penobscot Bay got started shortly after 1900, when gasoline-powered ngines made it possible to tow a drag over scallop grounds. In his 1908 eport, the commissioner of Sea and Shore Fisheries described the "advent f the motor boat for dragging and the motor engine and drum for hoist-ng the dredge." Prior to these developments, "the scallop fishery was not rosecuted in Maine on account of the great depth of the water in which hey are taken." The 1908 report went on to describe in some detail the Knox County scallop fishery, which comprises most of Penobscot Bay. "In December there were 57 power boats, two men to a boat, averaging 30 gal-ons [of scallops] per boat, with an average market value of 90 cents per allon. It is believed that a close time should be enacted for the waters of Penobscot Bay in Knox County, this close time to cover the summer months, say from April to November, which is the period when the fish as the least food value and the smallest market value. I am informed that callop fishermen are preparing a petition to the legislature asking for a lose time and I recommend a law be enacted." A law was enacted the fol-owing year, and the closed season from April through November is still the rimary strategy for managing scallops.

Scallop landings in Penobscot Bay have fluctuated dramatically hroughout much of this century. Between 1909 and 1912, an essentially irgin population of scallops in Penobscot Bay was harvested, with local ishermen taking between 12 and 14 million pounds, a level not reached efore or since.

By 1916, the commissioner's report describes the increased depth at vhich scallop draggers were working — from 10 fathoms at the turn of the entury to as much as 50 fathoms by 1915. Except for a brief mention of tudies showing a high mortality rate for scallops in west Penobscot Bay some unknown disease had afflicted them), throughout much of the 930s Penobscot Bay scallop landings fluctuated between the comparative-y healthy levels of four to six million pounds.

Landings in excess of five million pounds occurred in 1956, and again in 1975, when a large percentage of the harvest for Penobscot Bay was concentrated in the area at the northern tip of slesboro. In December alone, it's estimated that more than a million pounds of scallop meats were

Figure 3: Scallops landed in Penobscot Bay from 1900 to 1993

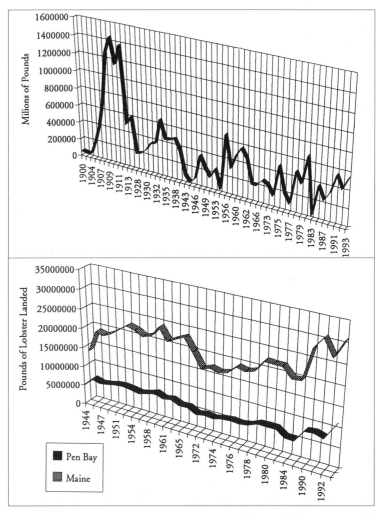

Figure 4: Percentage of lobsters from Penobscot Bay vs. state from 1944 to 1993 (Charts by Wendy Norden)

taken out of this small portion of the bay. Perhaps predictably, the harvests for 1976 and 1977 were a fraction of 1975, which was clearly a banner year. Populations rebounded by 1981 and 1982, followed by the lowest harvests in half a century in 1983, when only 41,000 pounds were landed. Harvests of scallops for the early 1990s have rebounded to between four and five million pounds, coinciding with a steep increase in prices and bringing Penobscot Bay winter fishermen a huge winter income of between $25 and $30 million, second only to lobsters in value.

It appears that scallop harvests along most of the remainder of the Maine coast are steadier than those in Penobscot Bay itself. Indeed, in those years which scallop landings are high in Penobscot Bay, upwards of 70 percent of the total statewide landings are harvested here. When a big population of scallops develops in Penobscot Bay, in other words, it is large enough to overshadow landings from the rest of the coast.

Herring

No other species so readily illustrates the immense productivity of the inshore waters of the Gulf of Maine as the herring. This fish has long been a mainstay of local firms producing canned sardines, smoked herring and pearl essence, as well as the chief bait fish for the lobster, groundfish and, recently, the salmon aquaculture industries. Ecologically speaking, herring is also the chief food fish for cod, haddock, pollock, silver hake and Atlantic bluefin tuna; the preferred food for finback and humpback whales as well as porpoises and seals. To call herring the ecological linchpin for the Gulf of Maine food web would not be an exaggeration.

For most of this century, herring have been managed primarily by a series of fishing closures during their spawning season, which progresses from the eastern sections of Maine and New Brunswick in June and July to the mid-Maine coast in August and September, and to the western part of the Gulf of Maine by October.

An 1898 report of the U.S. Commission on Fish and Fisheries by H. F. Moore provides the first comprehensive description of the spawning grounds of herring along the Maine coast. "Until about 1880 spawning herring were unknown at Matinicus Island," Moore wrote, "but now they come regularly about September 1 and remain for three or four weeks. No herring are known to spawn at Monhegan Island, but on the opposite shore in Penobscot Bay they arrive in September and remain until the end of October, although it is probable that a few are spawning during the latter part of their stay." A century later, we still do not know a great deal more about the location of herring spawning grounds in Penobscot Bay, except that the waters at the outer edge of the bay surrounding Matinicus, Criehaven, Seal and Wooden Ball Islands are significant. According to state biologist Richard Langton, Penobscot Bay is thought to be an important over-wintering ground for juvenile herring.

Decimated by foreign fishing 20 years ago, populations of herring have rebounded. (Christopher Ayres)

Landings data for herring from Penobscot Bay during this century (using extrapolated numbers for 1928-39) reveal large fluctuations that fisheries biologists assume mirror the uncertainties of recruitment during any given year. As mentioned earlier, the lowest landings of herring during the 20th century occurred in 1913. During the period between 1943 and 1993, herring landings in Penobscot Bay have fluctuated between 25 and 50 million pounds. (see Fig. 5) Since the early 1970s, herring landed in Penobscot Bay have generally comprised half or more of the statewide landings.

The domestic demand for canned herring has declined during the last several decades. A great deal of the Penobscot Bay herring is used to supply the lobster industry. A smaller percentage is canned for food, mostly for export.

Contrary to what many people believe, the canning of herring on the Maine coast is still an important industry. Although the herring cannery in Stonington had closed down by the early 1980s when Port Clyde Foods Company was sold, canneries in Rockland and Belfast still pack tens of thousands of cases per year.

Populations of herring on Georges Bank, decimated by foreign fishing 20 years ago, have rebounded. The National Marine Fisheries Service has been encouraging displaced groundfishing boats to "rig over" for midwater herring trawling, and has authorized sales of Gulf of Maine herring to international joint ventures. But this policy has led to a sharp debate over how separate the local spawning stocks are in places such as Penobscot Bay. There may indeed be a large herring biomass on Georges Bank, but if Gulf of Maine stocks are separate and distinct from offshore stocks (as many fisheries biologists now believe), allowing increased fishing pressure inshore could have negative effects on local stocks such as those in Penobscot Bay.

Figure 5: Herring landed in Penobscot Bay from 1900 to 1993 (Chart by Wendy Norden)

River fisheries: salmon, shad, smelt and alewives

Perhaps no species have suffered more intractable declines than those that spend their lives at sea but return shoreward to spawn in fresh water. Collectively referred to as "anadromous" fish from the Greek phrase meaning "up-running," these species were the mainstay of early colonists as well as the Native Americans who had been living in the Penobscot region for millennia.

The reasons for the decline were no secret even as they were occurring: the power of falling water over rapids was more valuable as an economic engine for growth in the 19th and 20th centuries than the potential catch of salmon, shad, smelt and alewives, and these species were sacrificed to the exigencies of industrial development of the Penobscot River.

The commissioner's report of 1907 contains the following reference to the salmon fishery: "The catch has been decreasing from year to year until it yields but a very small portion of its former return... The explanation of the present failure of this industry [is] that the fish are unable now, except in a few localities, to reach the spawning beds in fresh water and that the pollution of our rivers by refuse from mills has practically driven them away. In this respect, the same condition exists as in the alewife fishery: a failure, which seems almost criminal, to provide suitable fishways whereby salmon can reach the spawning beds."

The effect of sawmill waste on alewives, a fresh water spawning herring which once appeared in stupendous numbers in the Penobscot River, was described in stark terms in the report. "A well defined cause for the gradual failure of this industry is the pollution of our fresh waters through chemicals and waters from our mills, especially from our sawmills, which gradually raises the bed of the stream and fills up pools below the dams, where the fish bunch-up before taking the fishways...."

Dipping for alewife in Warren, Maine, in 1870 (Frank Claes collection)

Relatively few residents of the region recognize that shad once made huge runs up the Penobscot River. The shad fishery was still operating at the time of the Commissioner's 1907 report, though "gradually diminishing in numbers until at the present time the catch is very small. This year large schools of shad have been found ten to twenty miles off our coast and many large catches have been made by seiners ... which furnish another reason why suitable provision should be made to allow them to reach their natural spawning beds." The problem, in the commissioner's view, was that "private interests in dams and water privileges are too often considered, where beyond a trifling expense, no harm could possibly be done if proper ways and course are provided."

Two decades later, the anadromous fishery had deteriorated even further. The commissioner's report for 1935 states that "the shad catch in 1902 was 731,000 pounds and in 1935 it was much less than 100,000. This species is rapidly growing extinct. Our salmon are thinning out and are now only obtainable in a few streams. The smelts are growing scarcer. We would like to see greater cooperation of mill owners in eliminating pollution from our rivers. We would also like to see several streams stocked with salmon and shad fry."

A salmon hatchery was established in Orland in the late 1930s in an attempt to restock the Penobscot River, but it was not until the 1970s, with the birth of the environmental movement, that the cleanup of the river began in earnest. Since then, some dams have been removed and new fishways have been established. But the results of all these well-meaning efforts are still disappointing.

Groundfish

On Vinalhaven in 1903, reports historian Sydney Winslow, "the Vinalhaven Fish Co. had the largest amount of business of any year up to that time, its organization having handled between seven and eight million pounds. It had become the largest fish curing plant in the State of Maine and one of the largest in the country."

The report of the commissioner of Sea and Shore Fisheries for the same year, however, complains that the "salt fishery has generally been most unprofitable and discouraging to owners and fishermen alike." In contrast, the commissioner writes, "the vessels which have been in the business of bringing in their fares fresh and preserved on ice, popularly known as 'shack' fishermen, have been successful and made good profits." Twelve million pounds of groundfish were landed in Penobscot Bay ports in 1903, by approximately 400 fishermen.

A few years later (1907-1908) the commissioner reported with evident satisfaction that "It has not been necessary for the State to pass any protective laws in reference to these deep-sea fish. The industry has heretofore taken care of itself." The report does describe, however, one effort to limit fishing pressure: "There is at present a special law prohibiting netting for codfish at the mouth of the Sheepscot River. The purpose of the law is to prevent the destruction of female cod, who school in large numbers going up the Sheepscot River to the spawning beds. For some unknown reasons this locality seems to be the only known point where large number of cod are collected at one time for this purpose." Apparently, other inshore spawning grounds had not yet been discovered by fishermen. A few years later, however, the commissioner's report suggests this situation was beginning to change, that "the industry promises to increase from year to year, as new grounds are being discovered all along the Maine coast."

In 1918, even though the fishery was "in a flourishing condition," the commissioner asked that the industry and Legislature "not disregard the urgent need of intelligent restrictions [for] the protection of cod in the spawning season." Dismissing the opinion of Professor Andrew Agassiz of Harvard University, who wrote that cod spawned in August, Maine's commissioner pointed out that "it is a well established fact that during the spring months that large cod heavy with spawn seek the bays and rivers on the coast of Maine to spawn, at which time the gillnet fishermen capture them in large numbers."

By 1930, there were clear signs that the fleet had grown too large in relation to the capacity of the stocks. In 1934, the commissioner reports "that most species of groundfish are growing scarcer in our bays, harbors and inlets is an established fact." His recommendation to the Legislature, however, was to exhort Maine's fishing industry to "get on the bandwagon" and emulate other states where "the fisheries are caught in a new tide of optimism that has expressed itself in a wave of vessel building, vessel modernization and replacement, plant construction and modernization and inspired merchandising" — in other words, gear up and go further offshore to find the concentrations of fish sufficient to supply shoreside plants. An accomplished politician, the commissioner noted that the otter trawl, a blessing to the industry because of its efficiency, is a necessary form of harvesting, but under the present form of operation causes the waste of hundreds of thousands of pounds of small, unmarketable fish. We believe that the adoption of a regulation allowing no boats to use a mesh of less than 4 3/4 inches in otter trawling in Maine waters is worthy of consideration." The first regulations on mesh size in Maine waters was not adopted until the 1960s.

The real remedy for declining groundfish stocks, the commissioner concluded in his 1934 report, was to be found in "closing certain inshore spawning grounds during the spawning season to all fishing." A decade and a half later, the commissioner's report mentions that "groundfish stocks have been depleted. To begin the process of determining how to prevent further depletion, spawning grounds were surveyed." However, no further detail is supplied and no records exist of where such spawning grounds were located.

For most of the period between 1930 and 1980, groundfish landings in ports around the bay

(Christopher Ayres)

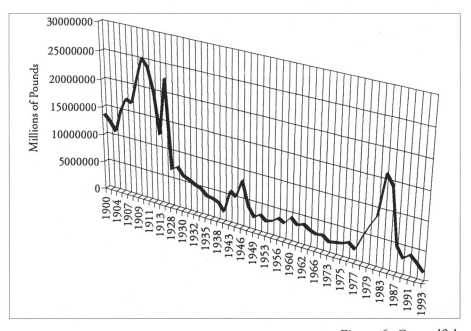

Figure 6: Groundfish landed in Penobscot Bay from 1900 to 1993 (Chart by Wendy Norden)

Fish await processing at the Vinalhaven glue factory in the 1920s. (Frank Claes collection)

hovered around two million pounds. This was also the period in which the fleet was composed either of beam trawlers under 60 feet or even smaller gillnet boats, both of which appear to have been harvesting the remnants of the spawning runs that had once come far up into the bay in the spring. These boats targeted other stocks of groundfish as well.

The last chapter of the long and sorry history of the Penobscot Bay ground-fishery began to unfold in the 1980s. Having chased foreign boats out of American territorial waters (newly defined under the Magnuson Act in 1977 as the zone within 200 miles of the United States coastline) Maine followed the lead of other New England fishing states and rapidly increased the size and efficiency of its fleet. The wave of modernization that the Commissioner had called for 50 years earlier was initiated with a vengeance. Large stern trawlers with larger nets, heavier cables and winches, larger rolling gear (to drag rough bottom) and an explosion of electronic technology transformed the industry almost overnight. The spike in landings that occurred in during the late 1980s and early 1990s in Penobscot Bay ports mirrored those throughout New England. For the past few years, groundfish landings around Penobscot Bay have averaged under two million pounds, contributing approximately $2 million dollars to the pocketbooks of local fishermen.

Spawning grounds of cod and haddock in Penobscot Bay

A more detailed account of the collapse of Penobscot Bay cod and haddock populations has been documented recently, through interviews with older fishermen. Piecing together this picture is part of a larger project to test the feasibility of restocking local spawning grounds with hatchery-raised young fish. It appears that some of the most significant spawning areas anywhere on the Maine coast are associated with deep water channels that run far up into the inner reaches of east and west Penobscot Bay over sand and gravel bottoms to Sandy Point in Stockton Springs near the mouth of the Penobscot River. (See map on opposite page.)

We have also tried to calculate the value of the historic groundfish resources from Penobscot Bay, based on historic landings from the period before such stocks went extinct locally.

While much has been written about the epic migrations of cod, such travel patterns do not reflect the behavior and character of local stocks. Many of the cod and haddock that once spawned in Penobscot Bay appear to have stayed in the general area throughout the year. An unknown number may have migrated from the area, but a great many simply changed their depth in response to seasonal changes in temperature or in pursuit of food.

Cod and haddock were abundant at a number of locations in the deeper channels and basins of both eastern and western Penobscot Bay, where they were caught for much of the year. In the first half of this century, fishermen rarely had to venture far to find them.

The former spawning areas of Penobscot Bay are so extensive that they increase the total known area of spawning grounds within the Gulf of Maine by nearly one third. The places where fishermen used to find "ripe" cod and haddock during spawning season encompassed more than 125 square miles of the bay. The magnitude of such a contribution to the fishery can only be imagined. Its loss is obvious.

The schools of cod and haddock that formerly congregated in Penobscot Bay every spring spawned in its numerous deep channels and depressions. Many of the spawning locations were basins and gullies with bottoms of mud and with sand or gravel located along the sides and edges.

These sites are also located in areas with complex tidal patterns that include gyres and eddies. Such currents tend to trap or entrain eggs and larval fish for longer periods of time than would otherwise be likely. Because of that, greater numbers of cod and haddock were probably allowed to reach the nursery areas. It may also be that the eddies distribute sediment in such a way that the proper-sized particles are there for young fish to use for shelter. Whatever the contribution, these tidal gyres may have played a key role in the productivity of Penobscot Bay groundfish.

The cod and haddock fishery

In west Penobscot Bay, boats and vessels would first encounter cod and haddock in the area between Metinic and Monroe Island in March. By early April, fish would arrive at the southern end of Islesboro. Soon afterward,

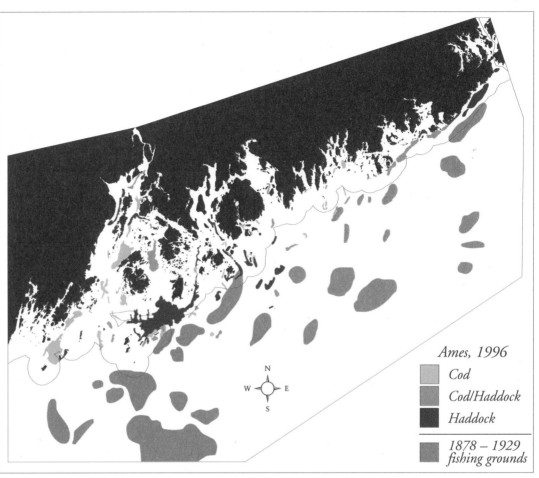

Ames, 1996

Cod

Cod/Haddock

Haddock

1878 – 1929 fishing grounds

Figure 7: Through extensive interviews with fishermen, it is possible to map the historical inshore spawning grounds for cod and haddock. This illustration also shows the larger coastal fishing grounds identified by G.B. Goode in the 1870s and W.H. Rich in the 1920s. Note that the historic cod and haddock fishing grounds offshore were separated from inshore spawning grounds 25 – 50 miles away.

schools of cod and haddock would appear off Lincolnville Beach and gradually continue northward until late May, when they reached the Castine-Stockton Springs area, the location of Penobscot Bay's northern-most spawning ground for cod and haddock. While larger vessels also fished these grounds, much of the catch was landed by smaller boats hailing from towns bordering the bay. Fishermen from Camden, Lincolnville Beach, North Haven, etc., sold their catch to smacks which then transported it to factories down the bay.

East Penobscot Bay offered comparable fishing. The grounds bordering Deer Isle and Little Deer Isle, Cape Rosier and Castine teemed with cod and haddock as the schools moved toward their spawning grounds.

Spawning grounds literally surrounded Vinalhaven and during the spring large numbers of boats and vessels arrived to fish them. Andrew Bennett, lighthouse keeper on Saddleback Light from 1915 to 1925, reported over 100 sails during the day, most of them belonging to cod fishermen.

Unfortunately, this wonderful circumstance did not last. Several calamitous events drastically reduced the fisheries of the bay. Some of the causes of these declines have been identified by fishermen, but it is not presently known whether there were other contributing reasons.

In 1935, fishermen reported that no cod or haddock were found above a line extending from Rockland to the Fox Island Thoroughfare and Saddleback Light, including Eggemoggin Reach. Fishermen insisted that it coincided with pollution from paper mills upriver. Virtually no commer-

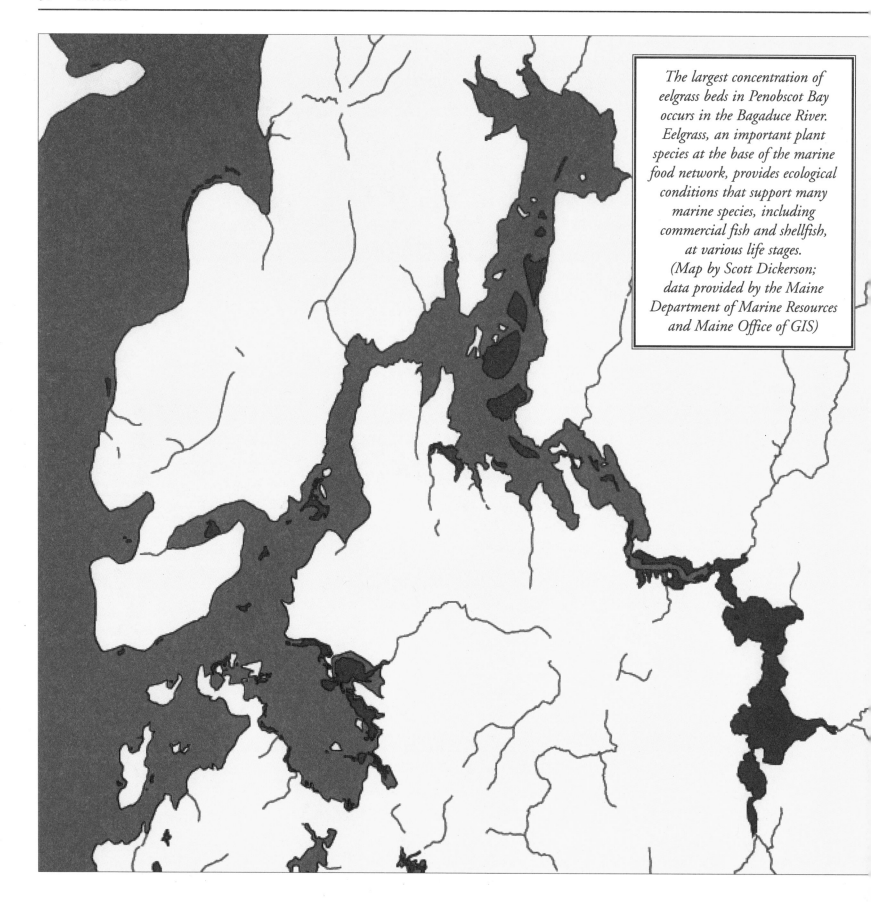

The largest concentration of eelgrass beds in Penobscot Bay occurs in the Bagaduce River. Eelgrass, an important plant species at the base of the marine food network, provides ecological conditions that support many marine species, including commercial fish and shellfish, at various life stages. (Map by Scott Dickerson; data provided by the Maine Department of Marine Resources and Maine Office of GIS)

cial groundfishing has occurred in the area since.

For a few years after 1936, fishing activity continued farther down the bay, centering in the area east of Monroe Island in the deep water, Perry's Ledge and the White Island grounds. This fishery was pursued initially by local fishermen using small boats (between 40' and 50') rigged with either tub trawls or the newly developed otter trawl.

Otter trawling proved so successful that fishermen quickly upgraded to larger vessels. By the late 1940s, however, the western bay was no longer producing commercial quantities of cod and haddock. During the 1950s, the eastern bay followed suit.

As late as the 1960s, there were still occasional, infrequent trips of cod and haddock caught inside Seal Island. But by the 1970s, the combined effects of dragging and the introduction of modern gillnetting had wiped out even these last remaining vestiges. Today, there is virtually no commercial fishing for cod of haddock anywhere inside of Jeffries Bank, 30 miles south of Vinalhaven.

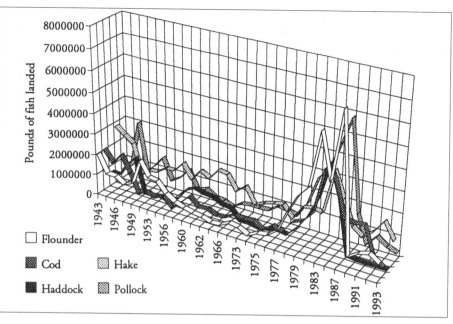

Figure 8: Groundfish species landed in Penobscot Bay from 1943 to 1993 (Chart by Wendy Norden)

The local stocks of groundfish in the Penobscot Bay area were lost piecemeal. Perhaps this fate could have been avoided if the bay's population of cod and haddock had been managed as a local stock segment, needing some protection during critical points in its life cycle; and if the biological communities the fish depended on for survival had also been protected.

New fisheries

Shrimp

The commissioner's report for 1934 describes the Department of Sea and Shore Fisheries' interest in developing a shrimp fishery in the Gulf of Maine. "Experimentation by the U.S. Bureau of Fisheries and the Department have demonstrated that there are many prolific shrimp beds in the Gulf of Maine," the Commissioner reported. "The shrimp taken are of marketable size and quality. With funds to do so, the Department would take the lead in the development of the shrimp industry."

Such efforts to identify the shrimp resource resulted in the gradual development of a small-mesh trawl fishery for shrimp in the 1940s and 1950s. Shrimp practically disappeared off the Maine coast in the mid 1950s, apparently in response to a warming of Gulf of Maine waters, but they returned in the 1960s as winter water temperatures again declined. Since 1973, Gulf of Maine shrimp have been managed by an agreement among Maine, Massachusetts and New Hampshire that regulates the mesh size of the nets and restricts the season. Since the late 1970s, when Japanese buyers began buying shrimp from local boats, the prices and the harvests have generally increased.

A troublesome problem associated with shrimping has been the large number of juvenile groundfish that were towed up by shrimp boats. A new requirement that shrimp boats be equipped with a so-called "Nordmore grate," a device developed in Norway that allows fish to escape, appears to have transformed shrimping into a "clean" fishery.

Although the year-to-year fluctuations of this species are still extremely variable – bouncing between 186,000 pounds in 1993 and 1.3 million pounds in 1995 – shrimp are a valuable winter

ishery for the small boats on the bay.

Mussels

A small volume of mussels had been harvested in Maine for decades, but no large-scale fishery for this species developed until the early 1980s when the Great Eastern Mussel Company established a processing plant in St. George. Since that time, a significant domestic mussel market has emerged. Mussel landings in Penobscot Bay today contribute between $350,000 to $500,000 to bay fishermen. Some 50 full- and part-time people are employed at the Great Eastern Mussel plant.

Urchins

The reproductive organs of sea urchins, prized in sushi bars, are associated with religious and cultural celebrations throughout Japan, which is the world's leading importer of urchins. In 1989, the Japanese taste for sea urchin roe began to influence Penobscot Bay fishermen's annual fishing strategies. Simply by hiring a diver and making a small investment in totes for boxing the spiny creatures at sea, virtually any boat owner could get into the "virgin" sea urchin fishery. Called "whore's eggs" for decades by lobstermen, who despised the creatures, which clog lobster traps and eat bait, the development of an export market for an abundant but un-utilized species is the most compelling example of the globalization of valuable marine resources in the 1990s.

By 1991, when 2.5 million pounds were harvested from Penobscot Bay waters, urchins had become a million-dollar fishery. Since that time, urchin harvests from Penobscot Bay have quintupled, and the average price received by fishermen has more than doubled. In 1995, urchins represented a $10-million fishery.

The Department of Marine Resources has run hard trying to catch up with this explosion. The coast has been divided into two management zones, there is a moratorium on new urchin licenses, and the harvesting season has been shortened at both ends. Nevertheless, in a clear sign of overfishing, urchin landings declined for the first time statewide in 1995. The 1995 harvest from Penobscot Bay also declined, but less than along other parts of the coast.

Urchins feed on kelps and appear to favor high-energy subtidal environments, suggesting that Penobscot Bay's abundance of windward island shores and exposed coastline provide ideal habitat. Surcharges on urchin harvesting, buying and processing licenses have recently yielded more than $625,000, which will be used to study the urchin's reproductive biology, larval settlement and growth rates.

Elvers

This newest fishery in Penobscot Bay appeared when the price Japanese buyers were willing to pay for tiny elvers reached the astronomical figure of $350 per pound in 1994. Suddenly another "gold rush" mentality was in progress as the Department of Marine Resources again struggled to develop regulations for a fishery that no one had ever heard of, and for which biological information is nearly non-existent. Even figures documenting landings are hard to come by, but it appears that elvers will be (if they are not already) a new million-dollar fishery for Penobscot Bay.

Elvers are baby eels, almost transparent in color, which are caught with bag-shaped fyke nets

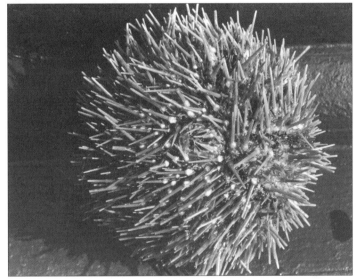

Urchin (Christopher Ayres)

Opposite page: This aerial photograph, taken at low tide in October of 1992, shows the rich zonation of intertidal and subtidal vegetation in Gilkeys Harbor, Islesboro. The darkest bands at the mouths of the coves are eelgrass beds, which remain submerged even at low tide. The rocky peninsula heads are covered with rockweed species, showing as yellow-brown. The gray-brown areas above the low-tide line are intertidal mud-flats. (Aerial photography by James W. Sewall Company, courtesy of Maine Department of Transportation)

Taking fish out of a weir, late 1800s (Frank Claes collection)

deployed at the mouths of fresh water streams. One could think of the life cycle of eels as the opposite of salmon and other anadromous fish, since eels spend their adult lives in fresh water lakes, ponds and rivers and then swim out to sea — all the way to the Sargasso Sea south of Bermuda — to spawn. The young larvae of eels drift for some months a sea before they develop the means to swim, at which time they head back to the streams where their parents spent their lives. How these tiny creatures navigate for thousands of miles and return to specific streams i part of a mystery that includes virtually all other aspects of eel biology.

Goose Creek, the tiny stream at the head of Rockport Harbor, first became choked with fyke nets in 1994. For millennia, tiny "glass" eels had been making their unfathomable journey up Goose Creek, headed for their fresh water habitats. During the past three springs, hundreds of thousands of elvers have been harvested before they reached their fresh water haunts. And because elvers are believed to live, on average, seven to ten years in fresh water before transforming themselves back into a marine species capable of tolerating salt water, we won't know what effects these harvests have on the Goose Creek population for another seven to 10 years. The same could be said of populations on several hundred other small creeks and streams in the Penobscot drainage.

The failure to frame the management of the eel harvest in its ecological context is another example of the shortcomings of marine resource policy. As elvers are ascending hundreds of streams in the Penobscot watershed on rising night tides, so are other species — smelt, alewives and brown trout. All are now unselectively caught in the fine mesh of fyke nets that line the channels of streams that have never seen such harvesting pressure. The Legislature struggled to develop regulations to keep mid-channel areas clear of nets to allow some elvers room to pass upstream, but it allowed the unintended effects of this new fishery on other species to go largely unnoticed.

Aquaculture

Farm-raised Atlantic salmon has recently become a $60-million industry elsewhere on the coast, mostly in Washington County. In Penobscot Bay a few mussel leases exist; a few town and volunteer groups are trying to cultivate clams on intertidal flats; and an experimental farm has recently been established to produce nori, a red seaweed used when dried to wrap rice and raw fish in Japanese sushi bars. But this record of attempts to culture species in Penobscot Bay has repeatedly failed to spark much interest among fishermen. At worst, it has produced virulent opposition from lobster fishermen and summer people, many of whom believed such farms would spread pollution throughout the marine environment. To say that the jury is still out on whether the cultivation of marine species has a future in Penobscot Bay is an understatement.

Ecological fisheries management

The fisheries of Penobscot Bay have astonishing economic importance. In 1995, the value of the marine resources harvested from the bay was nearly $75 million. Almost 90 percent of this value is attributable to just three shellfish species — lobster, scallop and urchin. And each of these species raises important questions for which answers are not readily at hand.

Despite our failure to manage successfully some potentially important marine resources — clam, salmon and groundfish stocks, for example — the inherent productivity and diversity of the bay have allowed fishermen to overcome resource declines time and again during the last half century. Huge fisheries for individual species have come and gone and sometimes come back again.

The biological diversity of its marine environments is the bay's most valuable asset. Yet we are woefully ignorant of some of the basic processes that drive this astonishing biodiversity: how do nutrient-rich, cold-water currents circulate through the bay, for example? Where do they come from? What ecological role do cobble and submerged aquatic habitats play? Where are the valuable nursery grounds?

It would not be asking too much to suggest that Penobscot Bay should become an important area for concentrating research dollars, given the immense value and importance of its resources to the economy of the whole coast.

The increase in lobster landings throughout Penobscot Bay during the 1990s (almost 50 percent greater than during the 1980s) suggests a powerful ecological shift. That this increase is occurring when almost all card-carrying lobster biologists believe the resource to be substantially overfished remains an enigma. Many lobstermen account for the increase of lobsters by pointing to the absence of cod, which feed on young lobsters. But populations of spawning cod have been absent from Penobscot Bay since the late 1930s.

Many steps could be taken to improve the management of marine resources in Penobscot Bay. Cod and haddock, for example, are not going to return to the bay unless and until we close their historic spawning grounds to dragging — a suggestion first offered in 1918. We know where the important scallop beds are and that if stock enhancement is likely to pay off for any species, it is for one that fetches $6 to $7 in the marketplace.

Bob Steneck's research suggests that the truly stupendous abundance of lobsters in Penobscot Bay depends on a subtidal cobble habitat that is easy to identify. We also know that the ecology and fate of lobsters and urchins are tightly linked, and that the cobble habitat critical to lobsters is also a target for fishermen who drag for urchins. We know that urchins feed on kelp, and that as kelp beds decrease, lobster-shedding habitat decreases; we also surmise that as kelp habitat decreases, juvenile groundfish and herring habitat also decreases.

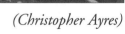

(Christopher Ayres)

The point is that marine species cannot continue to be managed on a species-by-species basis; we must develop management strategies that explicitly recognize those ecological links that we understand.

We will never be able to predict which species are going to develop a market overnight. The explosion of markets for urchins or elvers was driven by forces beyond our control, but our recent experience with them demonstrates the need to make constant (not necessarily large) investments in our understanding of marine biodiversity in a place like Penobscot Bay. For fishermen in Penobscot Bay, merely building larger vessels to exploit ever more distant resources will no longer suffice.

Improving marine resource management means managing specific habitats and harnessing the immense store of knowledge of specific bottom habitats that is collected daily by fishermen. New management structures are about to be tested by lobstermen who are in the process of setting trap limits and new management "zones" in specific areas that are tailored to ecological and historical conditions. We must continue to bring marine management and decision-making down to the local level if we are to have any hope of overcoming the boom-and-bust history of our fisheries.

Landings information was compiled by Wendy Norden.

Notes on the fisheries data used in this chapter:

Defining the region

Penobscot Bay, for the purpose of this report, was defined as all of Waldo County and Knox County, and one-third of Hancock County, because Hancock County goes beyond the boundaries of Penobscot Bay. Fishery landings data was separated by county, with the exception of the 1920s through the 1930s (see "Extrapolated numbers" below).

Collection of data

In January of 1996, landings data was collected from the Sea and Shore Fishery Reports, located at the Maine State Library in Augusta. These reports list the landings data by date and county. The fishery reports are available in this format until 1970. Post-1970 data was obtained from the Maine Department of Marine Resources (DMR).

Once all of the landings data was collected and entered into an Excel spreadsheet, further calculations were made as to the price per pound for each species. Total Maine landings and Penobscot Bay landings were compared. The percentage that Penobscot Bay landings increased total state landings was calculated as well.

This study of the fishery landings of Penobscot Bay was completed in March, 1996.

Extrapolated numbers

Fisheries landings data was not found listed by county for the 1920s and 1930s. There was, however, total landings data for the state for those years, and these numbers were extrapolated to characterize Penobscot Bay landings during the missing years.

Five years prior and five years just after the missing data points were used as the base for the extrapolation. These numbers (representing the total pounds of each species landed) were averaged over a ten-year period. The average was then applied to the total pounds of each individual species landed. The average number was used to predict what the total landings would have been for Penobscot Bay between the years of the 1920s and 1930s.

It is important to note that this number is simply a prediction of the total and does not reflect social or economic situations of those years for which extrapolated data was used.

Chapter 5: **Transportation and Energy**

By Lloyd C. Irland

"A community narrows down and grows dreadful ignorant when it is shut up to its own affairs, and gets no knowledge of the outside world except from a cheap, unprincipled newspaper. In the old days, a good part o' the best men here knew a hundred ports and something of the way folks lived in them. They saw the world for themselves, and like's not their wives and children saw it with them. They may not have had the best of knowledge to carry with 'em sight-seein', but they were some acquainted with foreign lands an' their laws, an' could see outside the battle for town clerk here in Dunnet; they got some sense o' proportion. Yes, they lived more dignified, and their houses were better within an' without. Shipping's a terrible loss to this part o' New England from a social point o' view, ma'am."

Sarah Orne Jewett, *The Country of the Pointed Firs*

As long as people and goods moved primarily by sea, midcoast Maine was close to capital for development and to markets for its goods. Maine's brigs of the 1820s could link the midcoast with the Indies, the Mediterranean and China. Its Downeasters and six-masters of later years could connect it to the coal, grain and guano trades that, in turn, stretched from the mid-Atlantic states to South America and the world.

At different times, economic life is shaped by dominant transport and energy forms. These periods overlap, of course, and seldom provide a simple scheme for interpreting a region's history, but they do help us identify important influences as they evolve and change. Interdependence is a major theme here: a region's commercial networks consist of complex economic and social linkages with other nations and regions. In this region, the links with Boston and nearby Canada are particularly strong.

The region's economy has always depended heavily on its land and water resources, and technology has been a driving force. But the region has always been on the periphery — connected to core cities by differing economic links, yet always at the edge. At the same time, it's important to remember the differences between moving people and moving goods — over most of the 19th century, people moved along the Maine coast by steamer while lumber, granite and provisions moved by schooner.

In some ways, getting around this region was easier 150 years ago. The Boston and Bangor Steamship Company was founded in 1833. In 1846, Henry David Thoreau paid three dollars for steamer passage from Boston to Bangor, a distance he puts at 250 miles in his classic account, *The North Woods*. At that time, the steamer left Boston at 5 p.m. and arrived at Bangor by the middle of

Opposite: Aboard the Vinalhaven ferry (Christopher Ayres)

the following day. Thoreau's trips to the Maine woods from Concord were taken entirely on public transportation, by rail, steamer, stage, Moosehead Lake Steamer, tramway at Northeast Carry. At the end of his trips, he could take public transit home. Traveling in this manner would not only be impossible today; it's almost unthinkable.

Sail

Midcoast shipbuilders of the 19th century were at the forefront of their industry. The clipper RED JACKET was built at Rockland in 1853. In 1885, Carleton Norwood in Rockport built the FREDERICK BILLINGS, at 2,600 tons the largest Penobscot square rigger ever built. The first six-master in the world, G. W. WELLS, was built in the Bean yard at Camden.

Launching of the LUCIA P. DOW at Rockland in 1919 (Courtesy of the Rockland Public Library)

A number of factors, all of which reinforced one another, conspired to end the days of sail. Efficient schooners could haul for competitive rates, but were more vulnerable to the weather than steamers. The opening of the Suez Canal shortened the haul to the Far East by several weeks, boosting steam because sailing ships had to be towed through the canal. In 1914, the Panama Canal opened East Coast markets to low-cost West Coast lumber and virtually ended the long Cape Horn voyages. Increasingly, sailing vessels were relegated to long hauls of low-value commodities like lumber or coal, and to coastal shipping of hay, lumber and granite.

World business was booming as the 20th century dawned: American grain exports rose 150-fold from 1855 to 1900, and the volume of world trade multiplied every decade during the same period. But other places were better suited to building and owning steamships, and the age of building and owning sailing ships, which previously had defined life on Penobscot Bay, swiftly passed away. When Thoreau visited in the 1850s, Bangor was a busy port serving cities around the world with its lumber.

"There stands the city of Bangor, fifty miles up the Penobscot," Thoreau wrote in *The Maine Woods* (1864), "at the head of navigation for vessels of the largest class, the principal lumber depot on this continent, with a population of twelve thousand, like a star on the edge of night, still hewing at the forests of which it is built, already overflowing with the luxuries and refinement of Europe, and sending its vessels to Spain, to England, and to the West Indies for its groceries, — and yet only a few axe-men have gone 'up river,' into the howling wilderness which feeds it. The bear and deer are still found within its limits; and the moose, as he swims the Penobscot, is entangled amid its shipping, and taken by foreign sailors in its harbor. Twelve miles in the rear, twelve miles of railroad, are Orono and the Indian Island, the home of the Penobscot tribe, and then commence the batteau and the canoe, and the military road; and sixty miles above, the country is virtually unmapped and unexplored, and there still waves the virgin forest of the New World." And Bangor's peak as a lumber port was still 30 years away.

Penobscot Bay's ties to the outside world changed from the original transatlantic linkages of colonial times, to the strong links to the Indies in the first half of the 18th century, to the coastal trades later on. The technology of marine shipping continued to change through the 20th century. Key improvements were the diesel engine, enabling ships to switch to more convenient fuel. Canneries, specifically, and containerization, generally, enabled the safe and economical movement of a wide variety of goods and permitted small shippers to use the regular liner services to move even small shipments from port to port. (For bulk cargoes, one still had to hire an entire ship.)

The coming of containers challenged ports to gear up for handling them or lose out. Halifax, Portsmouth, Portland and Montreal did so, and considerable Maine cargo moves overseas through these ports today. Lacking a port capable of handling containers, Penobscot Bay remained in a marginal position. A rail connection became critical; today, the ability to handle double-stacked containers brought on flatcars is a major competitive advantage for a port.

Steamship passenger service along the coast outlasted the age of sail by only a short time. Eastern Steamship Lines' service from New York to Bar Harbor ended in 1936, done in by the Depression and by the automobile. The major islands are now served by a ferry system operated by the state as part of its subsidized transportation infrastructure. The Maine State Ferry Service carried 400,000 passengers in 1994, serving Islesboro, North Haven, Vinalhaven, Swan's Island, Matinicus and Frenchboro. Ferry services also link Bar Harbor and Portland with Nova Scotia.

Railroads

The railroad shaped American life for decades, not least by steadily driving down the cost of moving people and goods. Together with other forces, this change created a nationwide market in chilled meat and fresh products, and made possible the creation of a concentrated food-processing industry, using huge plants located near the most productive farms. The effect on the Maine coast was dramatic: the centralized food-processing plants largely drove out the small, local canneries and poultry operations that had become a part of small-town life.

Like most major shifts in the nation's economy, this nationwide system had benefits as well. It enabled Mainers to enjoy fresh fruits and vegetables year-round, with-

(Christopher Ayres)

out their even thinking how remarkable this was (and is) in a place with only 143 frost-free days each year at the coast (125 at Bangor).

Railroads made possible the large-scale importation of grain that supported the Penobscot region's important poultry industry and provided feed grain for the shrinking base of dairy farms.

Overall, states like Maine that served customers by water lost an advantage. Railroads made it possible for distant mills to serve the lumber needs of the nation's vast interior, far from ports. Ironically, Maine's lumber industry had stimulated the construction of its first railroad in 1832, not as a replacement but as a supplement to water-borne commerce in Maine. The line was built to connect General Samuel Veazie's lumber mills with tidewater loading facilities to load his lumber onto schooners.

Bangor's rail connection to Saint John, New Brunswick, was completed in 1866, and the Maine Central arrived in 1881. The Bangor and Aroostook Railroad was extended into the lumber and potato country to the north in the 1890s. Maine's peak rail mileage was reached in the early 1920s.

Today, the Penobscot region is served by branch lines reaching along the coast to Rockland (the right of way is now state-owned); by the Belfast and Moosehead Lake Railroad, a former grain transporter which now carries only tourists; by the Bangor and Aroostook to Searsport, and by the Springfield Terminal (formerly Maine Central) branch serving Bucksport.

(Christopher Ayres)

Highways

Roads were primarily for local use in the 19th century, and they were, for the most part, terrible. Traveling by stage for any distance was an ordeal. The Camden Turnpike was built as early as 1802, and stage service from Boston to Bangor began in 1816. By 1825, the Bangor-to-Portland coach trip took 36 hours and cost $7.50.

The development of a modern highway system brought monumental social change. Practical road transport for goods and people depended on a whole series of other improvements: bridges to replace the ferries; all-weather construction techniques; a system of fuel and service stations. The region depended on improvements to the south such as the Carleton Bridge (1927) in Bath, and the completion of the Maine Turnpike to Portland by the late 1940s. The Waldo-Hancock Bridge across the Penobscot between Prospect and Verona was built in 1931, and the Deer Isle-Stonington bridge opened in 1939.

Completion of the highway system quickly re-oriented patterns of movement for people and goods. Autos and trucks drove out the ferry services. Islands and points that had been crossroads in he old system for moving eggs, milk, hay and fuelwood to Boston became isolated. The large inns hat stood by the ferry terminals were now a long drive down a narrow road from Route 1. (The ormer ferryman's house at the Deer Isle end of the Deer Isle-Stonington Bridge is now a bed and breakfast.) Small-scale farming and other enterprises withered as the major travel route shifted nland to the Route 1 corridor. Highways became a key element of state government policy sup-porting economic growth, and little attention was paid to businesses and lifestyles left behind or pushed aside as the system expanded.

It is a telling point that Maine's state government in 1960 spent three times as much on high-ways as it did on education. From the 1970s to the early 1990s, total vehicle miles driven in Maine doubled, generating controversy over the best methods of coping with escalating congestion at peak imes. The Interstate 95 corridor became the growth region of the state, a shift that was reflected in everything from farmland conversion to other uses, to income levels, to traffic counts. From being at the center of a busy worldwide transportation net as they had been in 1900, Penobscot Bay and much of its region were left behind. Waldo County, former ship owning center, was increasingly mentioned as Maine's poorest county.

By the early 1990s, trucks carried 80 percent of all the freight tonnage in New England (New England Governors' Conference, 1995). Planners and transportation departments saw escalating highway congestion in the future. They grappled with ways to divert some of this freight traffic to he rails and waterways, in hopes of conserving scarce highway capacity and shifting tonnage "at the margin" in terms of its cost toward more energy-efficient modes.

Air travel

By 1937, there were 11 airports in the state; the federal Works Progress Administration (WPA) eems to have been a major funding source. The nation's fascination with airplanes and air travel provided support for air mail and for federal programs to build airports and traffic control systems, ncluding much of the airport construction in Maine.

The Bangor International Airport has shown gratifying growth based on a good location and hrewd marketing; its traffic volume exceeds Portland's. At least part of this growth has resulted from the gradual improvement of containers that ship live lobsters over greater and greater dis-ances. As a result, the slumps in summer prices that used to plague the industry are more modest, and the value of the catch has continued to climb. Other local airports are busy, at least seasonally. But air travel has not become a significant influence on the region's tourism industry, which is built around automobile access.

Ports

As the center of lumbering moved west and the Panama Canal brought low-cost western lum-ber to northeast ports, vessel clearances from Bangor sputtered out. Construction of the St. Regis later Champion) paper mill at Bucksport revived movements of wood and pulp, pulpwood was driven on the Penobscot until 1953, and large loads of spruce pulpwood were cut on the islands hrough the mid 1960s. But for the past 20 years, waterborne commerce on Penobscot Bay has been dominated by imports, mostly oil and related products, and by the coastwise movement of a variety of goods.

In the late 1980s, the U.S. dollar exchange rate fell against major currencies, touching off a significant boom in U.S. exports. Cargo traffic along Maine's coast increased as well. Increases at Portland were dramatic, and Searsport participated in the growth as well. The major role played by oil in the Penobscot region's commerce leads naturally to the larger role of energy in the region's economy.

Maine state government began pursuing revitalization strategies for the Maine Coast in the 1970s, as studies were done for fish piers and cargo ports. From this process emerged a "three-port strategy" supporting cargo ports at Eastport, Searsport and Portland. This strategy has repeatedly been endorsed by the State, most recently in a comprehensive 20-year transportation plan, and has been supported by other groups, including most recently the Governor's Advisory Council on International Trade (1995).

The purpose of the three-port concept (which accompanied a less publicized effort to improve fish piers along the coast to support fishing and maintain public access to increasingly costly shore-fronts) was to provide access to modern port facilities in all portions of the state, including the under-served midcoast region.

Facilities currently existing at Searsport receive considerable use but are deteriorating and inadequate to support efficient and high volume operations. In recent years, the state has promoted a Sears Island development concept including a port with a wharf on the island, with the balance of the island preserved as open space. This proposal attracted severe regulatory scrutiny and was criticized by some for its environmental impact, its use of the island and its high cost. There was much debate over whether a mainland alternative (at nearby Mack Point) would be as effective. Wood chips were advanced as a major cargo for the proposed port, and the volume of chip exports projected made some observers nervous about effects on the forest. In early 1996, citing escalating requirements by regulatory agencies, the State

*Sears Island
(Christopher Ayres)*

dropped the Sears Island plan. What developments or repairs may be proposed at Searsport, and what the fate of the island's undeveloped land will be, are both uncertain. A proposal by Governor Angus King for the State to purchase the land was dropped when it received a cold reception in the Legislature.

The new owner of the Bangor and Aroostook, Iron Road, Inc., has discussed ideas for improving the facilities on Mack Point to build traffic on its tracks. As of mid 1996, there was no way to judge the potential or implications of this idea.

From fuelwood to coal to cheap oil

In 1880, the local economy on Penobscot Bay was relatively self-sufficient in terms of energy, relying on renewables such as wood and small-scale water power. The key mode of transport — the sailing ship — was powered by the wind, but was rapidly being overtaken by steam. (Steam-powred transport for passengers dates to the 1830s.)

In the pre-Civil War years, fuelwood was an export product for this region. Thoreau refers to wood sold in Boston from ports along the river below Bangor. Historian Edward Hutchinson Rowe notes that Belfast had 0 wood-transporting schooners "at one time." In Boston, firewood etched twice what it did in Maine. "Kilnwooders" carried 30,000 to 0,000 cords per year to fuel the lime kilns of Camden, Rockport, Rockland and Thomaston, and were supplied by coastal forests.

The woodlots of this region were far less extensive in 1880 than they re today, and were being cropped heavily for the 20 to 30 cords of wood hat the average farmhouse needed for cooking and warmth. Imports of coal and then oil took the pressure off the forests, and as farm tractors replaced horses, many acres of pasture could "go back" to brush and pines r hardwood sprouts to grow wood for the future. The oil wells of Oklahoma and Texas — and eventually the Persian Gulf — contributed greatly to saving the Penobscot region's forests.

As coal became the staple residential and industrial fuel in the New England cities, it slowly spread along the coast until it became a staple of the coastal schooner trade. Later, coal was brought in to fuel the paper mills. Schooner routes were built around routings to Newport News and other coal ports.

The replacement of wood by coal eliminated a longtime export and began the Penobscot region's 20th-century dependence on fuels imported from elsewhere. The communities of Penobscot Bay and upriver now required a vital raw material produced across the globe, often in unstable nations. Economic networks were re-woven once again. U.S. coal consumption per capita peaked around 1920, at about the same time that Maine's rail mileage did.

Today, coal provides only 1 percent of Maine's primary energy requirements. The coal piers and coal dealers with their rail sidings have gone from the waterfronts and industrial districts. Because of its waterfront location and distance from gas fields, Maine skipped the natural gas age that reached the rest of the country when gas consumption exceeded coal usage in 1960. Gas, like coal, accounts for less than 1 percent of the state's energy usage now.

(Christopher Ayres)

Discovery of huge, low-cost oil fields in East Texas and the Middle East remade the world's energy map. Oil swiftly became the fuel of choice for steamships and for industry. Availability of low-cost gasoline literally fueled the growth of the automobile industry and the tourism economy dependent upon it. State revenues from gasoline taxes financed roads and bridges. A better example of faraway (and seemingly unrelated) development affecting a region would be hard to find.

Electricity

Electricity is almost the symbol of the modern industrial age. The impact of electric power on the quality of everyday life is largely forgotten until the occasional power outage reminds us of how we depend on it for our daily light, cooking and water supply. Growth in electricity consumption has been strong, and electricity production now accounts for 37 percent of the nation's primary fuel usage (SAUS, p. 575), up from 19 percent in 1960. Electricity is a way to move and to use energy, but it must be produced from some primary source. Maine's leading sources of electricity are nuclear (32 percent), wood (25 percent), hydro (22 percent), oil (9 percent) and imports (6 percent).

Electricity is a flexible, adaptable form of energy. Today the Penobscot region depends on it, importing electricity as a basic energy form for its homes, industry and commerce. This has re-worked the nature of the region's trade links once again, and enhanced the ability of a small number of corporations to control the economy, in contrast to the far more decentralized system in place when the region depended on wood.

Transportation and energy links

Transportation and energy are strongly linked in the history of this region. Transportation accounts for 30 percent of the end-use energy used in Maine. Energy products (formerly coal, now chiefly petroleum) have long been a major cargo for the region's shipping industry and its ports. Changes in transport technology and energy sources have rebuilt the bay's commercial, social and cultural networks several times since 1880. Finally, both energy and transportation depend on costly infrastructure improvements — for example, the Maine Turnpike, pipelines, and powerline interconnections – funded and approved in distant places.

Self-sufficiency

Measured in terms of basic materials, energy, capital and local jobs, the Penobscot region has a low to moderate level of economic self-sufficiency. Levels of self-sufficiency are largely imposed by geography, but can be affected by consumer, business and governmental choices at the margins. Major policy questions about the region's future will be debated in that context.

Maine's midcoast is likely to remain a region dependent on imported energy, and especially dependent on water movements of its key petroleum fuels, and on truck movements of its goods. Its tourism industry is now served almost completely by automobile. This will make the area more sensitive to rising costs of energy, espe-

Brewer shipwrights, late 1800s (Frank Claes collection)

cially for its lower income households. Is there more natural gas in Maine's future? If Sable Island gas is ever developed, and if other gas pipelines ever spread further into Maine, then natural gas could play a growing role in the energy mix of the state and of the Penobscot region. Gas-fired combined-cycle power plants are the emerging approach to low-cost, clean, electric generation. As more of these plants are built elsewhere in the region, their electric output will find its way into regional grids and to the shores of Penobscot Bay. An "age of gas" will arrive, though it will be invisible to the region's residents, who seem to prefer having their electricity generated someplace else. Commerce in the region's needed oil products promises to remain an important part of the waterfront activity in the area's ports for some time to come.

It seems reasonable to assume that Maine Yankee and the nuclear plant at Point Lepreau, New Brunswick, will be closed at the end of their licenses. (Maine Yankee's license expires in 2008.) When this occurs, the large nuclear component of the state's energy mix will be lost. Whether or not the market prices of oil and coal rise, clearly the appreciation of the social costs associated with heavy dependence on these fuels is increasing. A transition to heavier reliance on conservation and on renewables is inevitable. How it will be managed, and how it will affect the Penobscot region is uncertain. But an area with limited production capacity of its own, in a state heavily dependent on nuclear and oil-fired electricity, will have to bear special burdens in this transition.

Evolving transportation and energy systems have shaped the economy and lifeways of the Penobscot region. As transport and commercial networks have changed, communities have sometimes experienced wrenching social changes.

At one time, energy and transportation decisions were incremental. The highway system was built one road, one bridge, at a time. Oil replaced coal, and one coal yard at a time went out of business. Shipping changed as one fleet after another scrapped its ships; one port after another turned away from its decaying waterfront or sold it to condominium developers. Today, the Penobscot region is affected by large projects that do not come in small doses. Debates about proposals to build a coal-fired power plant at Bucksport, a dam at Basin Mills, a cargo port at Sears Island are all fraught with major consequences, yet they are argued out in faraway corporate and governmental offices.

Sears Island reflects this history. Once a farm, it "went back" to brush and woods in the early 20th century. In recent decades, it has been considered and promoted as the location for an oil refinery, a nuclear power station, a coal-fired power plant. It could still become a cargo port and passive park, a housing subdivision, or a "wild" reservation. Our society is characteristically gridlocked over these decisions with their manifold implications for the region's communities, the local environment and the state. The economic interdependences will change, and new technologies will arise. But the facts of economic interdependence, resource dependence, economic self-sufficiency and peripheral geographic position will remain.

Chapter 6: Changing Patterns and Trends

By Bob Moore

Looked at over time, a region's population statistics provide a picture that is of great interest and importance to residents, educators, employers, government officials or anyone seeking a place to work, retire, set up a business, sell something or buy something or even come to the area for a summer vacation.

The Penobscot region's residents, on average, are slightly older and better educated than the population of the rest of Maine. But they are less wealthy and less mobile, and a higher percentage of them live in poverty. Averages conceal many differences among diverse communities, however, and within the region one finds stark contrasts among east, west, river and island communities.

Ancestry

People inhabiting the Penobscot region are principally of western European heritage, descended from individuals who arrived between the 17th and 19th centuries. With few exceptions, about a third of the people living in the region's towns are of English descent; a third are of Scotch-Irish origin; while the rest reflect a mix of ancestries including Swedish, Italian, and Polish, French and German. These last two nationalities account for 16 percent and 10 percent of the population, respectively.

People of French ancestry live primarily in the interior portions of Penobscot county, where early French influence was strongest at the time when Maine was divided (at the Penobscot River) between British and French jurisdictions. Today, the Penobscot region's largest contingent of residents with French ancestry inhabits the towns along the river, such as Bradley and Old Town. Most of Maine's French population, however, is of French-Canadian ancestry, having migrated to Maine in the late 19th century to work in mills.

With a few exceptions, there is scarce representation of black African, Latin, or Asian ancestry.

Fluctuating numbers

At the end of the 1860s, the prospects in Penobscot Bay appeared bright. The regional economy was booming: Bangor's lumber boom was at its height, and the populations of many of the coastal and island communities reached peaks they have never attained since.

After the boom period of the late 1860s and early 1870s, the population in the region began a declining trend that for many communities continued well into the 20th century. The decline was most severe in island towns — Penobscot Bay communities such as Criehaven, the Mussel Ridge

Opposite: Shift change at Champion International paper mill, Bucksport (Christopher Ayres)

Plantation and Eagle Island lost their entire year-round populations as the number of islands with permanent residents dropped from 300 to less than two dozen statewide.

For many towns in the region, the next upward trend would not begin until about the time of the national census of 1940. During the 70 years between 1870 and 1940, the population in the Penobscot region remained nearly stable, increasing slightly from 84,726 to 88,640.

Just as the population of the Penobscot region has fluctuated over decades, its communities swell and contract over the four seasons of the year. Ridership aboard Penobscot Bay ferries rises and falls with the seasons. In some areas, the size of the workforce changes dramatically as well. (Joanne Ciccarello)

Around 1880, a difference developed between rural and urban communities in Penobscot Bay. Cities continued to grow, albeit slowly compared to the growth during the boom years, while the decline in rural populations persisted. Between 1880 and 1940, Bangor's population nearly doubled as outlying rural communities declined.

While the Penobscot region's population increased 4 percent between 1880 and 1940, the population *without* Bangor actually decreased by 10 percent: with the exception of Rockland, Belfast, Bangor, Brewer, Orono and Verona, every community in Penobscot Bay lost population over the period 1880 to 1940.

The U.S. Census Bureau defines "urban" areas as being over 2,500 in population. Of the 39 towns around Penobscot Bay, only 12 have a population of over 2,500: Bangor, Belfast, Brewer, Bucksport, Camden, Hampden, Orono, Orrington, Rockland, Rockport, Searsport and Winterport. By most yardsticks, however, the Penobscot region today remains rural. Many of the towns surrounding urban areas are better classified as "suburban" than rural, since they act more as bedroom communities for commuters than independent village centers.

The seasonal flux

As the population of Penobscot Bay fluctuates over decades, so too does the bay community swell and contract over the four seasons of the year. Estimating the degree of seasonal flux is imprecise, since the seasonal population is highly mobile and migrates to Maine for varying lengths of stay.

Using Census Bureau reports of the number of vacation homes by town, a crude estimate of seasonal populations can be obtained by multiplying that number in each town by an average occupancy rate for such homes, according to Richard Sherwood of the Maine State Planning Office.

While the average occupancy for a year-round residence is just over two persons, Sherwood assumes a vacation house has three or four people occupying it. The usefulness of this method is limited because the Census reports "seasonal, recreational or occasional use"[1] for only 11 towns in Penobscot Bay with over 2,500 inhabitants: Bangor, Belfast, Brewer, Bucksport, Camden, Hampden, Orono, Rockland, Rockport, Searsport and Winterport. (Orrington was not included in this list despite the fact that the 1990 census reports its population as 3,309.) The total number of vacation homes for these towns was 874.

Assuming a minimum of three and a maximum of four inhabitants per vacation home, and assuming they all visit in the summer, the seasonal population of these towns expands by 2,622 to

,496 people. A look at where the seasonal dwellings are concentrated is revealing: Camden listed 314 homes for seasonal, recreational or occasional use, while the river towns combined listed fewer than 100. Bangor, with more than six times the residential population of Camden, listed 37 homes for seasonal, recreational or occasional use.

The importance of seasonal population surges in Penobscot Bay to the region's economy and infrastructure, as well as its culture and environment, is enormous. Unfortunately, there is no single reliable method to calculate the impact. Counting homes for seasonal, recreational or occasional use ignores the substantial number of transient visitors to the region. Gathering even a rough estimate of these numbers would entail tabulations of the number of beds occupied in lodging places throughout the region, the number of meals served at restaurants, changes in retail sales, and a town-by-town examination of tax assessment data to determine the number of vacation homes in smaller towns not included in the Census Bureau reports.

Many of the smallest towns in Penobscot Bay experience the most dramatic increases in summer population. For example, according to Vinalhaven town manager Susan Lessard, the summer population there "is stable at 3,000 additional people." But Vinalhaven is no Mecca for tourists - there are a few bed-and-breakfast establishments and only one hotel. "The people coming out on the ferry leave at the end of the day," Lessard said, "except the summer folk."

Determining how many people are enjoying any Penobscot Bay community during the summer will entail sorting out the transients, the longer-term summer visitors and the year-round residents.

Age

The age of the local population helps determine where and how government will allocate its time and attention, whether it be elementary schools or nursing homes. Every age group has characteristics that separate it from the others, a fact that plays a major role in how a community takes care of itself: young parents are concerned more about raising children and the school budget than senior citizens, who may be more focused on health care and cultural issues.

The U.S. Census Bureau divides population into five age categories: 0-4, 5-17, 18-44, 45-64 and 65-plus. The divisions are logically placed at stages in life in which changes typically occur. At the time of the 1990 census, the Penobscot region was, on average, slightly older than the Maine population. Combining the two youth categories into one (age 0-17), the region's **youth** comprised 23 percent of the population, compared to the state average of 25 percent. In the **young adult** category (18-44), the Penobscot region's figure was 45.2 percent compared to the state's 42.5 percent.

The proportion of Penobscot Bay residents in **middle age** (45-64) was the same as the state's (19 percent). In the **senior** category (65-plus), Penobscot Bay was close to the same as Maine (13 percent).

The boundaries that separate the east bay, west bay, river and island regions are geographically defined, but each area also has distinct population characteristics that are closely linked to the economy, culture and quality of life in Penobscot Bay. A good way of presenting a comparison of geographic regions is by age class.

Youth

The Penobscot region has a low proportion of youth (0-17) compared to the state as a

The importance of seasonal population surges in Penobscot Bay to the region's economy and infrastructure, as well as its culture and environment, is enormous. Unfortunately, there is no single reliable method to calculate the impact.

At the time of the 1990 census, 23 percent of the Penobscot region's residents were under age 18, compared with the statewide average of 25 percent. The west bay had the highest percentage in the region – a statistic with implications for local school budgets.

whole. In this age category, the west bay has the highest proportion.

High youth populations require services from their towns, and the school budget makes up the lion's share of every community's annual appropriations. Because youth are dependents, their well-being is a reflection of the ability of their parents or guardians to care for them. Their parents are normally the ones who decide where they live, go to school and often whether they will continue on to college.

These youngest members of the population do not invest in homes or cars, and are not considered eligible members of the work force. If youth represent the future, then it is not only the percentage of youth in the region, but also their welfare, that is important.

Working age

The young working age population (18-44) is the largest in number. These residents are forming families, raising children and starting jobs. They are net borrowers, buying cars and insurance, buying and furnishing homes, paying for education. They work at the lower end of the pay scale because they are younger, at the entry level of the work force.

The senior working-age group (45-64), is made up of the "empty nesters" — their children are leaving home, they are at the peak of their earnings, they own their homes. They have no child-care expenses; they are net savers.

The Penobscot region has a slightly lower proportion of working age population (18-64)

MAKING A LIVING: *Caretaking*

In Penobscot Bay towns where a summer colony is deeply rooted in the fabric of community life, caretaking is a significant part of the local economy. For some rural communities, it is the principal way to make a living and a force of stability in a time when fishing and agriculture have become risky vocations.

"Around here, you're working for summer people," said Ralph Gray. A longtime caretaker on Islesboro, Gray recognizes the symbiotic relationship between island residents and summer families, some of whom have been coming to his community for generations. Most of Islesboro's workers stay on the island and work in building trades and landscaping, supported by the many large summer places on the island. "Unless you're a lobsterman, just about everything you do, whether you're a painter, carpenter, or electrician, is for summer people," said Gray.

It is difficult to compile economic statistics about the importance of caretaking to the Penobscot Bay economy, since most of the caretakers are self-employed. Statistics for "county business patterns" and similar pictures of local employment do not include self-employment in their calculations. "It's a substantial component in Penobscot Bay, particularly where you have a summer community, like the islands and in the east bay," said Richard Sherwood of the State Planning Office. Janet White of the Maine Department of Labor keeps employment statistics in a "private residence" category, but caretaking falls between the cracks here, too. "Most of what we deal with is 'covered employment,' where the employee is covered by health insurance, even in the 'private residence' category," said White. Here again, self-employed workers are not included in the state's overall economic picture.

Thus the process of gauging the economic importance of caretaking as a way to make a living in Penobscot Bay is sketchy and anecdotal. In some places it is a significant contribution to the local economy; in others, caretaking does not even exist.

compared to the state (59.7 percent vs. 61.4 percent). Those statistics conceal wide regional differences, however. The river region has the highest proportion of working-age population compared to other regions (67.6 percent).

Young couples raising families locate near affordable housing that is within a reasonable commute to their jobs. Property values are high along the coast, generally more expensive than what younger people are able to afford. They tend to live instead in inland towns or along the river. For example, over two thirds of the region's early to mid-career-age population (18-44) live in river towns.

The younger age of residents of the towns in the river region is not surprising. The pattern is largely suburban; houses and land there cost less than they do in urban centers or on the coast. Bangor/Brewer, with its high concentration of businesses and professional services (legal, medical, financial), attracts professionals who live within a reasonable commuting distance. The fact that the 18-44 age group is augmented by a high student population further helps to explain why about half of the people living in the river region are between 18 and 44 years of age.

Retirement age

The Penobscot region's age 65-plus cohort is similar to the state as a whole, but again this average belies some striking contrasts.

The babies born in the Great Depression reached age 65 in 1995. Birth rates in that era were low — the 65-plus age group is only 12.7 percent of the 1990 Penobscot region's population — but the Census Bureau projects that it will rise to nearly 22 percent by the year 2030. This 65-plus age cohort will increase because of the high number of people now aged 45-64. The size of this group is expected to grow due to in-migration as well, especially in the east and west bay regions.

Island towns have the highest percentage of population in the 65-plus category in the region (18.6 percent). Only Matinicus and Isle au Haut had less than the state average of 13.2 percent.

The work a caretaker is expected to do varies with each place. In the spring, it's usually cleanup, putting in gardens, planting flower beds, growing vegetables and opening up the house. In the summer, it could be chauffeuring, sailing or boating, or taking the family out on picnics to an island in the bay. In the fall and winter, tasks typically include draining water pipes and closing down the house, and seeing that any needed maintenance is completed before winter.

"Looking after summer homes, you get paid, not a big lot, to be responsible, pay attention and do what needs to be done," said Gray. "You did everything, and I got so I could." In the off season, Gray would cut pulpwood, go clamming, cut ice — anything to earn a living.

In Islesboro's heyday as a summer colony, one caretaker might look after only one place. It was his job to maintain the gardens and look after the buildings (although painting and carpentry always required a crew because of the size of the cottages). Today, one caretaker might have the keys to eight or ten places, earning a partial salary from each. He is more of an overseer or general contractor, responsible for what needs to be done, while the owners hire the subcontractors.

Mainland contractors are now competing with island workers for jobs in the summer communities, either because there is more work than the island labor force can keep up with, or because the families are choosing to find more competitive work rather than stay loyal to a local person. Each morning on the 7:30 a.m. Islesboro boat to Lincolnville, there are a few people that leave the island, but coming over on the ferry's return trip at 8 a.m. are electricians, carpenters, painters, plumbers and masons. "Some island people are very good contractors, but they went off lobstering," says Gray. "It got to be that there wasn't enough here to handle the work."

The rest were all over 16 percent, topped by Islesboro at 21 percent. The case is similar in the west bay, where the 65-plus group in all 11 towns is greater proportionately than in the state as a whole. There, 18.2 percent of the population is 65 years or older, the highest after the islands. The town of Camden leads the entire Penobscot region with 25 percent of its population aged 65 or older.

In the east bay, 17 percent of the population is 65 or older. Only Orland has a smaller percentage (12 percent) than the state; the other towns are higher, topped by Brooklin with 21 percent.

The river towns' 9.4 percent of population aged 65 and older stands in sharp contrast to the rest of the Penobscot region. Only three river towns have a higher proportion of elderly citizens than the state: Bangor (14 percent), Brewer (15 percent) and Verona (15 percent).

Bangor's population of 33,180 makes up 44 percent of the river region's total population base, and 63 percent of this area's 65-plus population. Without the weighty influence of Bangor, the river region's 65-plus group drops to 6.2 percent, which is less than half of the percentage for the state as a whole.

Urban centers tend to have large elderly populations and the percentage of the elderly is augmented by youth who leave in search of employment opportunity and less expensive housing. "The elderly are in Bangor for low-income rental housing," said Anne Gardner of Atlantic Retirement Communities in Newburyport, Massachusetts, a hospital consultant and development marketer that has studied the Penobscot Bay region extensively. Having Bangor nearby is a huge plus to the elderly population in other parts of the Penobscot region. "Eastern Maine Medical Center, the symphony, Maine Center for the Arts in Orono are positive resources used by the elderly," Gardner said.

By age 65, people usually are living on fixed incomes. "They'll be fiscal conservatives on tax issues," commented Sherwood of the State Planning Office. "They don't have kids in schools, so there may not be as much support for school levies from this age group compared to the age 18-44 cohort."

Retirees also have more time to devote to volunteer activities and can share their expertise with such community groups as committees and boards, Boy Scouts and churches.

Camden storekeepers are hard hit, however, when the retirees with money to spend head for the Sunbelt during the winter months. "Retirees have a lot of knowledge and experience to lend," said Sherwood, "but many of them also tend to go to Florida for three months in the winter, leaving no one to serve on boards and organizations. How the positives and the negatives balance out, goodness knows".

"The mailbox economy"

According to some experts, senior citizens tend to bring in money while making few demands on local budgets. The major costs of elderly care, Social Security and Medicare are state and federal expenses. Retirement is an "export industry" for a town, where "age" is the "export commodity" and retirement income flows in from out of town.

Social Security and retirement income is received in 48 percent of Hancock County households, 49 percent of Knox County households and 43 percent of Waldo County households. However, over half of all income in Knox County in the mid 1980s was unearned income from pension checks, Medicare and Medicaid payments, interest and dividend income, Social Security and rent, according to the State Planning Office. Typically, unearned income is about a third to a quarter of total income.

This retirement income is independent of local economic fluctuations. Dubbed the "mailbox economy," it means that even if the local economy suffers a downturn, income will continue to flow in from outside the region. Camden, with a quarter of its population over 65, would be buffered from the worst of a local or regional recession because Social Security and pension checks from out of town would continue to arrive in local mailboxes. "Around Penobscot Bay, the large number of elderly brings in a large number of Medicare dollars," said Sherwood. "How many small places like Camden and Rockport could support the medical facilities they have if they didn't have high Medicare payments in the region? Those payments help pay for the Pen Bay Medical Center, and support doctors, equipment and services."

The retirement business

Retirement has become big business in Penobscot Bay, both because of the large number of elderly people living in the region and because of their socio-economic status. "This age bracket wants support systems in place and available, while at the same time maintaining their freedom and independence," said Mark Biscone, administrator of the Waldo County General Hospital in Belfast.

Health services were the second or third largest industry in Penobscot region counties in 1990. The waiting list for existing units in the region's elderly care facilities is already years long. Two new residential facilities for the elderly are underway in Belfast: Penobscot Shores, 47 independent living units affiliated with Waldo County General Hospital, and Harbor Hill. They will join a growing array of options from Camden to Blue Hill affording seniors in Penobscot Bay the full range of options, from acute care hospitalization to assisted or independent living.

Migration

Between 1980 and 1990, the population in the Penobscot region grew by 6,467 people, from 114,874 to 121,341 — a 5.6 percent increase. Except in the river towns, migration accounted for a significant proportion of the change in population over the decade.

In the east bay, 95.4 percent of the increase was due to newcomers. According to the Maine Department of Labor, this trend will continue: future changes in population will be more the result of migration than natural increases or decreases.

Two west bay communities, Rockland and Camden, demonstrate how population trends can highlight the differences between two neighboring towns. Rockland's high natural *increase* in population (286, fourth in Penobscot Bay) was eclipsed by a high out-migration rate (-233, second in Penobscot Bay). Camden, on the other hand, experienced a natural *decrease* (-211, highest in Penobscot Bay) which was eclipsed by a massive in-migration (687, highest in Penobscot Bay). In one decade, two towns separated by six miles of Rockport shoreline diverged completely in age and growth patterns.

Camden's in-migration trend was a function of older, wealthy people moving in and buying desirable real estate, driving up property values. Young families couldn't compete for housing and moved out, likely heading for inland towns where land and housing were more affordable.

Health services were the second or third largest industry in Penobscot region counties in 1990. The waiting list for existing units in the region's elderly care facilities is already years long.

Island populations declined over the decade, experiencing a natural decrease that was augmented by out-migration. The 65 people who moved to Islesboro accounted for the only positive number in the migration category for the region's seven island towns during the 1980s.

Of the seven island communities in Penobscot Bay, only Vinalhaven suffered the twin effects of a natural decrease (-33) coupled with a loss of 106 island residents to out-migration. "On Vinalhaven, if working-age people don't fish, they leave," explained town manager Susan Lessard. "There are no jobs. There's not a lot of choice here — if you're not fishing, you're either a teacher, you work for the town, or in the store."

According to Lessard, many of the families who leave eventually come back to Vinalhaven when work and school pressures have subsided. She suggests this is one reason why the island's older population is relatively high (19 percent).

Striking among the east bay communities is the strong influence migration played in the region's population increase in the 1980s, when 95.4 percent of the increase was due to migration: births accounted for only 29 of the 643 people who boosted the population in these towns.

Brooklin and Deer Isle, which together had a modest natural increase of 20 children in the 1980s, also saw 483 people move to town. Brooklin and Deer Isle both have a high retirement-age proportion (20.5 percent and 19.3 percent, respectively), and the high in-migration rate during the 1980s suggests that many of the newcomers were retirees moving in. Penobscot and Brooksville show similar trends.

Neighboring Stonington, on the other hand, experienced a net population decrease over the period, the exodus of residents (-98) outweighing a relatively high natural increase (77, more than the other east bay towns combined). The younger working-age segment (18-44) in Stonington is smaller than the surrounding towns and well below the statewide percentage. Stonington's working-age people move away when employment opportunity is limited, as they do in Vinalhaven.

Where do the migrants come from, and where do Mainers go when they leave? The Maine Department of Labor has statistics from the five-year period between 1985 and 1990 showing that, of newcomers to Maine of all age groups, the highest number came from Massachusetts (about 28,000), followed by New Hampshire (about 15,000) and "elsewhere" (meaning immigrants from outside the U.S.; in Maine's case, probably most came from Canada.

The destination for the highest number of out-migrating Mainers is Florida (about 14,600), followed by Massachusetts (about 13,800) and New Hampshire (about 11,600).

Seeking "quality of life"

The retirement group migrating to Penobscot Bay is affluent and in search of a high quality of life. "Their money enables them to move," said Anne Gardner of Atlantic Retirement Communities. "Many are relocating from elsewhere in New England, escaping from pollution, overcrowding and crime."

These seekers offer a sharp contrast to retirees who live in urban centers for reasons of affordable rental housing, public transportation and accessible social services. Penobscot Bay's retirees are active volunteers in their communities and share their expertise readily. "Look at the boards of Penobscot Bay hospitals — Waldo County General, Pen Bay, Blue Hill Memorial. Their boards are volunteers over age 65," said Gardner. "Look at hospital auxiliaries -- 90 percent are women age 65 and over. Many want to give back what they grew up appreciating in Penobscot Bay in summers."

Waldo and Hancock counties are now the fastest-growing counties in the state. Much of the growth is in the elderly age sector.

The region's retirees tend to be ardent promoters of the arts and cultural programs, and very environmentally conscious. While the retirees Gardner described seek places that offer a comfortable lifestyle and scenic appeal, "having water just to look at isn't enough. They are birders and naturalists. Above all they don't want problems such as pollution to follow them from the cities," he said. These retirees spend two-thirds of their income in the region, on housing, transportation and food.

Waldo and Hancock Counties are now the fastest-growing counties in the state, according to Sherwood. Much of the growth is in the elderly age sector. "Belfast is experiencing now what Camden did in the 1970s and 1980s. Land values have been run up in the southwest coast, and Belfast now appears attractive and affordable," Sherwood said. The trends of the 1980s are still alive, they are simply shifting around Penobscot Bay. Gardner agrees, referring to Belfast as "a bud waiting to bloom."

The burgeoning health care facilities in the area provide an example of the commercial muscle a high elderly population wields. "What we're seeing is the exercise of economic power," said Mike Bush of the Eastern Maine Development Corporation. "Not with evil intent, it's just happening. [The elderly] purchase at local stores, and hire local contractors, because they are interested in service rather than getting the best deal at the time of purchase."

There may be consequences. Property values tend to appreciate, since many newcomers are accustomed to seeing higher real estate values in other states. "They could cash out a house in Connecticut and buy four of them in Belfast," said Gardner. An influx of wealthy retirees can also make community less diverse, as younger, less economically advantaged residents get pushed out to adjacent communities where housing costs are lower.

When land prices shot up in the 1980s, said Vinalhaven town manager Susan Lessard, "some people were valued out of existence and sold out to the 'from away-ers.' More change occurred in valuation and population shifts than in any recent decade, and it caused a real change in the complexion of communities." But Vinalhaven, while it experienced the same trends as the mainland did, was steadied by the influence of a traditional and inter-generational fishing industry. "Nowadays, people are staying on Vinalhaven with their kids," said Lessard. "I'm betting we're back up to 1980 population levels. There are thriving supermarkets, restaurants, hardware stores, newspaper shop, a clothing store and 1,000 names on the voter lists now."

Income and poverty

Next to education, income is one of the best indicators of social and economic health, and differences in age and education within the population most heavily influence income. The number of wage earners, the type of industry in an area and the occupational mix in an area also influence median incomes.[2] Just as variations in age distribution around Penobscot Bay are related to economic and cultural opportunities and preferences within the region, so, too, are income and poverty related closely to those patterns.

The median annual household income in Penobscot Bay is $24,949, which is below the state median of $27, 854.[3] Castine has the highest median income ($35,104); Isle au Haut the lowest ($16,000). East bay and island communities are lower on average.

Statewide norms for income distribution generally apply in Penobscot Bay. Suburbs in Maine, for example, are primarily middle- and upper-middle-class communities that have higher median incomes than either urban centers or rural areas. This pattern holds true for the Penobscot region, which in addition has coastal retirement communities with high median incomes. For example, Owls Head, Camden and Rockport, each having high percentages of population over age 65, average a median income of $30,872.

As a rule, the Penobscot region's urban and suburban populations have higher incomes than those in rural areas. The river towns' average median income of $28,887 surpasses both regional and state median incomes, reflecting its more urban-suburban character. (The one notable exception is rural Frankfort, where the median income is $22,163.) Towns near Bangor and Bucksport that serve as bedroom communities for skilled and professional workers typically exhibit higher incomes and lower poverty rates.

Rockland and Belfast had the *lowest* median incomes in the west bay area, as well as high poverty rates.

In east bay rural towns, all but Orland and Castine had higher poverty and lower median

MAKING A LIVING: *Boatbuilding*

Boatbuilding has been a part of the Penobscot region as long as people have lived here, and like most enduring occupations it has weathered many cycles. Builders have survived through their resilience, their ability to embrace technological change and their willingness to take risks.

The region's concentration of boatyards attracts buyers who are looking for a custom boat and know they can find it in any one of the competing shops in the area. "They like the 'Downeast' look of the boats," said Kent Lawson, division manager at Atlantic Boat in Brooklin. "They can get what they want because it's custom."

Boatbuilding is subject to economic cycles and government policies. In the early 1990s, a federal luxury tax dragged what had been a region-wide economic slowdown to a standstill in the boatbuilding industry. The theory behind the tax was that it would affect only the rich, but it proved devastating to boatbuilding. The tax was repealed in 1993.

Since the repeal of the tax, the recovery of this industry has been slow and steady for the boatbuilders that survived. "It put a few companies out of business that never will come back," says Lawson.

Other changes in tax policy have affected the industry as well. Maine boat buyers were formerly required to pay taxes only on material and labor. Now, they must pay a 6 percent sales tax on the entire selling price of a boat, a considerable increase. Builders of smaller boats are hit especially hard because people wanting to use a new boat in Maine can travel to tax-free states like New Hampshire or Rhode Island to buy a boat, then trailer it to Maine.

Suppliers and builders in Maine now say the boatbuilding market is active, but much different from several years ago when the industry placed a heavy reliance on constructing fishing boats. Today, orders in the pleasure marine industry surpass orders for fishing boats. "It's a very fickle business," says Dave Norman, salesman for Hamilton Marine, which supplies gear and hardware to boatbuilders throughout the country.

In contrast to ports Downeast, where fishing is the primary purpose of building a boat, builders in Penobscot Bay have typically sold their boats and services to people "from away" as well as to fishermen.

"Penobscot Bay has a long heritage of yachting, and lots of summer folk with money," says John Hanson, editor of *Maine Boats and Harbors* magazine. "Penobscot Bay is where people started selling Maine-built boats to people from away, and the trend continues today. The market is active, and it's yachts."

Building cruisers and other types of pleasure boats makes a healthy contribution to the rural economy of the Penobscot region, since a major portion of the money comes from out of state. Not all of it, however: Hanson notes a growing number of pleasure boat orders from local customers.

The service sector of the marine industry is a strong component for many of the yards working in Penobscot Bay. Steve White of the Brooklin Boat Yard keeps 24 people on the payroll busy by offering customers a mix of services, from new construction to repair, service and storage.

comes compared to the region and the state. Orland had a high percentage of the local work force commuting to skilled jobs at the Champion International paper mill in neighboring Bucksport; Castine had the Maine Maritime Academy. Five of the eight towns in east bay had higher child poverty than the state average.

No island community had a median income as high as the state. Thus, the average of island median income levels was lower ($20,744 compared to the state's $27,854). But there was great variability in poverty rates among the islands: North Haven, Monhegan and Matinicus had no children in poverty, while Isle au Haut had a 50 percent child poverty rate — the highest in Penobscot Bay.

One might suspect that communities with higher median incomes would have lower poverty levels than poorer rural areas. In the Penobscot region, however, the inverse is the case: regions with the highest percentages of people in poverty also had the highest median incomes.[3]

Possible explanations include the fact that areas in the Penobscot region with higher median incomes are also more densely populated, and poverty assistance and social service programs can be more readily attained there: social services such as Meals on Wheels or Aid to Families with Dependent Children are more easily delivered where the recipients of the services are closer together. Penobscot Bay's urban communities of Rockland, Belfast and Bangor all had high poverty

Boatbuilding in Penobscot Bay today is a blend old and new. Builders are using new techniques and materials. Many boats that are now being constructed primarily of wood are no longer planked, but are constructed of multiple veneer-thin layers of cold-molded wood and epoxy resins. Builders of fiberglass boats, such as Flye Point Marine (which merged with Brooklin's Duffy and Duffy in 1995 to form Atlantic Boat), usually build boats from layup to finish, but frequently send hulls to other builders for them to finish off. Today, builders range from big operations to small crews with a shed in their doorway.

Brian Robbins, a contributing editor at *Commercial Fisheries News,* has witnessed as many boat launchings as anyone in the region. "Years ago, you had guys at Beals Island, or the Riches and Stanleys in Mount Desert — wooden-boatbuilders that hired big gangs of guys to build them," says Robbins. "Today, the fiberglass world has opened up the market to more builders. You have hull-molding shops, and then a ton of small finish shops that finish off the hulls. Hulls and tops can disappear down the road and show up in anybody's dooryard."

The boatyard gamut in Penobscot Bay runs from yards such as Billings Diesel Marine Service in Stonington and Wayfarer Marine in Camden — high-tech yards that have the capability of servicing boats of lengths well over 100 feet — to small, one- or two-person finishing shops where pre-made hulls and cabins are completed. Low overhead and payroll responsibilities like insurance and health care allow some of the smaller operations to survive economic downturns and market fluctua-

tions, such as a shift from fishing boats to pleasure boats. "Most of the yards around Penobscot Bay are pretty flexible in what they're willing to take on and what they'll do," says Brooklin Boat Yard's White. Duffy and Duffy was more in the pleasure cruiser market, but spent the winter of 1995-96 building two lobster boats, one clammer and a science research boat for an out-of-state university. Robbins cites one builder, Wade Dow at Bridges Point Boat Yard, who, like many, started out finishing lobster boats. He is now building Joel White design sailboats.

Boatbuilding specialties are well represented in Penobscot Bay. The internationally recognized Robert H. Eddy & Associates of Camden constructs design models, using computer technology and lasers for cutting some of the parts.

At the other end of the spectrum is the WoodenBoat School in Brooklin. Approximately 600 students from Canada, Europe and the United States pass through its boatbuilding school during an 18-week season. Not all of the 87 courses taught there have to do with adzes and planes; students have choices ranging from half-models and lofting, surveying, engine repair, electronics, photography and seamanship.

Regardless of their niche in the industry, boatbuilders and allied tradesmen are constantly looking over their shoulders, because profit margins are tighter than they were in the 1980s when disposable incomes were high and fishing boats were still in demand. Today, new construction, repair and maintenance businesses are strong.

rates. The exact reason why poverty in Penobscot Bay's rural regions is lower than suburban and urban regions, however, is unclear.

Education: confounding the statewide averages

As more complex urban and technological commerce has reduced agriculture's dominance in Maine, there has been an increased emphasis on and demand for higher education. The "information age" has made hitherto-rural areas such as the Penobscot region more attractive to businesses for various reasons, including the quality of life. In a 1994 Eastern Maine Development Corporation survey of manufacturing in Hancock County, 77 percent of respondents said they located in the county because of the quality of life or because the business owner lived there.

Business activities considered "new," such as financial services, make location and quality of life as important a consideration as telephone and transportation networks. (The growth of MBNA in Camden and Belfast is a case in point.) According to the Maine Department of Labor, the educational "proficiency" of a community indicates its quality of life and prosperity better than any other social indicator. For every $10,000 increase in household incomes nationwide, there is a corresponding increase in Scholastic Achievement Test (SAT) scores of about 14 percent.

According to the Maine Department of Labor, greater economic opportunity in urban and suburban areas tends to draw residents with higher educational attainment to those places, because high level professional positions there have correspondingly high qualification requirements. The Penobscot region, however, confounds typical urban-rural patterns of educational attainment: all four regions have markedly higher levels of educational attainment compared to

MAKING A LIVING: *Recreation*

Twenty years ago, Gordon Bell could remember the face of every person who came to Camden Hills State Park for the day. The crowd would amount to only six cars a day, so it wasn't difficult. "These days, we have to turn cars away during the summer because the parking lot is full," says Bell, who is now the park manager.

The Penobscot region's attraction is magnetic for outdoor recreation activities. It has long been recognized as a scenic place to drive and cruise, and now the growing popularity of kayaking, bicycling and hiking has resulted in more people reaching more distant and remote areas.

Not that the traditional haunts are empty: parks and preserves are experiencing record numbers of visitors. Part of the reason is a growing recognition of Penobscot Bay as a destination rather that a stopping place for tourists on their drive up to Acadia National Park. "We call ourselves the Jewel of the Maine Coast," said Debbie Stressing, office manager at the Rockport-Camden-Lincolnville Chamber of Commerce.

Much of the recreational opportunity consists of day trips around the area, on foot, bicycle or by boat. Day trips are profitable for guides because it is possible to handle a large number of paying customers in a shorter time period, compared to trips of three or six days with the same clients. Camden Hills State Park's Bell estimates the park gets about 30-35,000 campers per year, and over 200,000 day use visitors. "Most of our use is people driving up to the scenic overlook on Mount Battie," says Bell. "You can see the stone tower at the top from the road into Camden, and people driving by often turn in."

The same is true for the windjammers sailing out of Camden and Rockland, many of which take out passengers on short harbor tours. The schooners combined take out approximately 5,000 people between mid May and October, averaging about 300 people a week.

The biggest wave in the Penobscot Bay recreation scene is sea kayaks. Maine Sport, a retail sporting goods and equipment store in Rockport, rents kayaks and leads guided trips varying from two hours to five days in length. The company also operates a training school on an

statewide averages.

Compared to the rest of Maine, Belfast and Rockland have low high school attainment; Rockland also has a relatively low proportion of college graduates. Bangor and Brewer have high levels of high school and college level attainment compared to both the region and state (24.4 percent and 21.1 percent, respectively).

Monhegan Island residents, on the other hand, have the highest high school *and* college level attainment in Penobscot Bay: 100 percent of people over age 25 are high school graduates; 40.9 percent are college graduates. Only the college towns of Orono and Castine have higher percentages of college-educated residents. Matinicus and Islesboro residents are also well educated, compared to the state as a whole.

Maine's suburban and coastal retirement communities tend to have higher educational attainment, probably because people with higher economic success generally are more flexible in their choices of where to live, and better education generally implies economic choice. A look at educational attainment in coastal retirement communities clearly demonstrates this trend: communities with greater high school and college attainment are Rockport, Camden, Brooksville and Brooklin.

The Penobscot region confounds typical urban–rural patterns of educational attainment: all four areas of the region have markedly higher levels of high school and college level attainment than Maine as a whole.

island base in Muscongus Bay where it teaches paddling, safety and rescue techniques. "We put thousands of people through guided tours in the summer," says Kristen Oehler, assistant director of Maine Sport's outdoor school. That doesn't count the short haulers — on the average summer day, 24 people take part in one-hour harbor tours.

Maine Sport is one of the largest kayak touring companies on the coast, partly because of its location in Rockport. "Being here with access to Penobscot Bay is a prime location," says Oehler. Maine Sport planned to host the American Canoe Association's annual instructor certification training, which is held on the east and west coasts every year. "People come from all over for that, and we've become a center partly because of it," says Oehler.

The boom in sea kayaking has brought a lot of new business into Penobscot Bay. Even inns and bed-and-breakfast establishments rent kayaks to their guests. Oehler says that makes her uncomfortable because many people will be paddling out into the bay without the benefit of safety training or education. Currently, Maine law requires trip leaders to possess guide licenses issued by the Maine Department of Inland Fisheries and Wildlife (IFW), but most Registered Maine Guide licenses are geared towards canoeing, rafting or fishing on Maine's interior freshwater lakes and streams.

In addition to sea kayaking, marina development is increasing steadily in Penobscot Bay. This is true especially in the upper bay, where there is demand from boat owners from the Bangor area who prefer to drive to the bay and put in, rather than power downstream to the bay from marinas in Bangor. According to Ken Rich, the Rockland harbormaster, the city's working waterfront is making the transition from working to pleasure boats. "We're a good jumping-off place for cruising in any direction" in Penobscot Bay, said Rich. Jim Chandler, executive director of the Maine Marine Trades Association, says pleasure boating "presents a good economic opportunity that we want to enhance, but not to the detriment of the fishing industry."

Richard Sherwood of the State Planning Office sees a distinction between east and west bay towns that is related to education. "If you live in a coastal west bay town you're still able to commute to larger and year-round regional employment centers such as Augusta. East bay towns are not close enough for commuting to Bangor or other regional employment centers."

Breaking the Rules

The Penobscot region defies many conventions that statisticians like to describe as "typical." It is also subject to trends no one in the region can control. Age is one such trend. People who were 65 years old in 1990 will be 75 in the year 2000 (provided they live that long). The percentage of people age 85 and over in Knox County is projected to grow 24 percent between 1990 and 1997, even if the in-migration of the elderly subsides (which is doubtful, considering the facilities under construction in Penobscot Bay).

The first of the people born during the Great Depression turned 65 in 1995. That number will be low compared to the first of the "baby boomers" (the population born between 1945 and 1960) will turn 65 in 2010. Across the U.S. there is a high number of people in the baby boom age class, and they are now having their own children. The surge of baby boomers' kids is what demographers call the "boomlet."

Interestingly, while the percentage of youth is high in the United States, baby boomers' children do not account for a large share of it: because of immigration and high birth rates, 52 percent of the so-called boomlet in the U.S. is non-white. Maine and the Penobscot region aren't experiencing the same immigration and birth rate surges affecting other regions of the country.

Maine's birth rate suggests young couples are having fewer children, and a majority of the Penobscot region's couples are past childbearing age. According to Cathy St. Pierre at the Maine Department of Human Services, the number of births per year is also falling, a remarkable fact because Maine's birth rate is already 49th in the U.S. In 1994, Maine saw the lowest number of births (14,300) since 1901. Though the actual number of 1994 births may have been close to the number of 1901 births, the birth *rate* is radically lower because the state's population today is larger

Footnotes

[1] The Census Bureau defines vacation homes, or "homes held for seasonal, recreational or occasional use," as those "intended for use only in certain seasons or for weekend or other occasional use throughout the year. Seasonal units include those used for summer or winter sports or recreation, such as beach cottages and hunting cabins...."

[2] "Median income" describes the halfway point between the highest and lowest incomes; half are above, half are below. The median is a good summarizing measure because extreme highs and lows do not distort the mid point.

[3] Poverty thresholds are revised annually to allow for changes in the cost of living as reflected in the Consumer Price Index. The average poverty threshold for a family of four persons was $12,674 in 1989, the year questionnaires were filled out for the 1990 Census. At the core of the Census Bureau definition is the 1961 U.S. Department of Agriculture "economy food plan," the least costly of four "nutritionally adequate" food plans. It was determined that families of three or more persons spend approximately one third of their income on food; hence, the poverty level for these families was set at three times the cost of the economy food plan.

PORT IN A STORM BOOKSTORE

MAIN STREET, SOMESVILLE
MOUNT DESERT ISLAND, MAINE 04660
TELEPHONE: 207-244-4114
TOLL FREE: 800-694-4114
WEBSITE: http://www.acadia.net/portbks
e-mail: portbks@acadia.net

A BOOKLOVER'S HAVEN

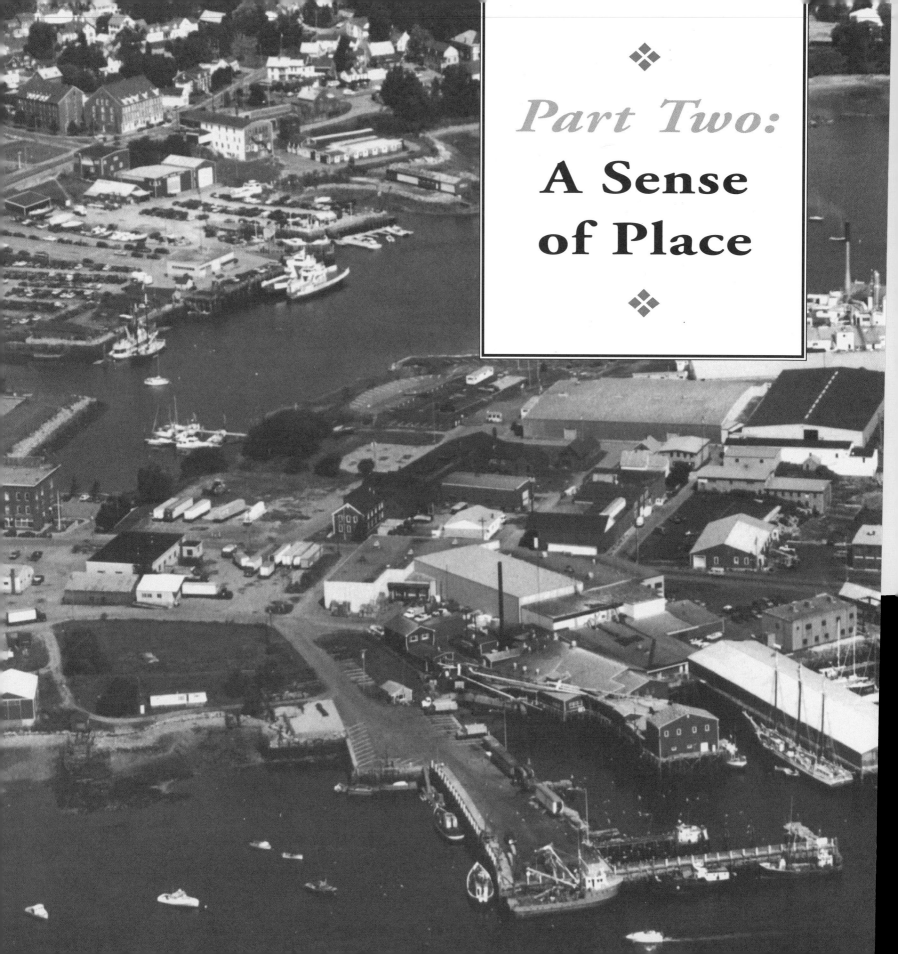

Part Two:
A Sense of Place

Chapter 7:
West Bay Towns

Opposite: Aerial view of Rockland today (Christopher Ayres)

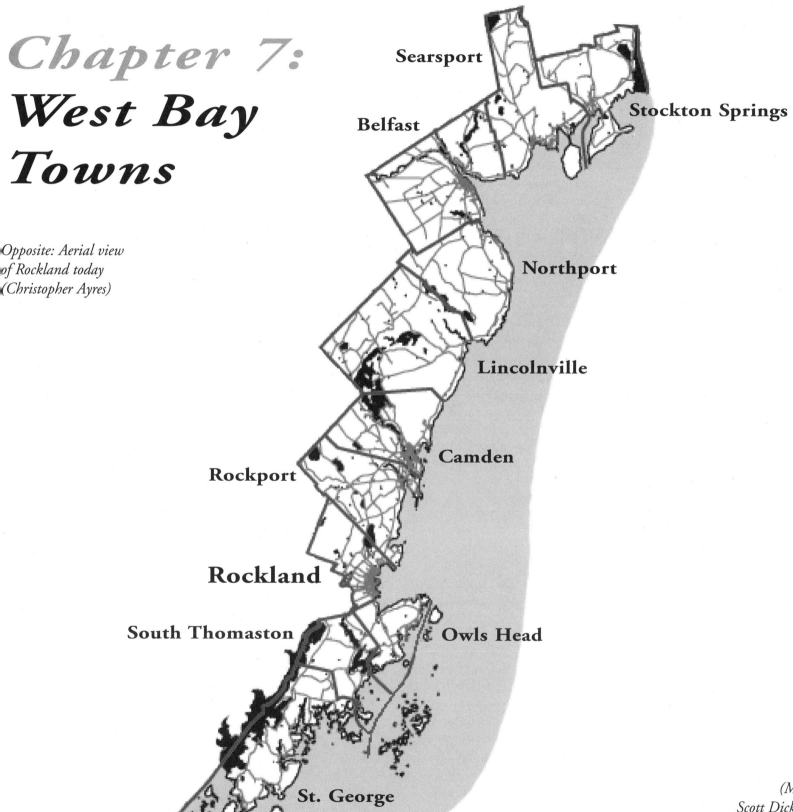

Searsport

Belfast

Stockton Springs

Northport

Lincolnville

Camden

Rockport

Rockland

South Thomaston

Owls Head

St. George

(Map by Scott Dickerson; data provided by Maine Office of GIS)

ROCKLAND

1882: Lime kilns, shipyards and the Red Jacket

Rockland, a city and the shire town of Knox County, is situated on Rockland Bay, on the western side of Penobscot Bay. Its harbor is enclosed by two headlands, Jameson's Point on the north and the long projection of Thomaston, terminating in Owl's Head, on the south. The environs abound in picturesque hill and marine scenery. The north-west is occupied by an extensive meadow. The only considerable sheet of water is Chickawaukie pond, lying partly in Camden, which, by means of an aqueduct, supplies the city with excellent water.

Rockland has three or more ship-yards, one marine railway, five sail-lofts, two boat-builders, three grain mills, two foundries, three carriage factories, six lumber mills, two machine ships, three cooperies. a tannery, twelve lime manufacturers, four granite and marble works, two boot and shoe factories, four printing-offices, etc. Formerly ship-building was the leading industry, but the lime business has now outgrown it. In 1854, Rockland ship-yards sent out eleven ships, three barks, six brigs, and four schooners. The "Red Jacket," registering 2,500 tons, was built here in 1853, being one of the largest and finest vessels ever sent out from our ports. In 1858 there were twelve lime quarries in operation, requiring 125 kilns of the old style to reduce the rock, turning out about 900,000 casks, upwards of 3,000 vessels being employed in conveying them to market. The amount now produced is 1,200,000 casks annually, the lime industry employing about 1,000 men.

There are three fine schoolhouses in the city proper, where the schools are graded. The number of public schoolhouses in the entire city is eleven. The population in 1870 was 7,074.

(A Gazetteer of the State of Maine, with Names and Illustrations, 1882)

1996: Bootstrapping into the future

As recently as 1990, Rockland was reeling from economic decline and a steady out-migration of its population and businesses. Government and citizen efforts to turn the tide were frustrated by the inexorable dwindling of the fishing industry, which for decades had been perceived as Rockland's economic and cultural foundation. Almost 500 fish processing jobs were lost in Rockland in a four year period, between 1988 and 1991. Ironically, George Goode's comprehensive treatment of Maine's fishing industry, published in the late 19th century, contained this arresting description: "Rockland has never been a fishing town, and has had very few fishing vessels sailing from its harbor. Even the 'boat fisheries' of the town are very limited."

The city was barely on the map for visitors to Penobscot Bay. The transformation of a backcountry road between Warren and Rockport into Route 90 created an effective bypass around Rockland, and made travel along Route 1 into the city a dubious option.

"Depression" so described both the economy and the mood in Rockland six years ago that few could have foreseen its transformation in the mid 1990s. Timing, national and global economic trends and circumstance certainly helped, but the story of Rockland's reversal of fortune is equally one of local initiative and determination to succeed. The Maine Lobster Festival, which had its 48th annual celebration in Rockland in 1995, drew around 70,000 visitors. Schooner Days and recent expansion at the Farnsworth Art Museum are welcome signs of interest and rejuvenation, both on the waterfront and on Main Street. Although the groundfishing fleet has virtually disappeared from the Rockland waterfront, urchins have become a very large winter fishery, while in the summer large volumes of herring supply the remaining herring packing plant and the prodigious lobster boat industry.

While Rockland's re-emergence into the sunlight has people literally dancing in the street (at the North American Blues Festival), some worry that the city may be placing too strong a reliance on visitors from away to feed the enthusiasm. Rockland tradition, after all, is blue-collar working town, not glitzy tourist center.

History

Originally a settlement of Thomaston, Rockland at the end of the 18th century was little more than a couple of houses on the shore of Lermond's Cove where the island ferries now load and unload. Eventually the settlement grew enough to require its own post office, and in 1820 the "Shore Village" was re-named East Thomaston. Government and services at that time still originated in the older Mill River Village of Thomaston, with teachers, constables and firemen based or at least paid there. Commerce in East Thomaston thrived with increasing demand for the primary local resource -- lime rock. By 1848, the population of East Thomaston was nearly double that of Thomaston, and in that year divided from the parent town and incorporated under that name. The name was changed to Rockland two years later, out of deference to the community's commercial dependence on its native lime rock.

For more than a century, the lime industry was the foundation of Rockland's prosperity. As American cities grew, so did demand for Rockland lime as a building material. There were 12 lime quarries in operation in 1858, with 125 kilns turning out 900,000 casks of lime. By 1880, the lime industry was directly employing a thousand workers and produced 1.2 million casks annually.

Main Street, Rockland
(Christopher Ayres)

Quarrying, burning and shipping limestone required the services of numerous trades and professions: barrels and casks to contain the lime, quarrying equipment and transportation were in high demand, and Rockland swelled with traders, laborers and artisans to meet it. In the 1890s, the Lime Rock Railroad had 12.5 miles of track servicing 39 modern kilns, and connected the quarries to kilns and the docks. The Knox-Lincoln Railroad connecting Rockland to Bath was built to facilitate transportation of lime to other parts of New England and markets to the south.

Shipbuilding began in the early 1800s to service Rockland lime kilns. Native forests had been depleted to supply charcoal for the kilns; ironically, wood had to be imported from Canada for both the kilns and shipbuilding. Over 2,500 ships were built in the Rockland area between the late 18th and early 20th centuries, peaking in the 1850s and 1860s. Rockland's most famous clipper ship, RED JACKET – was launched from the Deacon George Thomas yard in 1853 — at 251 feet the largest Maine-built ship of its day. RED JACKET was also the fastest clipper, setting the record for the shortest sailing trip from New York to Liverpool – just over 13 days.

Manufacturing and tourism took hold early. Blocks of brick buildings along the city's main street reflected permanence and prosperity. Two iron foundries and several manufacturers of fittings for Rockland's shipyards sprang up; the Rockland Steam Manufacturing Company and other steam mills were founded there. Penobscot Bay's granite quarrying was headquartered in Rockland, and Livingston Manufacturing Company produced stone-working tools and equipment. The Bodwell Granite Company operated quarries on Vinalhaven, St. George and Spruce Head. Bodwell Company granite went into the Rock-land breakwater, the Brooklyn Bridge and the Cathedral of St. John the Divine in New York.

The Bay Point Hotel opened in 1889 on a peninsula overlooking Rockland harbor. Its commanding views of Penobscot Bay and the islands drew guests from around the world. As the Bay Point Hotel expanded, it was renamed the Samoset, whose splendid wood frame structure, which figured prominently on the Rockland shoreline for nearly a century, burned in a spectacular fire in 1972. The resort has been rebuilt near the original location, and operates prosperously today.

Rockland's shoreline developed into a working waterfront that endured longer and perhaps more seriously than some of its sister towns around the bay that took to recreational boating and tourism early on as their maritime connection. By the mid 1900s, though, the Rockland waterfront smelled more like trouble than prosperity: a fish-rendering plant in the harbor inspired the slogan, "Camden by the Sea, Rockland by the smell."

Loading fish at a Rockland wharf for the Vinalhaven glue factory in 1921 (Frank Claes collection)

"Based on what I saw when I grew up, Rockland is very different today. This was a grimy fishing and industrial town," says Gil Merriam, a Rockland native and retired historian who grew up in town. "I liked it, it had a vibrant downtown." Merriam wrote a history about Rockland during the war years entitled *Home Front on Penobscot Bay*. But the gritty fishing and industrial town of Merriam's youth began to decline in the 60s. The 1970s were "pretty rough," says Merriam. Three sardine factories, lobster-processing plants and the fish-rendering plant lined the harbor. As a commercial fishing port and station to national fish dealers, Rockland served as landing for most of the island and west Penobscot Bay boats. But traditional groundfishing was in decline. Many commercial wharves were sold, and Rockland harbor was left a derelict reminder of better days. Young people, seeing little future in traditional industries, left to seek opportunity elsewhere.

The long road back

Rockland's population declined steadily from the 1950s straight through to the 1990 census. Even during the 1980s, a boom period for much of the Maine coast when many surrounding communities experienced significant population growth, Rockland saw a significant out-migration — the highest in the Penobscot Bay region. Today, Rockland's population is stable at about 8,000.

Rockland stands out as having a relatively high percentage of its population age 65 and over (17.3 percent vs. the state's 13.2 percent), a statistic that translates into high demand for services and care for the elderly, and strain on the municipal budget. Rockland also has a high poverty rate among its residents: according to former city manager Cathy Sleeper, 49 percent of Rockland's poplation was in the low- to moderate-income range. Just as troubling is the percentage of Rockland's children aged 18 or under who were at or below poverty: 21 percent in 1990, compared to the state's 13.2 percent.

But Rockland's impoverished residential population may not reflect its economic level, because many of the people who own Rockland businesses live in "bedroom" communities (representing an area that roughly incorporates Owls Head, South Thomaston, and parts of Thomaston and Rockport). Sleeper said that while Rockland's population has not increased much overall, the community has grown significantly, both economically and socially.

The city has a limited amount of land for new development, and new housing has been built on the perimeter of the city. In 1995, the city's unemployment rate was lower than the state's. While 23.5 percent of Rockland's workers held seasonal jobs, Sleeper said these were not typically summer tourism jobs. "Some are seasonal fish-processing jobs, but not just summer," Sleeper said, citing a local seafood-processing enterprise that processes mid summer to December.

Today, after the recent decades of downward-spiraling trends, attitudes in the community have changed, and community spirit appears feisty and alive. Ask a local what sparked the current revitalization, and the answer is likely to be "Rocklanders." Ed Komolsky, who volunteered to help organize the Maine Lobster Festival, says that enthusiasm is what keeps people working to improve Rockland. "Local people can still make a difference," Komolsky says with conviction. "We're not going to wait for someone to move here and take care of things for us. We're going to take charge and do it ourselves."

Take charge they do: with an army of 1,000 volunteers, Rockland has put on a series of carnivals, festivals and parades that keep the region looking forward, year-round. Private citizens and weekend volunteers from civic groups painted a filling station and a store, and manned booths at the Lobster Festival. "Keep something going all the time," says Komolsky, and people start to believe the positive energy is working.

Over 4,500 people attended the 1995 North American Blues Festival as part of the Schooner Days celebration. Rockland was featured in articles in the *Philadelphia Inquirer*, *Columbus Dispatch*, and *Boston Globe*, among others. Fueled by national media attention, Rockland's success at drawing an estimated 70,000 visitors to the Lobster Festival swamped the local lodging industry. "We sent people to Bath and Augusta to find rooms," says Merriam.

"Lobster Capital of the World"

The Lobster Festival does its share of warming people up to the celebrity crustacean: no less than 15,371 pounds of lobster were cooked. The Maine Tourism Office estimates the Lobster Festival translates into a $7.3 million pulse into the midcoast area economy.

In 1994, Knox County landed the most lobster of any place in the United States. The Maine lobster catch in 1994 of 40 million pounds, worth over $100 million, was the highest in 130 years of collecting landings data. Over half of those lobsters were caught in Penobscot Bay, according to the National Marine Fisheries Service.

Lobster remains the mainstay of the Penobscot Bay fishery. Regulations to protect the industry were promulgated in 1995, always with the hope that they were not "too little, too late." With declining opportunities in other fisheries, lobstermen and regulators feared increased pressure on their resource in Penobscot Bay if fishermen in other fisheries took to lobstering.

Even in Rockland, waterfront dockage is becoming an expensive commodity. Now that the harbor is clean, it has become a destination for recreational boats. Merriam has a new moniker for Rockland, "Gateway to Penobscot Bay," to promote its proximity to some of the best sailing grounds in the world. Rockland has already begun to shift from a working waterfront to recreational marinas, says Peter Marcoon of the National Fisheries Service in Rockland. "Pleasure boater have found Rockland," he says. "Camden and Rockport were filled, and Rockland was the next-best stop." Schooner captain John Foss, based in Rockland, says he has been watching tourism since the mid 1960s, and confirms the trend toward commercial recreation. "The west side of Penobscot Bay is bound to be the service side of the bay," says Foss. "The type of shoreside facilities are changing, with more marinas and fewer boatyards."

"Lobster ports like Rockland will always be there," says Bob Morrill of the National Marine Fisheries Service in Portland, "but competition for dock space will tighten. Dockage fees will rise to a point only a yachtsman can afford. The natural tendency will be to go where the money is, and that's recreation and marinas." Southern Maine is an example. There were 75 finfish boats in York County in the early 1980s. Now there are 14 left. "They went to Portland, or got out of business, or went into whale watching," says Morrill. The same process has long been underway in Penobscot Bay

In the future, communities such as Rockland will need to find ways to keep harbors and fishermen working. Maine still has 9,000 vessels that it considers commercial fishing boats. "You don't just get off your boat and go to work at McDonald's," says Morrill. "Maine is one of the last bastions of independent fisheries."

Ken Rich, the Rockland harbormaster, sees a bright future for Rockland's working waterfront. Next to lobstering, Rich envisions aquaculture as the most viable "fishery" in Rockland's future. "Aquaculture for cod and haddock will play well for Rockland," says Rich. "Rockland would be a good place to stage and supply aquaculture businesses, for distribution of feed and gear, as well as processing." Still, Rich sees Rockland harbor heading more in the direction of its tourist-oriented neighbors, with marinas surpassing other types of working wharves in importance. He has adopted Gil Merriam's "gateway" slogan. "We're a good jumping-off place for cruising in any direction," says Rich. "Rockland is like a century plant that's about to bloom." And each petal on the flower is shaped like a pleasure boat.

Rockland has one of the largest deep-water harbors on the coast. Gil Merriam likes to cite the impression this feature made on the Friendship Sloop Society, which had been holding its regatta in Boothbay Harbor. "When they found out they could hold their races inside the harbor, it blew their minds," says Merriam. It also impressed some of the windjammer schooner captains, who are able to sail out of Rockland harbor— something undreamed-of in Camden. Schooners were entirely based in Camden, but space there began to get tight at about the time Rockland harbor was being cleaned up. Now, the Rockland schooner fleet is the largest in the United States.

The trend in Rockland may be toward recreational marinas, but the traditional working waterfront in Rockland is still holding on. Sleeper, the former city manager, would retain the culture and economics of a commercial harbor. "I still feel we're a working waterfront, not solely tourism based. A lot goes on here" said Sleeper, reeling off a long list of waterfront enterprises lining Rockland harbor: the Rockland Municipal Pier, a busy place for urchin and lobster buyers; the former F.J. O'Hara fish processing plant, leased by Oak Island Seafood; the Port Clyde Canning Company, bought out by Connors Brothers of New Brunswick in the mid 1980s; Stinson's wharf, taken over by Dragon Cement Company for shipping by barge (to make this practical, the Atlantic rail line connecting Thomaston to Rockland was reactivated); the former Snow's Shipyard, now Rockland Marine; North End Marine, fabricating fiberglass parts and designs.

Striking a balance

Can Rockland retain its character against the crushing momentum of a tourism boom? Gil Merriam thinks that won't be hard. "People appreciate the diversity of Rock-land. We try to strike a balance, and the majority of people here hope to keep it. Traditional businesses need to stay healthy — we have to promote other kinds of economic development as well as tourism. It's a delicate balance."

Rockland's diversity is a source of strength. Traditional manufacturing jobs declined in the late 1980s and early 1990s – National Sea Products left, and Stinson's and O'Hara's fish-processing plants closed. But new ones have arrived: Van Baalen Pacific Corporation's Nautica Enterprises chose Rockland for its national sports clothing distribution center. FMC-Marine Colloids, makers of seaweed products, is growing and diversifying, and Fisher Engineering, the snowplow company, has grown up on the Rockland waterfront. Small but stable businesses are the mainstay of the local economy, and Rockland is being pro-active in seeing that their needs are met.

1995 Rockland Lobster Festival (David Grima, courtesy of Rockland Courier)

The city's active and full industrial park includes the first and largest dogfish processing plant in Maine, a composting facility and small manufacturers. "Rockland is unique because it's more like a traditional city," says Cathy Sleeper. "We're not isolated in a particular niche — Rockland has always been a diverse place. We have a working-class base. The changes are happening in places like culture and tourism, which Rockland hasn't had and now does. We're growing into it."

Three key institutions are the cornerstones of the Rockland area's cultural revival. The Farnsworth Art Museum has new galleries and a museum shop on Main Street, and recently bought a former church building to be used to store its collection of Wyeth family works. The Owls Head Transportation Museum and the Shore Village Museum (which houses extensive lighthouse exhibits and memorabilia) are experiencing growth as well.

If the role of cultural center is a new mantle for a blue-collar industrial town, it is one Rockland is wearing well. Sleeper attributes Rockland's changes to market forces, creativity and people promoting the city's positive attributes. "Pent-up demand wasn't being met in other places," she says. "Rockland was discovered as a viable new location."

Whether Rockland retains its diverse heritage or reaches for the lure of prosperity in the tourist economy remains to be seen. For now, the city is slowly and deliberately progressing down the path of its choice. Community leaders have placed local needs at the top, keeping the focus on a diverse Rockland culture and economy so that year-round residents can have a high-quality lifestyle. It is a strategy that could work: if the city heeds the priorities of its residents, perhaps visitors will like Rockland as much as the locals do.

— **By Bob Moore**

ST. GEORGE
1882: Canned lobsters, granite and marine railways

St. George is the most southerly town of Knox County. It embraces the southern and larger part of a long and broad peninsula formed by St. George's River on the west and the ocean on the east. It includes Metinic, Elwell and Georges Islands. Tennant's Harbor is the principal village. Others are St. George, South St. George, Martinsville and Clark's Island. At South St. George some ship-building is done; other productions are ice and canned lobsters. At Tennant's Harbor, is a large sail loft; and in the vicinity the Long Cove and the Clark's Island granite companies, and others, have their business. Tennant's Harbor and Port Clyde each have a marine railway.

St. George originally was part of Cushing, from which it was set off and incorporated in 1803. The woods are chiefly of spruce. The soil is a clay loam, good for potatoes, which is the crop chiefly cultivated. St. George has 16 public schoolhouses, and its school property is valued at $5,000. The population in 1870 was 2,318.

(Maine Gazetteer)

1996: Tourism, fishing, lobstering

Today, St. George incorporates the villages of Tenant's Harbor, Martinsville, Wiley's Corner, Hart's Neck and Port Clyde. The economic base in St. George is tourism, fishing and lobstering.

SOUTH THOMASTON
1882: Tidal power on the Westkeag

South Thomaston is the most south-eastern town of Knox County, extending southward in the form of a peninsula, and into Penobscot Bay in the form of a promontory. The surface of the town is rough and rocky along the coast, but back some distance there are many excellent farms. Hay is the principal crop. Westkeag River is the principal stream. Its pond, confined at South Thomaston village by a dam, furnished the chief water-power in town. It is a tide-power mainly. Upon it are a grist-mill, three polishing machines for granite, and a lumber-mill.

There are fourteen public schoolhouses in south Thomaston, and the school property is valued at 6,300. The population in 1870 was 1,593.

(Maine Gazetteer)

1996: *Farming, fishing and summer visitors*

South Thomaston also includes Spruce Head and Spruce Head Island. The economic base is still lobstering and some fishing (primarily for scallops and shrimp). Summer residences and tourism play an important seasonal role in the South Thomaston economy.

OWLS HEAD
1882: *Lighthouse, harbor, village*

Owl's Head, a promontory bearing a light-house on the west shore of Penobscot Bay in south Thomaston, a short distance below Rockland. Also a small harbor and village just south of the promontory.

(Maine Gazetteer)

1996: *Lobstering, retirement, construction*

The lobster fishery continues to be a mainstay of the Owls Head economic base, but today, much of the Owls Head labor force commutes to businesses outside of town.

There is little in the way of commerce. Over 22 percent of Owls Head residents are aged 65 or older. As is typical in most retirement communities, building trades provide steady employment for carpenters, painters, plumbers, electricians, etc., who maintain, renovate and remodel the old homes in Owls Head.

Tourism is a big component of the Owls Head economy. The Owls Head Transportation Museum draws visitors from throughout Maine to see the air shows and antique auto auctions held there. The regional airport for the midcoast area is located in Owls Head.

SOUTH THOMASTON

Cultural institutions
- South Thomaston Historical Society and Library (at the old schoolhouse).

Important natural features
- Muscle Ridge Islands (off-shore)
- Weskeag River and Ballyhoc Cove
- St. George River
- Pleasant Beach
- Waterman Beach

OWLS HEAD

Incorporated 1921; originally part of South Thomaston

Population in 1990: 1,574; 73.6 percent born in Maine 1940: 609

Cultural institutions
- Owls Head Lighthouse
- Owls Head Transportation Museum
- Owls Head Grange

Important natural features
- Owls Head Harbor
- Crescent Beach
- Holiday Beach
- Birch Point Park

ROCKPORT

(In 1882, Rockport was still part of Camden.)

1996: A thriving year-round cultural center

In 1881, Rockport consisted of "a post-office and village in Camden Knox County." Today, while still sharing resources with its parent town, Rockport has grown. It is a both a retreat for a large summer population, who enjoy the benefits of Rockport's cultural offerings, and a rural, coastal setting for the strong retirement population. Rockport is a thriving year-round cultural center in the midcoast.

The economy revolves around visitors to the town, many of whom attend the Rockport Apprenticeshop to learn traditional wooden boat building, or the Maine Photographic Workshops.

The picturesque harbor, a favorite subject of budding photographers, also functions as a port for local lobstermen.

CAMDEN

1882: "The Indian name, signifying sea-swells, is properly descriptive"

Camden is situated on the west side of Penobscot Bay, and is the north-eastern town in Knox County. The surface is broken and mountainous, and the Indian name of the place (Megunticook) signifying great sea-swells, is properly descriptive. There are grouped within the town five mountains, spoken of in early times as Mathebestucks Hills. They range in general from north-east to south-west, and were more or less clothed with forest trees quite to their tops. The summit of Megunticook affords one of the noblest of marine prospects, embracing Penobscot Bay with its islands, Mount Desert at the east, and a vast sweep of the ocean on the south-east. They are visible 20 leagues distant.

Camden was a part of the Waldo patent, and the township passed into the ownership of the "Twenty Associates," becoming Megunticook plantation. The first settler was James Richards, who

---

ROCKPORT

Incorporated 1891, formerly part of Camden

Population in 1990: 2,854; 58 percent born in Maine
1940: 1,526

Launching of the ship FREDERICK BILLINGS at Rockport, 1885 (Marine Research Society)

Cultural institutions

- Rockport Opera House, Bay Chamber Concerts
- Rockport Public Library
- Maine Photographic Workshops
- Maine Coast Artists Gallery
- Vesper Hill Children's Chapel – gardens
- Indian Island Lighthouse

Important natural features

- Harbor Park
- Rockport Harbor

commenced a settlement at the mouth of the Megunticook in 1769. Robert Thorndike together with Peter Ott, Paul Thorndike, Harkness and Ballard, about the same time commenced one at what is now Rockport village.

Camden has six ponds, Lily, Hosmer's, Canaan, Grassy, Rocky, and Oyster, ranging from 65 to 900 acres. There are five considerable streams and twenty-one water-powers. Fourteen of these are on Megunticook Stream, the outlet of Canaan, or Megunticook Pond, situated about 2 1/2 miles from Camden Harbor. The stream is, however, some 3 1/2 miles long, and in this distance has a fall of about 150 feet.

The manufactures at Camden village consist of foundry products, railroad cars, woolens and paper-mill felting, anchors, wedges, plugs and tree nails, planking, powder-kegs, excelsior, mattresses, powder, barrel-head machines, tin-ware, oakum, wool-rolls, carriages, boots and shoes, leather, flour and meal, ships and boats. At Rockport, the manufactures are ships, boats, sails, capstans and wind-lasses, lime, bricks, tin-ware, meal, boots and shoes, patent clothes-dryers; and a considerable business done in ice. At West Camden, are made corn-brooms, carriages, cooperage, meal, lime, etc. At Rockville, the products are carriages, and boots and shoes. There are operated in town sixteen lime-kilns, three shipyards, four grist-mills and six saw mills. Limestone is the principal rock underlying the soil.

The "Camden Herald" is a spirited and ably conducted sheet, a good collector of local as well as national and foreign news. At this date it advocates the measures of the greenback party.

Camden furnished 300 men for the armies of the Union during the war of the Rebellion, of whom 90 were lost. The town has sixteen public schoolhouses. The total school property is valued at $11,650. The population in 1870 was 4,512.

(Maine Gazetteer)

1996: A greater percentage of retirees than Florida

Today, Camden's three biggest employers are MBNA, a computer-based credit card services company, employing approximately 550 people; Wayfarer Marine Corp., employing 85; and Tibbetts Industries, makers of hearing aid components, employing approximately 150. The Camden Tanning Company runs a tannery occupying an old woolen mill on Washington St. (Rt. 105) and employs 65 to 70 people.

While considerably grown up since the 1882 account, Camden continues to experience grow-ing pains. A former lime quarry, once it closed, was used as a dump for 40 years. Today, there is an active regional transfer station. The quarry is being drained, with the leachate pumped into the Sewer Treatment Plant. Polluted storm water poses water-quality problems; the expensive process of separating it from the sewer lines is in progress.

The town has a greater percentage of retirees than Florida. Both Camden and Rockport have become home to many retirees from the CIA and the State Department, people who have lived across all continents and decided that Camden offers remote, small-town quality of life, scenic geography, the ocean and an active cultural base. The annual Camden Conference, nine years old in 1995, is dedicated to bringing to the town speakers and stimulating discussion on international issues.

CAMDEN

Incorporated 1791

Population in 1990: 5,060; 58.3 percent born in Maine
1940: 3,554
1880: 4,386

Cultural institutions
- Camden–Rockport Historical Society
- Camden Public Library
- Bok Amphitheater
- Camden Historical Society: Conway House
- Mary Meeker Museum
- Curtis Island Lighthouse
- Windjammer fleet

Important natural features
- Fernald's Neck Preserve
- Shirttail Point
- Laite Memorial Beach
- Mount Battie
- Camden Hills State Park
- Merryspring Horticultural Nature Park
- Bay View Beach
- Camden Harbor
- Harbor Park
- Camden Snow Bowl

LINCOLNVILLE

LINCOLNVILLE

**Population in 1990:
1,809; 61.8 percent
born in Maine
1940: 892
1880: 1,706
Comprehensive plan
last revised: 1993**

Cultural institutions

- Lincolnville Town Band
  (a privately funded group)
- Lincolnville Historical
  Society and Museum
- Schoolhouse Museum
- United Christian Church
  (1821) is one of the oldest
  meeting houses in Maine,
  and on National Register
  of Historic Places.

Important natural features

- Fernald's Neck Preserve
- Knight's Bog (quaking bog)
- Ducktrap Mountain
- Megunticook Mountain
- 5 ponds: Coleman, Norton,
  Moody, Pitcher and Leven-
  seller
- Megunticook Lake
- Camp Tanglewood (2,200
  acres in Lincolnville, 4-H)
- Ducktrap Point state/town
  park on Ducktrap River.
  The mouth of the Ducktrap
  River is the only area in
  west Penobscot Bay with
  water quality good enough
  to allow shellfish harvesting.
  The river also has a run of
  Atlantic Salmon.

1882: On the stage line from Bangor to Rockland

Lincolnville forms the south-eastern point of Waldo County, being about 7 miles in length and 4 in width. It lies on the western shore of Penobscot Bay, 12 miles south of Belfast, and is on the stage-line from Bangor to Rockland. Pitcher Pond extends along the northeastern line, lying partly in Northport. Its outlet, Ducktrap River, is the principal stream in the town. The town has six lumber mills, a grist mill, a tannery, several lime and granite quarries, the last material being of superior quality. There are also manufactured here in small quantities tinware, boots and shoes and carriages.

The number of public schoolhouses is fourteen. The value of the entire school property in the town is $9,989. The population in 1870 was 1,900.

(Maine Gazetteer)

1996: Fewer farms, more tourists, more computers

Lincolnville's economic activity has quieted down since the 1882 report. The single manufacturer in town is Andy Hazen, purveyor of "Andy's Beer" (available in kegs only). Lincolnville's only other industry, Duck Trap River Fish Farm, recently moved to the Belfast Industrial Park.

What little agriculture used to be here has dwindled to one dairy farm and two sheep farms. Today, tourism and retirement generate most of the economic activity in town, and that primarily from late spring to early fall. Lincolnville Beach is a major attraction. Restaurants, inns and motels serve the transient tourist population. There are also a number of antique shops. The summer vacation camps on Lincolnville lakes are gradually being converted into year-round residences for retirees.

MBNA, the computer-based credit card services company in Camden, began construction on a conference center in Lincolnville in the summer of 1995, as well as "executive homes" for visitors and guests. MBNA's activities have proven a boon to the regional construction industry.

Along the waterfront today, between seven and ten lobstermen and several urchin divers operate out of Lincolnville.

NORTHPORT

1882: Cool sea breezes, 300 cottages and a large hotel

Northport, in Waldo County, lies on the west side of Penobscot Bay, and adjoins Belfast on the south. The town projects somewhat more than its neighbors into the bay, and its eastern part, therefore, enjoys more of the cool sea-breezes. There are 9 miles of sea-coast, and the width of the town is about 4 miles. There are three small villages, all on the coast. Brown's Corner occupies a cove near the northern line of the town, and Saturday Cove is a pleasant little village in the more southern part. It has its name from the landing here on Saturday, it is said, of a company of the early settlers of Belfast. Wesleyan Camp Ground is a picturesque collection of summer cottages in a pretty grove on a projecting portion of the shore, about half a mile south of Brown's Corner. There are now about 300 cottages and a large hotel which, in the summer of 1878, entertained upwards of 3,000 guests; and while the annual religious meeting in August still remains the leading feature, the place is becoming a popular watering place.

The manufactures of the town consist of two saw-mills, one of which manufactures lumber, and cooper's wares, and the other adds treenails to these productions. There is also a boat builder, and furniture, cooperage and carriage factories. The Northport Cheese Factory produces large quantities of cheese that finds ready sale. Farming and fishing are the chief occupation of the people.

There are 9 public schoolhouses; and the school property is values at $2,700. The population in 1870 was 902.

(Maine Gazetteer)

1996: Farming has declined, but the summer people still come

The "three small villages" referred to in the 1880 account are still active: Saturday Cove is an extension of Temple Heights, and Browns Corner is just above the Bayside settlement. Birchcrest is the third settlement, but is more a collection of cottages than a village. Summer cottages abound at Bayside, Temple Heights and on Pitcher Pond. The "large hotel" in Bayside (the Bayside Inn), was renovated to its original architectural style in 1993 and converted to private condominiums. The Temple Heights Spiritual Camp (no denomination) is still active in summer.

Tourism and summer folk keep the local economy going. Northport's population more than doubles in summer, and motels and bed-and-breakfast establishments stay busy on a seasonal basis. Vacationers come for only few weeks, not the whole summer as they once did. Northport has a large elderly, retired population, although there are no retirement communities in town.

The traditional agriculture, fishing and lumber industries mentioned in the 1882 account have only a fraction of their former economic importance today. The only manufacturing in Northport is Peter Ratcliffe, boatbuilder.

NORTHPORT

Incorporated 1796

Population in 1990: 1,068; 62.3 percent born in Maine
1940: 485
1880: 872

Cultural institutions

- Saturday Cove, the site of an early Northport settlement, is the most sheltered place for vessels to land, and the site of a former brickyard and wharves.
- The Blue Goose Dance Hall is rented by local organiztions for dances on Saturday nights year-round. Auctions are often held on weeknights.
- The "gingerbread" style architecture of Bayside's houses is distinctive.
- The Northport Community Church in Saturday Cove is the only church in town.
- The "nine public schoolhouses" have been consolidated into one elementary school. The town will celebrate the bicentennial of its incorporation in 1996.

Important natural features

- Pitcher Pond (shared with Lincolnville)
- Knight's Pond
- Herrick's Bog and Knight's Bog. Town owns oceanfront beach on Saturday Cove.

BELFAST

Incorporated 1773

Population in 1990: 6,355; 73.5 percent born in Maine
1940: 5,540
1880: 5,308

Cultural institutions

- Belfast Museum depicts the early history of the city.
- Belfast Historical Association
- Belfast Opera House
- Belfast Free Library
- Belfast Curling Club
- Artfellows cooperative gallery
- Frick Gallery (contemporary and applied art)
- Marvin Jacobs Gallery
- Gallery 68 (contemporary fine art)
- Institute of Advanced Thinking (outdoor sculpture, indoor art)
- Belfast Community Band
- Belfast Dance Studio, modern dance
- The Belfast Maskers
- Colonial Theatre
- Penobscot Bay Singers
- Myth Weaver Theater
- Belfast Bay Festival (formerly the Belfast Broiler Festival) held in July in Belfast City Park; a five-day event attended by people from all over Waldo County, with parades, music

Local agriculture consists of two beef farms and one sheep farm. Some forestry is conducted on a small scale. Several lobstermen go out of Northport.

The auto is a necessity in the town. Residents drive to Belfast (10 minutes) or Rockland (30 minutes) for necessities, work and groceries. Northport workers commute to Rockland, Bangor, and Augusta (a one-hour drive).

Businesses in town include two general stores, motels and bed-and-breakfast establishments, antique shops, and four year-round restaurants.

BELFAST
1882: Shire town of Waldo County

Belfast, a city and shire town of Waldo County, is situated at the north-western angle of Penobscot Bay, about 20 miles from its mouth, and 10 west of the mouth of the Penobscot. This portion of the large bay is known as Belfast Bay.

The soil is loamy and quite fertile. The principal crops are hay and potatoes. The forest trees are mostly maple, beech and birch. The streams are the Passag-assawa-keag, having its origin in a pond of the same name in the town of Brooks; Goose River which rises in a pond in Swanville; and Little River, rising in Belmont.

The Passagassawakeag is navigable to 3 miles from its mouth at which point is a small village known as the "Head of the Tide." At the mouth of this river on the western side of the bay, is the compact portion of the city. Goose River, which empties into the bay opposite the city, furnishes the larger part of the water-power in use. On this stream are a paper factory, two axe-factories and a grist-mill. Little River also has powers which are improved. The city has several grain mills, a sash and blind factory, employing from 30 to 50 persons, and a shoe-factory, employing from 150 to 200. Other manufactures are ships and boats, blocks, pumps, brass and iron castings, sails, spars, staves, men's clothing, tanned wool-skins, bricks, etc.

Belfast and Moosehead Railroad, which connects with the Maine Central at Burnham, has its terminus in the city. Belfast has a steam-boat connection through the year with Portland and Boston, also to Castine and other towns eastward. In former times shipbuilding was a large business in this city, and many residents are still largely interested in navigation.

The city lies along an undulating acclivity that rises gradually from the water, each successive street along the hillside having a little greater altitude than the last, until at the summit of Congress Street, the elevation is 178 feet above tide-water. From this point the eye commands a beautiful view of Penobscot Bay with its islands, with Blue Hill and the lofty peaks of Mount Desert in the distance.

It is democratic in politics. The "Republican Journal," published in this city, has long held the reputation of an able and witty sheet. It has always done effective service for whatever cause it espoused. It is now republican in its affiliations. Belfast was made the shire town of the county in 1828. The population in 1870 was 5,278.

(Maine Gazetteer)

1996: The chickens came — and went

In the 1800s, Belfast had 11 shipyards, which turned out hundreds of vessels and were responsible for the town's early prosperity. At one point, 300 whaling ships sailed out of Belfast. A customs house still operates in the post office. During its early, prosperous years, Belfast built most of the beautiful downtown buildings, including the triangular building at Post Office Square. Ship owners and captains constructed ornate Victorian, Federal, and Greek Revival mansions.

Between 1940 and 1988, poultry processing was the area's largest industry, with two big poultry plants, Maplewood and Penobscot Poultry. Belfast now has seven or eight manufacturers employing over 1,000, about equal to what chicken plants employed in their last decade. Some principal manufacturers include Matthews Windows and Sash, which just celebrated its 140th year of continuous operation in Belfast. Before the advent of modern manufactured windows, Matthews made ships. Penobscot Frozen Foods (potato processing) is now Belfast's largest employer (225 employees). Searsmont-based Robbins Lumber employs approximately 320. Stinson's Seafood, the only remaining seafood processor in town (a sardine cannery), was purchased by a New York firm that kept the Stinson name.

Duck Trap River Fish Farm, makers of smoked seafood, moved to the Belfast Industrial Park from Lincolnville. Harborside Graphics employs 75 people to make T-shirts with nature graphics.

Between eight and ten commercial fishing vessels, mostly lobster and shrimp, anchor in Belfast, but fishing is not the major enterprise it used to be here. The port's location at the top of the bay is a disadvantage.

Tourism is a growing economic sector in Belfast. Lodging, restaurants and retail have grown with the demise of the poultry plants and the resulting change in the town's image. Still, Belfast is a stopover — not a destination — for tourists on their way through to Acadia National Park or other points. The 135-year-old Belfast and Moosehead Lake Railroad is a major tourist attraction, connecting with the VOYAGER excursion boat for "rail and sail" trips out of Belfast harbor.

Retirees are a growing sector in Belfast's population.

BELFAST

Cultural institutions

- Belfast Winter Carnival in February
- Church Street Festival in October
- Sarsaparilla was first made here, and the first sarsaparilla factory ever was established in Belfast.

Important natural features

- Harbor, Belfast Bay
- Belfast City Park (1904)
- Moose Point State Park

Passagassawakeag Valley, from the belfry of Belfast's Methodist Church, late 1800s
(Courtesy of the Rockland Public Library)

SEARSPORT

1882: "The neatness born of the pride of the seaman"

SEARSPORT

Incorporated 1845

**Population in 1990:
2,603; 74.1 percent
born in Maine
1940: 1319
1880: 2323**

Cultural institutions

- The Penobscot Marine Museum, the oldest of its kind on the East Coast
- The Stephen Phillips Memorial Library, located at the Marine Museum
- Carver Memorial Library
- Searsport celebrated its Sesquicentennial in 1995.

Important natural features

- Moose Point State Park
- Searsport Harbor
- Swan Lake Park
- Mosman Municipal Park
- Sears Island (900 acres), a nearly undisturbed island of wetlands, forests and woods, connected to the mainland by a causeway (permission is required from the state to visit)

Searsport is situated at the head of Penobscot Bay on the western side of the river. The surface of the town along the shore is quite uneven, but farther back it is more level, and many fine farms are found. The manufactories of Searsport consist of a spool and block factory, a lumber and a grist-mill, an iron foundry, three ship-yards, a boat-yard, and other small establishments.

This town was set off from Prospect and incorporated February 13th, 1845. With that town, it had originally been part of Belfast. The name was chosen in honor of David Sears, of Boston, one of the proprietors. His family retained Brigadier's Island until it acquired the new name of Sears Island. It is now owned by David and Henry F. Sears, of Boston, great-grandsons of the first mortgagee. The area of this is land is about 1,000 acres, largely covered with wood. It is two miles long and one broad, and is used as a summer residence by the family. There are in the town 111 persons above 70 years of age, 33 over 80, and 2 over 91. The social tourist will often be surprised to find the farmer with whom he stops to chat, indulging in reminiscences of far-off regions, of hurricanes in the western tropics, and of cyclones off the Asiatic coast, and other strange and thrilling experiences of port and sea. Such incidents bring out the fact that among the independent yeomen of the town are many whose early years were spent upon the sea, and some who acquired handsome properties in maritime pursuits. Often their houses will be found adorned with natural and manufactured articles of strange beauty from many climes; while about the grounds, as well as buildings, is the neatness born of the pride of the seaman in the trim appearance of his ship.

The population in 1870 was 2,282.

(Maine Gazetteer)

1996: Cargoes, tourists and antiques

Mack Point in Searsport Harbor is a dry bulk cargo port, with Irving Oil, Sprague Energy and Bangor and Aroostook Railroad Piers receiving petroleum and dry bulk cargoes. General Alum and Chemical (formerly Delta Chemical) is situated on the shore, and represents the entire manufacturing sector in Searsport.

Because of its tourism industry, many people in Searsport don't want more heavy industrial development. Many of the large sea captains' houses in Searsport have been converted into bed-and-breakfast establishments; the Searsport B&B Association brochure lists 17 members in town. Another attraction for visitors is the antiques trade centered in Searsport. An Antiques Mall, a conglomerate with 25 dealers, and many private antique stores are open year-round.

Lobstering is the dominant fishery although the nearby waters are not as productive for lobsters as further down the bay and around the islands. Agriculture is no longer a significant portion f the Searsport economy. Hamilton Marine, which sells marine equipment and supplies, claims to e the largest marine supply store north of Boston, conducting most of its business through mail-rder catalogue sales.

The state abandoned its plan to build a cargo port at Sears Island in 1996, after a decade of attles over environmental permits.

STOCKTON SPRINGS
1882: Nine schoolhouses, a shoe factory and an excellent summer hotel

Stockton lies at the head of Penobscot Bay on the western side of the river in Waldo County. The ock is generally granitic in character; and the soil, though rocky, is productive. The forests are of rock naple, beech, birch, spruce and some hemlock. The manufactures consist of Stockton shoe factory, tockton and Prospect cheese factory, a door, sash and blind, lime-cask and fish barrel and clothing actories.

There are good harbors at Sandy Point, Fort Point Cove and Cape Jellison. The latter is a large eninsula extending southward. Fort Point is a smaller peninsula extending eastward from Cape ellison, now occupied by an excellent hotel for summer visitors. A light-house erected on this point n 1837 marks the entrance of Penobscot Bay. It was refitted in 1857.

Stockton was set off from Prospect and incorporated March 13, 1857. It was first settled about 1750. Stockton maintains a high-school and has nine public schoolhouses, with school property val-ued at $8,800. The population in 1870 was 2,089.

(Maine Gazetteer)

1996: Commuters, tourism and a fine harbor

Stockton Harbor, nearly landlocked by Sears Island, is nearly ledge-free, and the mud bottom rovides excellent anchorage; it is claimed to be one of the most secure harbors in the state. The economic base is tourism. Most of the Stockton Springs work force commutes to Belfast, Bangor nd Bucksport to work. There are three bed-and-breakfasts and a handful of restaurants that cater o the seasonal tourist trade. The town is also attractive to retirees. One manufacturer in town nakes ice creepers.

STOCKTON SPRINGS

Incorporated in 1857 as Stockton, the town was originally part of Prospect. "Springs" was added when mineral springs were discovered and developed for bottling the waters.

Population in 1990: 1,383; 71.7 percent born in Maine
1940: 905
1880: 1,548

Cultural institutions
- Stockton Springs Historical Society
- Fort Pownal State Park: Fort Pownal (1789), an earthworks fort located on Fort Point
- Fort Point Lighthouse

Important natural features
- Beaches and harbors at Sandy Point, Fort Point and Cape Jellison

Chapter 8:
East Bay Towns

Opposite: Stonington
(Christopher Ayres)

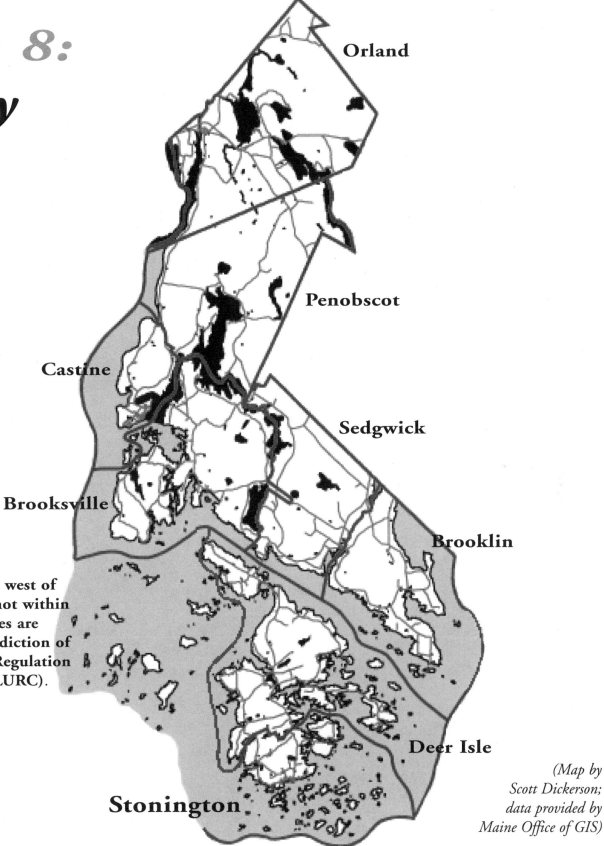

Orland

Penobscot

Castine

Sedgwick

Brooksville

Brooklin

Smaller islands west of Deer Isle and not within town boundaries are under the jurisdiction of the Land Use Regulation Commission (LURC).

Deer Isle

Stonington

(Map by Scott Dickerson; data provided by Maine Office of GIS)

STONINGTON

Incorporated in 1897
Population in 1990: 1,252
1940: 1,493

Fending off the trend seen on the mainland coast toward service and tourism economies, Stonington is fighting fiercely to retain its working link to the sea.

STONINGTON

(In 1882, Stonington was still Green's Landing in the Town of Deer Isle.)

1996: Will the sea urchins last?

Walking through Stonington on a bright, cold December day, you're likely to see vehicles parked along the street with license plates from both coasts of the United States. The people driving them aren't the typical camera-toting tourists normally seen jaywalking local streets in the summer — the newcomers are urchin divers and their crews, come to Stonington to capitalize on the opportunity to supply the Japanese with urchin roe.

For Stonington it's only the latest boom. At the turn of the century, Stonington granite was a global commodity, quarried on local shores and islands and shipped to cities worldwide. By 1910, the local population had swelled to 2,038 and consisted largely of immigrant stoneworkers, some of whose descendants still remain in the area. Today, only a handful of stoneworkers are employed in Stonington and nearby Crotch Island. Stonington's population of 1,252 reflects a gradual decline that even the current economy, based on fishing, has been unable to stem. And signs are evident that fisheries are becoming a risky vocation even for the most steadfast fishermen in Stonington.

In the face of declining groundfish stocks, the Stonington fishing fleet has had to be flexible, making the transition from the cod and haddock fishery to scalloping and lobstering, and now shrimp and sea urchins.

The number of fishing boats using the Stonington Fish Pier provides a measure of fishing's predominance in Stonington's economy: in 1986, the then-new Fish Pier served 65 boats. Today, that number is up to 103 boats, a 58 percent increase. It is significant to note that not a single recreational boat uses the pier.

Traditionally a town with a small-boat fleet, Stonington has been able to adapt to emerging fisheries like urchins and, more recently, sea cucumbers. Constructed in the mid 1980s, the pier enhanced fishermen's access to buyers who bid competitively for their catch. It changed the traditional relationship between fishermen and their buyers, who usually ran their own dock, provided bait and set prices for the catch.

Competition for space at the pier at least indicates a robust catch being brought in, and the town is proposing to expand the pier to accommodate more traffic.

Economic booms are often followed by busts. For now, Stonington fishermen are depending on the strong work ethic that has kept them going through hard times in the past. "You're only going to die once," says lobster fisherman Brent Jones, adding that it's preferable to work harder doing what you like than to give up and do something else. With his bait and fuel expenses on the rise, Jones sees his margins narrowing. "Then your engine up and quits," says Jones, with hardly a hint of despair, "it's part of goin' fishin' — you think you're making a living, but you never do."

Skip Greenlaw, who runs the Stonington Lobster Co-op, sees the fisherman's work ethic as something to admire, but he questions whether working longer and harder is enough. He has a saying: "It's no longer enough to work hard, you have to work smart."

Quarrying and fishing represent the first two transition periods in the life of Stonington since 1900. A third wave, real estate, arrived in the 1980s. Within four years in the latter part of the decade, Stonington housing prices rose 66 percent. Waterfront property and houses with views of the harbor sold to newcomers, primarily for seasonal use. "Year-round residents are relegated to living along interior roads in town," says Nat Barrows, proprietor of the *Penobscot Bay Press,* which publishes three weekly newspapers for towns in east Penobscot Bay, including Stonington.

"People here get frustrated by flocks of tourists in the summer," says Barrows, referring to the traffic of sea kayakers, sailors and windjammers descending on the town, and the visitors heading for Isle au Haut. "But," he adds, "the population of the island drops by half in the winter." The Stonington comprehensive plan refers to a "ghost town" effect, created when neighborhoods empty out in the fall as summer folk head home.

Still, some of the new arrivals to Stonington have integrated themselves into the community fairly well, according to George St. Amand, who runs Green's Landing Realty in town

(Christopher Ayres)

(named after the original settlement that became Stonington). "It's a different kind of person that's come here," says St. Amand. "They like the simplicity here. They're not trying to generate a tourist flow of traffic, like Cape Cod or the strip heading toward Mount Desert Island. They are willing to roll up their sleeves and participate in town life — sometimes overzealous, wanting things to change faster, but meshing with the native population."

Barrows notices two types of tourists in Stonington. The first type is the summer resident, or the vacationer who comes to stay for a few weeks or a month. The second type is the day-tripper. Since motels, parking, gift shops and restaurants on the island are few, so are day-trippers.

One reason there will be few additions to the short list of amenities for day-trippers is the lack of space to put them in the crowded Stonington downtown area. To make growth more complicated, the town just completed installing a $3-million sewer that was designed to handle only existing capacity, so future construction in town must locate its own means of sewage treatment.

(Constructing the sewer through Stonington posed a challenge, because a large portion of the line had to be blasted into ledge. "Practically every house had to be set back on its foundation," remarked one local resident.)

A third deterrent to Stonington's becoming a tourist destination, next to space and development restrictions, is the fact that Stonington is a dry town. Town manager Roger Stone was deadpan when he remarked that he didn't see much push to develop Stonington. The biggest recent change in Stonington? Tarring the airfield, Stone said. "I don't have people pounding the door of the town office down," he added. "When they come, I point out the restrictions of sewer, space and alcohol. We'd rather promote fishing and more traditional businesses, as long as they're viable."

How long traditional employment sectors remain viable is a key question for Stonington. In a trend that began during the same period as the 1980s real estate boom and continues today, traditional fishing employment dropped off 10.9 percent, with a 5.1 percent decline in processing, handling and labor jobs (much of the latter related to the shutdown of the sardine processing plant in town). The Stonington economy is still very heavily dependent on fishing, with 16 percent of the population employed in the industry, compared to 5.7 percent for Hancock County and 2.8 percent for Maine as a whole.

The sloop NOKOMIS out of Boston, unloading its fish catch at a Stonington factory in 1901 (Frank Claes collection)

But as traditional jobs were declining, new sectors of the area economy expanded. The number of professional specialty occupations grew by 9.1 percent, the number of service jobs grew by 5 percent. A new medical care facility and the Haystack Mountain School of Crafts are drawing professionals and artists to the area. There is an uneasy sense in Stonington that fishing can't last the way it is forever. Skip Greenlaw had his best year ever in 1994, and he is not alone in his worry that fishing is a bubble about to burst. "There are too many people in lobstering already," says Greenlaw, echoing a sentiment around the harbor that lobstering won't be as good for long if fishing pressure increases. More and more ground-fishermen are switching to lobstering, and many urchiners take to lobstering after the winter urchin harvest is over.

But sea urchins are not expected to last, especially at current harvesting rates. On one day in

December, 1994, Joe Grego harvested 1,090 pounds of urchins. But with 25 to 30 boats going out of Stonington for urchins, the pickings are getting harder. "You've got to jump and fetch, but there's still some out there," says Grego. "It's kind of like extreme diving out there now."

George St. Amand, whose office overlooks the Fish Pier, sees urchins going the way of groundfish in what he likens to a harvesting frenzy. "It'd be nice if it became a reasonable, locally sustainable harvest instead of a gold rush," says St. Amand. "But now, urchin divers are coming in from all over the east and west coasts, renting houses or motel rooms for the season. They have no place to park so they park on the street, and everybody grumbles. But there's no question they do add to the economy."

North Lubec Manufacturing and Canning Company, Stonington, 1923 (Frank Claes collection)

Diversifying the local economic base can only help Stonington residents keep their options open in the long run. Few like the idea of working in service or tourism jobs, because of the lack of opportunity for steady, year-round work in these sectors. Fending off the trend seen on the mainland coast toward service and tourism economies, Stonington is fighting fiercely to retain its working link to the sea. With both the local population and traditional fishing employment gradually declining, the future poses big challenges to Stonington's resourcefulness in dealing with the boom and bust cycles it has always known. "The booms and busts aren't terrible," says St. Amand. "As long as people are willing to work hard, they'll survive."

St. Amand looks over the harbor out to the bay, and sees the health of Penobscot Bay playing a strong role in the life of Stonington for a long time to come. "When the lobster traps and draggers disappear," he says, "something else will come, like aquaculture. Pollution is the worst part of it."

— **By Bob Moore**

DEER ISLE

Incorporated 1789

**Population 1990:
1,829; 71.8 percent
born in Maine
1940: 1,303
1880: 3,267 (including
what is now Stonington)**

Cultural institutions

- Haystack Mountain School
  of Crafts
- Deer Isle Library
- Island Historical Society
  and Museum (Salome
  Seller's House)
- Shakespeare Hall

Important natural features

- Naskeag Harbor
- Center Harbor
- Salt Pond with reversing
  falls (Brooklin/Blue Hill
  boundary)

DEER ISLE
1882: "Its public schoolhouses number twenty"

Deer Isle, in Hancock County, is a group of three islands lying between the northern part of Isle au Haut Bay and Brooklin and Sedgewick on the mainland. It is 35 miles south-south-west of Ellsworth. The town includes Little Deer Isle, Great Deer Isle, and Eagle Isle. The first mentioned and most northerly of the group has an area of 1,000 acres, which is well suited to agriculture. Great Deer Isle is about 10 miles in length, from north to south, and near 5 miles in width.

The soil is loamy, and the largest crop is potatoes. The forest trees are principally spruce and fir. The manufactures consist of sails, wrought granite; while at Oceanville and at Green's Landing, are establishments for the packing of the various kinds of fish.

Deer Isle was incorporated in 1789, being the fourth town in the county.

The climate is quite salubrious, as is apparent from the number of old people, there being 10 between eighty and one hundred years of age. The roads are good, and the buildings are generally in good repair, and a look of thrift prevails. There is a nice town-hall, three stories in height. Deer Isle has three high-schools, and its public schoolhouses number twenty. The school property is valued at $8,810. The population in 1790 was 682; in 1870, 3,414.

(A Gazetteer of the State of Maine, with Names and Illustrations, 1882)

1996: A growing in-migration

If population age is any indication of climate, then the air of east Penobscot Bay is as salubrious as ever: over 19 percent of Deer Isle's population is over age 65, and word about Deer Isle's attraction is getting out. In the decade of the 1980s, the town's population increased by 321 souls, almost entirely due to in-migration.

Deer Isle is steeped in maritime tradition. Boatmen from Deer Isle were once considered the most desirable crew aboard any ship or yacht. Fishing (for lobster, urchins, scallops, finfish) is still a large component of Deer Isle's economic base, although the building trades have become a significant employment in support of summer residents and retirement homes. As was the case in the 19th century, there is much work, fishing or processing fish, found in Stonington, formerly a part of Deer Isle originally called Greens Landing.

Quarrying, once a significant Deer Isle industry, is still carried out on a small scale (for granite, silver marble and roofing slate). A vital arts and crafts culture on Deer Isle keeps many employed, at least seasonally. Professional services (Haystack School, Deer Isle nursing home) are a growing employment sector for Deer Isle.

Including Stonington, the area's population is only slightly less (about 5 percent) than what it was a century earlier.

BROOKLIN

1882: Nine general stores and a large town hall with a mansard roof

Brooklin is the most southerly part of the mainland of Hancock County, being also near the western side. Sedgewick bounds it on the north-west, from which it extends south-eastward into the sea, and north-eastward toward Bluehill Bay. In 1856, a lighthouse was erected on Flye's Ledges, but it does not now appear in the list of the national lighthouses. The town is rather rugged in its appearance, and its rocks show evidence of paying deposit of phosphate of lime. The soil is gravelly, but strong and productive, and the inhabitants are giving more attention to agriculture than formerly. Hay is the principal crop; and porgy chum has been largely used for dressing the land. There was formerly a large porgy business, but little is done in it at present. Smoked herring are produced in considerable quantities; there is a lobster-canning factory, a barrel-factory, and the manufacture of boots and shoes is also quite a business. Naskeag Point is frequently mentioned in documentary history, and there are said to be "signs" of its occupation at a time and by a people now unknown.

There are in the town nine stores of general goods, one of fancy, and one of millinery goods. The town-hall is a large building of three stories, crowned with a mansard roof. Brooklin has nine public schoolhouses, valued at $4,500. The population in 1870 was 966.

(Maine Gazetteer)

1996: Seven boatyards

The existing Brooklin town hall is small – so small the town fathers are moving into the old elementary school building (a new K-8 school is being constructed).

While the lobster cannery and herring smoker have long since disappeared, fishing (for lobster, mussels and scallops) is still actively pursued by a number of Brooklin residents.

Brooklin is probably best known as a center for boatbuilding: there are seven boatyards in town, and numerous individuals working in the trade.

Brooklin is also home to numerous summer residents and also has a high retirement population (21 percent of Brooklin residents are over the age of 65). Building trades are strong, possibly because of the demand to keep up the many seasonal homes.

BROOKLIN

Incorporated 1849

Population 1990: 785; 55 percent born in Maine
1940: 656
1880: 977

Cultural institutions
- WoodenBoat School
- Friends Memorial Library
- Flye Point Light (Green Island)
- Rockbound Chapel
- Home of E. B. White
- Historic stone cattle pound

Important natural features
- Naskeag Harbor
- Center Harbor
- Salt Pond with reversing falls (Brooklin/Blue Hill boundary)

SEDGWICK

1882: Connected with the sea

Sedgewick is situated in the south-western part of Hancock County, having Bluehill on the north-east, Brooksville on the north-west, Brooklin on the south-east, and Eggemoggin Reach (a part of Penobscot Bay) on the south-west. Benjamin's River and Sargent's Stream each has a grist-mill. Other manufactures are ship building, tanning and cooperage. The town has two excellent harbors. A large part of the town is suitable for sheep-grazing rather than for cultivation. Along the shore of Eggemoggin Reach, from Sedgewick to Sargentville, the soil is easy of cultivation and quite productive. A large part of the occupation of the inhabitants is connected with the sea.

Sedgewick has 10 public schoolhouses, valued at $5,000. The population in 1870 was 1,113.

(Maine Gazetteer)

1996: A varied economy

Sedgwick's economy is small but diverse. Much of the local workforce is employed in a variety of building trades, building new homes or renovating, restoring and remodeling old homes in town for the growing retirement sector in Sedgwick's population. Although there are a handful of B&B's, tourist accommodations in Sedgwick are few. Most of the visitors to Sedgwick come to stay in houses they own or have leased for a portion of the season. During the summer the Sedgwick population expands considerably. Sedgwick's "productive" soil is primarily blueberry barrens, which supply the Allen Brothers' freezer plant on Route 15 in adjacent Orland.

Sedgwick's population, though 20 percent less than a century earlier, has been slowly increasing in recent years.

BROOKSVILLE
1882: "Being almost an island"

Brooksville, the most south-westerly town of Hancock County, is bounded on all sides by Penobscot Bay and its connected waters, except on the south-east where it joins Sedgewick, — being almost an island. The south-western projection bears the name of Cape Rozier, in honor of James Rozier, the companion of Weymouth in his voyage to the coast in 1805, and the historian of that voyage. The Indian name of this cape was Mose-ka-chick, signifying a moose's rump. Mr. A. W. Longfellow, of the Coast Survey, gives this legend respecting the locality. In very early times, as an Indian was pursuing a moose over the peninsula upon which Castine is situated, it came to the shore, and leaping in, swam toward the opposite side of the harbor. The dogs were unable to follow the game, but the hunter himself followed in a canoe, and succeeded in killing it upon the shore. On his return, he scattered the entrails of the animal upon the water, where they may be seen even to this day, in the shape of certain rocks strung along at intervals.

The waters of Castine Harbor and North Bay wash its shore on the north, and Bagaduce River, running northward from its ponds in Sedgewick, forms the boundary line on the east. The granite quarry at the foot of Kench's Mountain affords a fine quality of stone. The clam shells lying high upon Dodge's and Haney's points, and the mound on Henry's farm, afford themes for the curious. Walker's Pond is said to be a sheet of enchanting loveliness. It is also one of the best alewife fish pastures in the country.

A large proportion of the male population of the town are engaged in coasting and the fisheries. There is a pogy-oil factory at Buck's Harbor; and in other parts of the town are two saw, two shingle, two grist-mills and a planing-mill, and one wool-carding, cloth and yarn-factory. The soil of the town is chiefly clay loam, and the principal crops are wheat and potatoes.

Brooksville was formed from parts of Castine, Penobscot and Sedgewick, having been set off and incorporated in 1817.

Brooksville has nine public schoolhouses, valued at $5,000. The population in 1870 was 1,275.

(Maine Gazetteer)

1996: Summer homes and retirement

Today, Brooksville's economic base is devoid of manufacturing; agriculture is nearly gone as well. Summer homes make up much of the business for local building tradesmen. There are several lobster fishermen harbored in Brooksville.

Tourism and retirement shape the local economy to a certain degree.

The population in 1990 was 760, less than half its population of a century earlier.

BROOKSVILLE

Incorporated 1817

Population 1990: 760; 64.4 percent born in Maine
1940: 805
1880: 1,419

Cultural institutions

- Brooksville Historical Society and Museum
- Brooksville Free Public Library

Important natural features

- Walkers Pond
- Holbrook Island Sanctuary
- Bagaduce River (reversing falls)

CASTINE

Incorporated 1796

Population 1990:
1,191; 41.4 percent
born in Maine
1940: 662
1880: 1,215

Cultural institutions

- Maine Maritime Academy
- Corning School of Oceanography
- Schooner BOWDOIN National Landmark
- Dice Head Lighthouse
- The Wilson Museum
- Witherle Memorial Library (1913)
- Fort George State Park (1779)
- Fort Madison (1808)
- Site of Fort Pentagoet, (circa 1626) National Landmark
- Castine Historical Society
- Castine Abbott School (Historical Society Headquarters)
- Cold Comfort Theater Group

Important natural features

- Wadsworth Cove Beach
- Bagaduce River and marshes
- Castine Harbor ("the second largest natural harbor on the east coast")

CASTINE
1882: "An air of elegance and repose"

Loading and salting herring aboard a fishing schooner at Castine, 1906 (Frank Claes collection)

Castine occupies a peninsula in the south-western portion of Hancock County, overlooking the eastern entrance of Penobscot River. The village of Castine occupies a commanding position on the eastern side of the peninsula, which gradually ascends from the shore to the height of 217 feet. On the north the shore is more precipitous. At the summit is a rectangular line of hillocks, the remains of Fort George. On the southward shore below are the nearly effaced ruins of Castine's fort, built as early, probably, as 1626; and at several points are the remains of batteries erected during the Revolution. Many of the dwellings are large and old, and there is an air of elegance and repose.

Before it spreads out the grand harbor, dotted with islands. The depth of the water and the movement of the tide, make it an open harbor for large vessels at all seasons, with rare exceptions. The business is chiefly related to the fisheries. There is one saw-mill and one grist-mill, a large brick-yard, two canning-factories for putting up lobsters, clams and other fish; a rope-walk, and a cod and mackerel line factory, the latter doing a business of $20,000 annually. For a quiet summer resort, Castine is equal to any point on the coast. The climate is very healthy, and old people abound.

The town of Penobscot, which included Castine, was incorporated in 1787. The town of Castine was set off and incorporated in 1796, and was also made the shire town of the county.

After the Revolution, Castine became rapidly settled; and for a long time it was the most important mart of business in the eastern part of Maine. Shipbuilding was formerly a leading industry, and the fitting out of vessels for the Grand Banks was carried on largely. In 1838 the courts were removed to Ellsworth; later the bounty act for fishermen was repealed and shipbuilding declined, all contributing to the commercial injury of the place.

The town has six schoolhouses, and the school property is valued at $10,000. The population in 1870 was 1,303.

(Maine Gazetteer)

1996: Home of Maine Maritime Academy

Today Castine evokes the same grace and elegance as it did in 1881, with its well-kept 19th-century homes and magnificent elms towering over the streets. Agriculture has nearly disappeared, save for one apple farm. Although once the mainstay of the local economy, the fishing industries, whether harvesting, processing, or vessel outfitting, have dwindled to only a handful of fishermen.

The climate is as friendly today as it was 100 years ago, and retirees remain a dominant factor in the local population and economy. Building tradesmen and suppliers stay occupied restoring, remodeling and caretaking the fine early 19th-century homes.

Castine is also home to the Maine Maritime Academy. Founded in 1941 as a training college for merchant marine officers, the Academy in recent years has switched its emphasis to oceanography.

The population in 1990 was about 10 percent less than its level a century earlier.

PENOBSCOT
1882: "Farmers' clubs and Temperance lodges"

Penobscot is situated in the southern part of Hancock County, having Penobscot Bay on the west, and South Bay (an extension of Castine Harbor) in the southern part. The surface is generally level, the greatest eminence being Togus Hill, which has a height of perhaps 300 feet.

There are in operation in town three stave, one saw and one meal and flour mill; other manufactures are bricks, fish barrels, lime casks, carriages, harnesses, coffins, boots and shoes. There has been quite a business done by a mitten factory, whose annual product has reached $12,000.

The plantation name of Penobscot was Major-bigwaduce. It was incorporated under its present name in 1787. Castine was set off in 1796 and a portion for Brooksville in 1817.

Farmers' clubs and Temperance lodges furnish the public entertainment. The number of public schoolhouses is twelve; and the school property is valued at $1,625. The population in 1870 was 1,418.

(Maine Gazetteeer)

1996: Fishing, blueberries, high voter turnout

Champion International in Bucksport is the major employer for Penobscot's labor force. Fishing (primarily for lobster and scallops) still comprises a small share of the local economy. Sarah Condon's famous Penobscot mittens are no longer manufactured, but Peninsula Weavers, a small local textile operation, employs a handful of people. There is also a small manufacturer of trailers in Penobscot.

Agriculture remains a vocation in Penobscot. There are two organic vegetable farms, and one farm that raises cows and hay. Low-bush blueberries are harvested from Penobscot hillsides. There are also a sawmill and stable in town.

Formerly, people passed through Penobscot on their way to Brooklin or Castine. Now, people are buying homes to retire to; retirement is a growing feature of the demographic and economic picture in Penobscot. The Penobscot Nursing Home is a large employer. It has been in service longer than many of the newer, upscale retirement facilities in east Penobscot Bay, and serves predominantly locals who have grown up in the region.

Residents of Penobscot like their opinions heard: the town is proud to claim the highest percentage of voter turnout in Maine.

PENOBSCOT

Incorporated 1787

**Population 1990:
1,131; 68 percent
born in Maine
1940: 680
1880: 1,341**

Cultural institutions

- Penobscot Historical Society

Important natural features

- Pierce, Wight and Toddy ponds
- The Great Heath, numerous peat bogs (mined until the 1970s)
- Bagaduce River
- Northern Bay
- Togus Hill

ORLAND
1882: Lumber, bricks and 30,000 yards of woolens

Orland is situated upon the Penobscot, being the most northerly town in Hancock County, except one. It is at the head of Eastern River, 15 miles west of Ellsworth. The surface confirmation of Orland is peculiar. The hills are conical and precipitous, while the valleys approach the gorge form. There is, in general, a tidiness about the farms that would indicate thrift; and many are supplied with mowing and other labor-saving machines. At Orland village are a lumber and grist-mill, a brick-yard, and a ship-yard. The woolen factory in Orland, when in full operation, turned out in one season 30,000 yards of repellants, at a cost of six cents a yard less than any similar establishment in the State.

Orland has fifteen public schoolhouses, and the school property is valued at $6,500. The population in 1870 was 1,701.

(Maine Gazetteer)

1996: A bedroom community, a fish hatchery

The only mill Orland residents work in today is the Champion International paper mill, seven miles away in Bucksport. There are no large businesses in town; Orland is largely a bedroom community for workers commuting to Bucksport, Ellsworth and Bangor (which is 35 miles up-river).

Orland's "conical and precipitous" hills and steep "gorge" valleys were never very hospitable to agriculture, and today only one organic vegetable grower remains. Orland's primary fishery is alewives. Recently, harvests have been curtailed — limited to dipnetting, as a conservation measure. There is only one alewife fisherman in Orland now. The other prinicpal fishery concern in Orland is the Craig Brook National Fish Hatchery, where salmon are raised. Orland's chief tourism attraction is its many lakes and ponds, where public beaches are a strong draw to visitors.

The population of Orland in 1990 was about 10 percent greater than a century earlier.

Salmon boats in the locks at the lower falls fish hatchery, Orland (Frank Claes collection)

Chapter 9:
River Towns

Opposite: Bangor cityscape (Christopher Ayres)

Penobscot
Indian Nation

Orono

Veazie

Bradley

Bangor

Eddington

Brewer

Orrington

Hampden

Winterport

Bucksport

Frankfort

Verona

Prospect

Solid black areas indicate open water (Map by Scott Dickerson; data provided by Maine Office of GIS)

BANGOR

Incorporated 1834

Population in 1880: 16,857
1940: 29,822
1990: 33,181

"Bangor has become the commercial gateway to the western mountains, Baxter State Park, Acadia National Park, the downeast region of Maine and Canada."

BANGOR

1882: "The booms to hold the logs extended for miles"

Bangor is situated in the southern part of Penobscot County, on the Penobscot River, about 60 miles from the sea and 30 from the head of the bay, and has a harbor deep enough to float the largest vessels.

Bangor stands midway between the great Maine forests and the sea. Her vessels span the latter, while her rivers gather in their branches, and bring down the vast product of forest and mills from a wide belt extending nearly across the State. The booms to hold the logs extend for miles along the river. Up to 1855, there had been 2,999,847,201 feet of lumber surveyed at Bangor; between 1859 and 1869, 1,869,965,454 feet of long lumber were shipped hence; in 1868, 274,000,000 feet of short lumber (clapboards, laths and shingles) were shipped; and in 1872, there were 246,500,000 feet of long lumber surveyed here. The total lumber crop of Maine in 1872 was about 700,000,000 feet of which 225,000,000 floated down the Penobscot. To transport these vast amounts of lumber to its markets, hundreds of vessels must ascend this great thoroughfare of Maine, the lordly Penobscot.

Besides the lumber manufactures within her own borders, Bangor is the common shipping-place for the numerous mills and quarries up the river and its branches, and has therefore extensive exports of lumber, roofing slate and agricultural products. The city has been the second lumber mart of the world. Besides her coastwide business, she has a large commerce with the West Indies and European ports; there are large entries as well as clearances at her custom house. No other large city of New England is the trade centre of so large a number of rural towns as Bangor.

Naturally, under such conditions, much wealth would accumulate in the hands of prudent citizens, and such we find to be the case with Bangor.

In 1771-2, the settlement contained twelve families, many of them from Woolwich and Brunswick, Maine.

Bangor furnishes the only all-land route from the westward to Mount Desert. Coaches are run daily (except Sunday), during the season, from the Bangor House to Bar Harbor, affording what is said to be one of the most beautiful drives of the country.

Bangor has a superior high school, and fifty-seven of a lower grade. There are thirty-six public school-houses, which together with their grounds, apparatus, etc., are valued at $125,000. The population in 1870 was 18,289.

(A Gazetteer of the State of Maine, with Names and Illustrations, 1882)

1996: Reconnecting to the Penobscot River

Perched at the head of tide, Bangor has always had a strong physical and cultural connection to Penobscot Bay, 30 miles down the Penobscot River. Until the advent of rail and, later, highway transportation, the river provided the primary link between communities along its banks, and between the wealth of the great interior forests of Maine and the rest of the world. The Penobscot carried logs down to mills in Bangor, where they were sawed into lumber and exported by ship.

From the mid to late 19th century, millions of board feet of lumber were exported from lumber mills operating in the Bangor area to coastal cities around the world. Bangor was also a cargo and passenger port until the 1950s, when railroads supplanted river traffic.

Bangor spent her youth as a booming lumber town, cosmopolitan from her connection to the world as an international port of call for steamship traffic, at the same time rowdy, often seamy, from the rough-and-tumble crews that came in with the great log drives.

Along with the surrounding towns of Hampden, Brewer, Veazie and Orono, Bangor has grown up and changed significantly since its 19th-century lumbering days, and while the log drives have disappeared, the city remains the cultural and economic hub for eastern, northern and central Maine. Today Bangor's ties to the expansive region it serves are stronger than ever, testimony to the city's adaptability and resourcefulness.

By the time the last Penobscot log drive was over in the 1960s, Bangor had turned its back on the river. The city had become an industrial center with factories, tank farms and mills lining the river. Rail corridors along the banks of the Penobscot further separated people from the river on both Bangor and Brewer shores. But that separation was a welcome blessing, for the river had become a polluted sewer of human and industrial waste. There was little protest over the lack of public access to a river that was for all practical purposes both ecologically and aesthetically dead. The ecological effects of this industrial legacy are still being studied, but reports have shown that the sediments in the river and bay describe a plume of toxic metals and chemicals gradually decreasing in concentration along a gradient progressing into the bay.

Many of the sources of pollution have been cleaned up or eliminated, and today's discharges into the river are a small fraction of the pollution the river received in its early industrial days. Major point-sources, such as pulp and paper mills and sewage treatment plants, have significantly improved the quality of their waste water before it reaches their outfalls in the river. Storm water runoff from urban and rural areas today accounts for a majority of the pollution entering the river, which, because of the diffuse nature of the sources, makes targeting cleanup a challenge. The fact that water quality in the river

Architectural detail, Bangor (Christopher Ayres)

continues to improve, even while bordered by a metropolitan area with a large industrial and manufacturing base and a regional population of 100,000, leaves hope for further improvement.

A regional downtown

With a resident population of 33,000 and a metropolitan population of 81,000, Bangor has a large work force from which to draw. The Bangor area's labor force of 48,000 is the highest concentration in Maine outside of Portland. In fact, Bangor is the only town in this sudy of the Penobscot region that has more than doubled in size since 1880. To entice new businesses, the Bangor Chamber of Commerce promotes the city's sprawling regional influence over three market sectors. The first serves 28 communities closest to Bangor, an area with a population of 96,000 and extending 40 miles from Winterport on the south to Charleston on the northwest side of the city.

The second market area claims a six-county area in central, eastern and northern Maine, and includes a population of 350,000. Michael Bush of the Eastern Maine Development District, a private non-profit development group in Bangor, sees Bangor's present role as a regional center as a natural outgrowth of the city's historical regional dominance during the lumber era. In what Bush terms the "agglomeration theory" of growth, activities become congregated, then tend to become more congregated.

"The area is so dispersed," says Bush, "that Bangor has become the commercial gateway to the western mountains, Baxter State Park, Acadia National Park, the downeast region of Maine and Canada." Thus, for medical, financial or legal services, persons from Greenville, Machias or Canada might travel as far as Bangor. While in the area, they might take advantage of the greater variety of services and retail shopping and restaurant choices in Bangor that they don't have in their home territory.

Serving such a broad geographic area has the reciprocal effect of making Bangor vulnerable to economic fluctuations in a wide area: if the outlying communities are economically depressed, people are less likely to travel to Bangor to spend their money.

"The economic health of the entire region, from Aroostook County to Waterville and Augusta to Hancock and Washington counties, has a big impact on the vibrancy of Bangor as a regional center," says Bush, describing the fragile balance between Bangor and its outlying communities. "Bangor wouldn't be Bangor if didn't have a large number of people commuting in from other areas. If they don't have a healthy economy there, it'll hurt Bangor."

What the local chamber of commerce describes as Bangor's "tertiary" market reaches out as far as the provinces of New Brunswick and Quebec. A recent decrease in Canadian business, prompted

Bangor Salmon Pool, early 1900s
(Bangor Historical Society)

by exchange rates and a provincial tax, has had a noticeable impact on Bangor's retail economy.

Bangor's rise as the dominant regional center has supplanted the role of smaller regional communities in eastern Maine such as Machias, Dover-Foxcroft and Calais. "They didn't have the critical mass," says Bush. Now, because Bangor offers so much, it will be more difficult for these formerly strong town centers to come back.

Bangor's largest employers are less subject to major employment shifts than many industries: three hospitals, including Eastern Maine Medical Center, the second largest in the state, employing 2,444; and six colleges, including the University of Maine in Orono, which employs 2,500. According to the Bangor Chamber of Commerce, the 48,000-member metropolitan labor force works in 26,000 retail and service jobs, including 10,000 local, state and federal government jobs.

Far from being strictly a service economy, however, the greater Bangor area has a strong manufacturing base, employing 4,600 workers, 28 percent of whom work in paper industry jobs at Eastern Fine Paper (Brewer), James River (Old Town), and Champion International (Bucksport).

Bangor's prosperity also depends on the natural resources of the region. "Look at the forests — we're probably cutting too much, and polluting lakes," says Bush. "But if the solution is to stop cutting, look at the probable impact it would have on the forest and paper industries. Go north to Old Town, Lincoln and Millinocket. Without those jobs, the whole region will collapse. The retail and service sectors in Bangor would be devastated if the big employers shut down."

Bangor has room to spread out and a city government with an aggressive intent to pursue growth. The city capitalized on the problematic closure of Dow Air Force Base in the late 1960s by developing the facility as an international airline refueling and customs stopover. When the base first closed, the city's population dropped 21 percent. Stan Moses of the Bangor Office of Planning and Community Development says, "Now cities across the U.S. facing base closures are being directed to Bangor to ask, 'How did you do it?'"

Moses answers the question by pointing out that it took "25 years and a significant amount of planning" to make the base area a busy commercial section of the city.

As a "central city," Bangor attracts regional enterprises such as non-profit organizations, hospitals, schools, churches, universities and colleges. The city provides water, sewer, fire and police protection to these institutions without being able to tax them, and financing those services is a big problem for the city. The city recently constructed a $22-million secondary sewage treatment facility to comply with the federal Clean Water Act. "Over the last five or six years, sewer-user fees have gone up 10 percent every time the bills go out to customers," says Moses.

"The Bangor downtown still has its problems," says Ken Gibbs of the planning department. "Only 10 percent of the Bangor work force works downtown. There are still a lot of empty shops, and downtown is not the economic force it used to be." The key, says Gibbs, is to "keep up with the infrastructure," to make it as attractive as possible. That means dealing with some of what Gibbs calls Bangor's "albatrosses" — enormous, empty retail stores occupying much of the downtown, but unable to bring in revenue.

Re-establishing the Penobscot connection

A few years ago, Bangor acquired a quarter-mile stretch of industrial shoreline that included a railroad switching yard, shoe factory, tank farm, coal yard, paper company and warehouse. "Economic times were changing, and the city had the opportunity to regain control of the water-

Bangor, Brewer and the Penobscot River (courtesy of the James W. Sewall Company)

front and give it back to citizens of the region," says Moses. Bangor cleaned out the contaminated soil, removed the warehouses, established a waterfront park and replaced an industrial waterfront wasteland with public open space.

It helps that the Penobscot itself has improved: there is no smell, and eel fishermen and bald eagles share the river, something few cities can boast. The money spent to clean up the river by building the new secondary treatment plant has awakened interest in the river as a recreational resource, and the city has improved access for pedestrians and boaters. "Rather than see the river as a barrier between Bangor and Brewer, the Penobscot River and bay are important to the region in so many different ways," says Moses.

Aside from the waterfront acquisitions, there is ample evidence of an awakening in Bangor: a riverside trail along the Kenduskeag Stream leading into Bangor, protected with conservation easements along both sides, follows steep wooded banks into the city from the northwest. In reviewing new development, the city focused on opening visual and physical access to the river, to the point that now the river is visible from the center of the busy downtown.

"Quality of life is one of the main advantages Maine has to offer long-range. You have to preserve the natural environment," says Moses, reflecting on the city's expense and effort to improve water quality in the river. "Comparing the cost of contaminating something and the cost of cleanup, it's a lot easier to keep it clean."

– **By Bob Moore**

BREWER

1882: "Seven water-powers, all on the Segeunkedunk Stream"

Brewer is situated in the southern part of Penobscot County, on the eastern side of the Penobscot River. Its dimensions are about 6 miles along with river, with a width of 3 miles. Brewer has seven water-powers, all on the Segeunkedunk Stream. The height of the falls, beginning with the first on the tide water, are 20, 14, 4, 12, 10, 14 and 12 feet respectively. There are five saw-mills in the town, one using steam-power. These cut in the aggregate about 4,000,000 feet of long lumber annually. There are at Brewer Village two grist-mills; and here in other parts are shingle and clapboard-mills, two planing and molding-mills, three or more shipyards, two mast and spar makers, one boat-builder, thirteen or more brickyards, and two makers of brick-machines, three carriage-makers, a churn and spinning-wheel factory, one machine-shop, one tannery, three shoe manufactures, two stove and furnace makers, three ice companies, a marine railway, etc.

The population in 1870 was 3,214.

(Maine Gazetteer)

1996: Linked to greater Bangor

The logging boom had already peaked by the time that account was written, and both banks of the Penobscot were lined with sawmills. Today, Brewer has a diversified economic base that relies far less on the river for water power and transportation, and far more on its close links to the services and transportation assets of greater Bangor. One traditional industry has survived on the banks of the Penobscot since the 1880s: the Getchell Ice Company still makes and sells ice in Brewer.

A strong manufacturing base remains in Brewer, anchored by Eastern Fine Paper (430 employees) on the site of the former Sargeant Lumber Mill. Brewer has two auto parts manufacturers, including Lemforder, a German automotive company manufacturing steering components with 300 employees. There is no commercial agriculture in Brewer today. Most employees in Brewer commute to work from out of town.

Retail sales are part of the urban economic mix, and there are three shopping centers within city limits. Marden's Company moved its operations into the restored Emple Knitting mill. Tourism is transient. There are five motels.

Upon her death in the late 1920s, Ellen M. Leach left a bequest of $10,000 in a trust to pay for constructing a home for the elderly in Brewer. The trust recently matured, giving the city an $8-million surprise gift. The 30-unit Ellen M. Leach retirement home opened in the spring of 1995, serving the needs of the elderly at a level of care between a nursing home and elderly housing.

The only notable fishery in Brewer is the Bangor salmon pool, located on the Brewer shore of the Penobscot River just below the breached Bangor Dam.

Brewer is the birthplace of Joshua Chamberlain, the Civil War hero of Gettysburg and later four-term govenor of Maine.

BREWER

Incorporated 1889

Population in 1990: 9,021; 79.9 percent born in Maine
1930: 6,510
1880: 3,170

Cultural institutions

- Joshua L. Chamberlain House, his birthplace
- Brewer Historical Society
- Brewer Public Library
- Brewer Home Town Band (plays Big Band music)
- Brewer Auditorium

Important natural features

- Penobscot River
- Riverfront Park
- Segeunkedunk Stream (rises from lakes in Orrington)
- Bangor Dam (breached)

ORONO

Incorporated 1806

Population in 1990:
10,573; 51.9 percent
born in Maine
1940: 3,702
1880: 2,245

Cultural institutions

- University of Maine

Important natural features

- Confluence of the Stillwater and Penobscot rivers, Basin Mills, situated between Orono and Veazie, is the site for a 43.7-megawatt hydro-electric generating facility proposed by the Bangor Hydro-Electric Company.

The Penobscot River winds past the University of Maine in Orono. (Christopher Ayres)

ORONO
1882: "College of Agriculture and Mechanic Arts"

Orono, in Penobscot County, lies on the west side of the Penobscot River, and adjoins Bangor on the western part of each. The land along the Penobscot is very productive, but the quality deteriorates as it recedes from the river. A large proportion of the people are engaged in agriculture. There are two considerable falls on this river in the town, and successive falls amounting to 31 feet on the western channel of the Penobscot between Ayer's Island and the village, known as "Ayer's Falls." The mills upon the privilege are known as the "Basin Mills." On this power are mills containing eight single saws, four gangs, two lath, two clapboard, one shingle, two rotary saws and a machine-shop. The village has something of the clutter usual to lumber towns, yet the houses are generally neat and attractive, and even elegant in some cases, while the streets are beautified by large numbers of elms and maples.

The State College of Agriculture and Mechanic Arts is located about one mile from the village on the east bank of the Stillwater River in a beautiful and commanding situation. The design of this institution is to give the young men of the State the advantages of a liberal education, by affording the student opportunity of applying practically the principles he learns in the classroom, and by his labor in this application to defray a portion of his expenses. The number of students in 1880 was upwards of 100. The population in 1870 was 2,888.

(Maine Gazetteer)

1996: University town

While Orono is regarded primarily as Maine's university town and the University of Maine is the major economic force there, a number of non-academic concerns are also located in town. Shaw and Tenney, makers of oars and paddles; the Striar Textile Mill, makers of textiles and woolen blankets; Byer Manufacturing, makers of cots, canvas bags, wooden lawn chairs and other items; and MBNA (the credit card processing company also located in Camden). A shopping center that has been half-vacant for the past five years was sold at auction in December, 1994, and is being renovated by the new owners.

The University of Maine contributes most of the community's cultural vitality. The Maine Center for the Arts incorporates the Hudson Museum and

Hutchins Concert Hall and draws audiences from a wide area. People from all over the region also visit the University of Maine Museum of Art at Carnegie Hall, Fogler Library, Page Farm Museum, Alfond Arena and the university planetarium.

Orono's growth, quintupling its population between 1880 and 1980, suggests the economic force of the presence of institutions of higher education.

VEAZIE
1882: Four stores and a hotel

Veazie, in Penobscot County, is a small town, with its eastern side resting on the Penobscot, and bounded by Bangor on the west, and Orono on the north-east, and the river on the east and south. The Penobscot, which separates it from Eddington and Brewer, furnishes the water-power. There is here a strong dam, upon which are located two blocks of saw mills. The "Upper Block" (so called), contains two gangs of saws, six single saws, and a lath-mill; the "Lower Block" has one gang of saws, three single saws, lath-mill, clapboard and shingle-mill, and others. At extreme low water, the power in this fall is 3,300 horse-powers, gross, for the 24 hours, or 133,000 spindles. The manufacturers are all sorts of lumber, coopersware, etc. There are four stores and a hotel.

Veazie has a very pretty village. The town was formerly the seventh ward of Bangor, but was set off and incorporated March 26th, 1853. It was named from General Samuel Veazie, who was the owner of the mills and privilege, and the chief portion of the property. There are three public school-houses, for 214 children of school age. The average attendance is about half that number. The population in 1870 was 810.

(Maine Gazetteer)

1996: Hydroelectric power and salmon

Veazie's position on the falls still makes the town a suitable site for "water-powers," but of a different sort: Veazie dam is a major hydroelectric facility owned by Bangor Hydro. There are two concrete-manufacturing firms in town, and several other smaller businesses.

Because of its location close to Bangor, Orono, the University of Maine, Bangor International Airport, Bangor Mall and Eastern Maine Medical Center, Veazie is an attractive residential community. Most of Veazie's growing number of residents commute to Bangor or Orono. Route 2 bisects the community from south to north, with the older, more densely developed neighborhood along the river, and the newer residential developments spreading west along the Chase Road.

Veazie residents benefit from the cultural offerings of nearby Bangor and Orono.

ORONO

Important natural features

- Pushaw Lake has a park and a beach. There are two other town parks in Orono, Webster Park and Marden Park. The Orono Land Trust maintains hiking trails.

VEAZIE

Incorporated 1853, formerly part of Bangor

Population in 1990: 1,633; 74.8 percent born in Maine
1940: 517
1880: 622

Cultural institutions

- The Veazie Salmon Club benefits from the Penobscot's restored salmon run.

Important natural features

- Penobscot River

BRADLEY

Incorporated in 1834

**Population in 1990:
1,136; 88.8 percent
born in Maine
1940: 716
1880: 829**

Cultural institutions

- Leonard's Mill: a working, water-driven saw mill from the 1800s, with covered bridge
- Great Works Dam

Important natural features

- Great Works Stream
- Blackman Stream
- Chemo Pond
- Widespread swamps and bogs

BRADLEY
1882: "Fire and the lumberman's axe"

Bradley is situated on the eastern bank of the Penobscot River, 11 miles above Bangor, and on the south-eastern border of the county. The surface is uneven, but without hills. A very small proportion of the land is suitable for cultivation, that portion lying principally along the Penobscot. Pine once grew here in large quantities, but fire and the lumberman's axe have swept it mostly away. Nicholas Pond, 3 miles long by 2 miles wide, is situated at the southern angle of the town. On the outlet are seven of the eighteen water-powers in the town, the other eleven being on Great Works Stream emptying into the Penobscot in the northern part of town. On these powers are one lumber, shingle and lath mill, one heading, stave and broom-handle mill, and five shingle mills. On the Penobscot just above and below the town, are also numerous mills. By a bridge near its north line, Bradley has access to the European and North American Railway, on the western side of the river.

Bradley was incorporated in 1834. There are four public schoolhouses, the entire school property being estimated at $1,000. The population in 1870 was 866.

(Maine Gazetteer)

1996: The jobs are elsewhere

Bradley's businesses are small, service-oriented shops usually employing just their owners, and serving the local population: a gun shop, auto body shops. The few dairy and hay farms are no longer in operation. The Bangor-Brewer market is where most of Bradley's work force is employed.

Much of the town's 49 square miles is swampy land, inaccessible except by snowmobile and canoe. The town owns 5.5 miles of road, and the state owns the remaining 10 miles of road. Many camps along the streams and ponds in Bradley are leased from paper companies, who own the majority of the land in town. Many of Bradley's residents are retirees from pulp mills along the Penobscot River. There is one family housing project, Hillside Apartments, which is federally subsidized.

EDDINGTON

1882: The Methodists at Eddington Bend, the Universalists at East Eddington

Eddington, in Penobscot County, lies on the eastern bank of the Penobscot, 5 miles E.N.E. of Bangor. The town is irregular in form, curving away from the river south-eastward to a distance of about 10 miles, while its width is scarcely 3 miles. The surface is uneven and in some parts broken. A broad-topped hill called Black Cap Mountain in the south-eastern part, is the highest elevation. At East Eddington, are saw, shingle and grist mills, and clothes-pin, spool, and axe factories. Other manufactures of the town are bricks, coopers ware, carriages, etc. The nearest market and railway station are at Bangor. Eddington Bend, on the Penobscot, is the other village. Both villages contain many tasteful dwellings, and the streets are numerously set with shade trees.

This township, at the recommendation of Congress, was granted to Jonathan Eddy and nineteen others, in consideration of their services and sufferings in connection with the Revolution. They were residents of Nova Scotia, but fled thence in 1776, on account of the persecution of the British. This grant was made in 1785, and the place was immediately settled. The town was incorporated in 1811, taking its name from Colonel Eddy, the principal settler.

The Methodists have a neat church at Eddington Bend, and the Universalists, at East Eddington. The number of public school houses in the town is seven, and the total school property is valued at $1,800. The rate of taxation in 1880 was two and a quarter percent. The population in 1870 was 776.

(Maine Gazetteer)

1996: Wood products and commuters

The active manufacturer in Eddington today is the Peavey Manufacturing Company, makers of wooden bats, billy clubs, and other turned wood products. Agriculture is no longer a livelihood, save for the four greenhouses in town which raise flowers and yard plantings. Of the four, only Hutchins Greenhouse raises vegetables. Eddington has become largely a bedroom community. Most of the work force commutes to jobs in nearby Bangor, Brewer or Old Town.

The local population has approximately tripled since its low point in 1940. Of all the towns considered here, Eddington has the highest percentage of its population from Maine – more than 82 percent, some native.

EDDINGTON

Incorporated 1811

Population in 1990: 1,947; 82.7 percent born in Maine
1940: 571
1880: 746

Significant cultural institutions

- Eddington Historical Society/Comins Hall (the original town hall)
- Eddington Salmon Club

Important natural features

- Penobscot River
- Davis, Holbrook and Chemo ponds (Chemo Pond has a public beach)
- Black Cap Mountain
- Cummings Bog
- Meadowbrook Stream

ORRINGTON

Incorporated 1788

**Population in 1990:
3,309; 78.1 percent
born in Maine
1940: 1,517
1880: 1,529**

Cultural institutions

- Orrington Public Library
- Orrington Historical Society and Museum
- The Orrington Pound, a circular stone enclosure once used to corral stray livestock

Important natural features

- Brewer Lake
- Fields and Swetts ponds
- Marsh Bog (at Fields Pond)
- The Penobscot River, where there is a public landing and picnic area situated on a high over-look with broad views of the river

ORRINGTON
1882: Settled by mariners ashore

Orrington is the most southern town in Penobscot County. It is situated upon the eastern bank of the Penobscot, about six miles below Bangor, on the Bucksport and Bangor railroad. The surface is rather hilly and rocky in many parts, but has a fair quality of soil which yields well under thorough cultivation.

Many of the first settlers were mariners, who had been forced by the approach of war to seek other business; but navigation reviving on the return of peace, many of these returned to their old pursuits, taking with them their grownup sons. The town has some excellent schoolhouses, the entire number being thirteen. They are valued at $4,875. The population in 1870 was 1,768.

(Maine Gazetteer)

1996: Industry and agriculture

Orrington has two large-scale industrial operations: the Penobscot Energy Recovery Company (PERC), a waste-to-energy incinerator producing electrical power, and Holtra-Chem Manufacturing (formerly LCP Chemical Company), manufacturers of sulfuric acid, chlorine and other chemicals supplying the paper industry.

Several Orrington residents are engaged in small-scale home occupations, and numerous local building tradesmen operate throughout the region.

There is still some agriculture in Orrington, though it is hardly the chief livelihood of its inhabitants. One farm operation in Orrington has existed continuously since colonial times: the Wiswell Farm, granted to the family by the King of England, is still intact, operating as a nursery and potato farm. The Howard Dairy Farm is a large-scale milk operation.

Fisheries, tourism and retirement in Orrington are small-scale to non-existent. The town serves as a bedroom community for people working in metropolitan Bangor, Bucksport and Orono.

PENOBSCOT INDIAN NATION

PENOBSCOT INDIAN NATION

The Penobscot Indian Nation is the oldest documented continuously operating government in North America. The succession of chiefs and governors has continued unbroken over the past 400 years of recorded history.

**Population (membership) in 1994: 2,055
1822: 277**

The earliest recorded contact with Europeans occurred in the spring of 1524, when the Italian mariner Giovanni da Verrazano sailed along the Maine coast under the flag of France. Subsequent 17th-century European explorers reported that the Penobscots numbered between 3,000 and 6,000. The population was decimated by disease introduced by the Europeans, apparently smallpox. The early Penobscot were semi-agricultural and cultivated maize, squash, beans and pumpkins. An ideographic writing system was used, although there was no true alphabet. During the American Revolution, the Penobscots under Chief Joseph Orono fought on the American side. Massachusetts assumed jurisdiction over the Penobscots after the Revolution, and jurisdiction passed to Maine at statehood in 1820. In the 1950s, the Penobscot governor hired a lawyer to research tribal land claims, leading eventually to the Maine Indian Land Claims settlement of 1980. The Penobscot Indian Reservation comprises all islands that existed on June 29, 1818, in the Penobscot River and its branches above Indian Island, excepting any island transferred to non-members after June 29, 1818, and prior to October 10, 1980. Several tracts of land have been acquired by the Penobscot Nation since the settlement act and are located in scattered parcels throughout the state of Maine. This land is held either by the Penobscot Nation or in trust for the benefit of the Penobscot Nation by the U.S. Government.

(Christopher Ayres)

WINTERPORT

1882: A fine harbor, usually open in winter

Winterport has a fine harbor, usually open in winter – hence the name of the town. The manufactures consist of cooperage (two factories), sugar hogsheads and glass-casks, lumber, cheese and butter (Winterport Cheese and Butter Factory), men's vests (four factories), harnesses, etc. Agriculture furnishes the chief occupation of the inhabitants.

Formerly what is now Winterport was noted for its ship-building and commerce. Its capacious wharves, large store-houses and deserted ship-yards bear evidence of the business which has now departed. Thirty or more years ago, Theophilus Cushing ran a steam saw-mill here, the usual annual product of which was 11,000,000 feet of lumber and 200,000 sugar-box shooks. The mill ran night and day, employing 100 men. At this period, also, large quantities of flour, grain and other commodities were discharged here from the vessels during the winter season, and hauled 13 miles to Bangor, thus making employment for farmers' teams for many miles around. These haulers were dubbed "Israelites," for their early rising.

Since 1870 there has been a large reduction of population, many mechanics having removed to the granite-quarrying localities in and about Penobscot Bay and River, and others to the Great West.

The number of public schoolhouses is sixteen, which are valued, with their appurtenances, at $9,000. The population in 1870 was 2,744.

(Maine Gazetteer)

WINTERPORT

Incorporated 1860

**Population in 1990: 3,175; 74.4 percent born in Maine
1940: 1,572
1880: 2,260**

Cultural institutions

- Winterport Memorial Library
- Winterport Historical Society
- Union Meeting House
- Winterport Dragway

Important natural features

- Penobscot River
- Marsh Stream
- Winterport harbor

Loading cargo at Winterport in the 1970s

1996: Fresh and frozen food

Shipbuilding reached its height in Winterport in the 1850s, with five yards active. Shipping is still an integral part of the town's economy, centered at the 270-foot Maine Terminals Pier. With 24.5 feet of depth at mean low water, the pier can berth vessels up to 550 feet in length, year-round. Most of the cargo handled at the port is fresh and frozen food products, such as meat, fish, vegetables, fruit and cheese. To accommodate such cargoes there is a 400,000-cubic-foot freezer-warehouse and a 180,000-cubic-foot dry storage warehouse at the port. Food brokers from throughout the United States and Canada use the facility.

The dock is nine miles from Interstate 95, 15 miles from the Bangor and Aroostook railhead in Searsport and 14 miles from Bangor International Airport, making Winterport accessible to markets and attractive to bulk haulers.

But most residents commute to other jobs in Bangor, Bucksport or elsewhere. Winterport's 3,175 inhabitants in 1990 are double the number of a half century earlier, and more than in its manufacturing heydays of the 1870s and '80s.

HAMPDEN

1882: "Soadabscook water power and two paper mills"

Hampden is the most south-easterly town in Penobscot County west of the Penobscot River. The area is 23,040 acres. Hermon Pond lies on the north-west corner, with which are nearly connected two small ponds, Stetson and Patten, lying wholly within the town. The principal water-power is near the mouth of the Soadabscook, at Hampden village. The manufactures of the town are paper (two mills), meal and flour, boats, barrels, coopers' ware and stock, etc. This and Hampden Corners, a short distance south on the river, are considerable villages. Both are ports, and have in time past had a large maritime commerce, and still have some business on the sea.

The number of public schoolhouses is eighteen; and the value of the school property is estimated at $10,000. The population in 1870 was 3,068.

(Maine Gazetteer)

1996: Two dairy farms left

Hampden's paper mills have long since disappeared. Today, the town has grown into a bedroom community for Bangor's busy commercial enterprises. The only manufacturing in Hampden is shoes, although the *Bangor Daily News* has a printing plant in Hampden. The U.S. Postal Service also has a regional postal office located in Hampden.

Two dairy farms still operate in Hampden, but the operations are small and said to be scaling back. Although there are a number of retirees in town, Hampden is not a retirement community on the scale or in the sense of other Penobscot Bay communities; instead of retirees coming from away to find a home, most of the retirement in Hampden occurs as local residents age.

Benefiting from the growth and development of Bangor as the commercial and professional center of eastern Maine, Hampden's population has never been higher.

HAMPDEN

Incorporated 1794

**Population in 1990:
5,974; 74.9 percent
born in Maine
1940: 2,591
1880: 2,911**

Cultural institutions

- Dyer Community Library
- Kinsley House Hampden
- Historical Society

Important natural features

- Penobscot River
- Soadabscook Stream
- Patten and Hammond ponds
- Hermon Pond borders Hampden.

FRANKFORT

Incorporated 1789
(Formerly encompassed
Winterport, Prospect,
Hampden and portions of
Stockton Springs,
Searsport and Belfast)

Population in 1990: 1,020
1940: 562
1880: 1,158

Cultural institutions

- Waldo Peirce Reading Room
- Frankfort Historical Society
- Site of former granite works

Important natural features

- North Branch of Marsh River; enters Penobscot at Marsh Bay
- Extensive tidal marshlands significant to migrating waterfowl
- Mendall Marsh Wildlife Management Area
- Mount Waldo (where the light gray granite was quarried)
- Northeast corner of Swan Lake

FRANKFORT
1882: "Three granite quarries from which immense quantities of granite have been taken"

Frankfort is situated on the western bank of the Penobscot River, in the north-eastern part of Waldo County. The surface is broken and rough. The soil is gravel in parts, in others loam. The principal crop is hay. Mosquito Mountain is an immense mass of granite, and is noted for the number of mosquitoes swarming about it from the stagnant marsh between its base and the river. Halley Hill is another elevation of land near the centre of the town. Each of these three eminences has granite quarries near it, from which immense quantities of granite have been taken. Frankfort has three companies engaged in quarrying granite, a saw, shingle and grist mill, etc. The buildings in the village and through the rural parts of the town give indications of thrift. Maple and birch trees prevail in the forests.

Frankfort has eight public schoolhouses, valued with their appurtenances, at $4,500. The population in 1870 was 1,152.

(Maine Gazetteer)

1996: A bedroom community

Although quarrying was the big industry in the mid 1800s, employing over 80 people, only McMillan Granite Monuments works the light gray Frankfort granite today. Stone from Mt. Waldo was used in construction of the Washington Monument, and was shipped to Boston, New York and St. Louis. Fort Knox in neighboring Prospect was constructed of Mt. Waldo granite.

Frankfort's commerce has faded with the quarries: there is little farming, and local industry is limited. William Doyle builds fiberglass dinghies at the Frankfort Boat Works. By local account, the town primarily serves as a bedroom community for workers who commute to Bangor and Bucksport.

The "stagnant marsh" referred to by the *Maine Gazeteer* is a 250-acre salt marsh that actually fertilizes the lower bay and is protected by the Department of Inland Fish and Wildlife as a migratory waterfowl feeding area.

PROSPECT
1882: "Rocky and mountainous"

Prospect lies on the Penobscot River, in the eastern part of Waldo County. Perhaps one-fourth the land is suitable for tillage, while the remainder is rocky and mountainous. In the north-eastern part of the town is a marsh, having an area of two or three hundred acres. The number of public schoolhouses is seven, valued at $4,400. The population in 1870 was 886.

(Maine Gazetteer)

1996: Home of Fort Knox

Most employment is out of town in Bucksport, where students also attend school. There is no manufacturing, agriculture or fishery. Tourists visit Fort Knox, situated atop the headland overlooking the entrance to the Penobscot River and Eastern Channel.

PROSPECT

Incorporated 1794

Population in 1990: 542
1940: 430
1880: 770

Cultural institutions

- Prospect Historical Society
- Fort Knox State Park, with Fort Knox, constructed of Frankfort granite. The fort's 140 guns have never been fired in anger.
- Prospect Community House

Important natural features

- South Branch
- Marsh River
- The marshes at the outlet of the Marsh River
- Halfmoon Pond and Stream
- Penobscot River

Fort Knox and the Narrows, viewed from Bucksport, 1880

BUCKSPORT

BUCKSPORT

Incorporated 1792

**Population in 1990:
4,825; 77.5 percent
born in Maine.
1940: 2,927
1880: 3,047**

Cultural institutions

- Orrington Public Library
- Buck Memorial Library
- Bucksport Historical Society and Museum
- Northeast Historic Films
- Buck Cemetery

Important natural features

- Bucksport waterfront park
- Silver Lake (water supply, not open to swimming)

1882: "18 miles from everywhere"

Bucksport is the westerly town of Hancock County, and its most northerly town on the Penobscot. It is beautifully situated on the east bank of the river at the "Narrows," forming a lovely picture, with its streets and houses rising gently on a slope from the water. The summit of the hill is crowned by the buildings of the East Conference Seminary, which, standing in bold relief against the sky, makes the most prominent figure of the village. The streets are very regular; for which the town is largely indebted to Stephen Peabody, Esq., one of the early citizens. Bucksport has the only railroad in the county, the Bucksport and Bangor Railroad, which, in the winter season, gives Bangor an open port.

A bridge of stone and timber 650 feet in length, connects it with Verona, formerly Orphans' or Wetmore's Island in the Penobscot. It is popularly said that Bucksport is 18 miles from everywhere, being that distance from Bangor, Ellsworth, and Castine. The majestic stream of the Penobscot forms the western boundary, its shore being fringed with a narrow village for almost the entire length of the town. The business in which the largest capital is invested is shipbuilding. Other manufactures are lumber in its various forms, carpentry-trimmings, ship pumps, blocks, plugs, wedges and wheels, boats, coopers' ware, carriages, leather, boots and shoes, stone work, etc.

The town was incorporated in 1792, as Buckstown, in honor of the leading citizen, Colonel Buck. The name was changed to Bucksport in 1817. The town furnished 367 men for the Union forces in the late Rebellion, 66 of whom were lost. The town has nineteen public schoolhouses, valued at $9,000. The population in 1870 was 3,433.

(Maine Gazetteer)

1996: Pulp and paper

Today it is the Champion International mill, not a seminary, which, "standing in bold relief against the sky, makes the most prominent figure of the village." Champion International is an employer of national significance, drawing workers from well beyond the Penobscot Bay region. Because Champion's pulp mill grinds wood up to produce pulp, unlike kraft mills which cook and bleach wood for pulp, its waste stream is much less toxic than other mills along the river.

Agriculture in Bucksport consists of a pick-your-own strawberry farm. Save for a few lobstermen, fisheries are also not a significant local enterprise.

The 900-foot south pier at the port in Bucksport, operated by Sprague Energy Corporation, handles petroleum products. It has road access, as well as rail connection to the Maine Central Railroad/Springfield Terminal on site. The 900-foot north pier, also operated by Sprague Energy Corporation, handles #6 and #2 fuel oil and has access to the same road and rail transportation routes.

VERONA

1882: Weir fishing for salmon and an excellent range for sheep

Verona, in Hancock County, is situated on the Penobscot River, just south of Bucksport. It is connected with Bucksport by an excellent bridge of stone and timber, 650 feet in length. The town is mostly high and rocky, and the soil hard, but affords an excellent range for sheep. Verona is said to have grown and shipped more wood to the acre than any other town in the county.

The chief industry is weir fishing; and during the "run of the salmon" there is but little sleep for the fishermen. Verona is the earliest settled locality on the Penobscot above Belfast. It was first mentioned in books as the island of Lett. Later, it was purchased by a Mr. Wetmore, and bore the name of Wetmore Isle up to the time of its incorporation in 1861. Its area is 4,600 acres. It was named for a town on the Po River, in Italy. Verona has four schoolhouses and the school property is valued at $2,400. The population in 1870 was 352.

(Maine Gazetteer)

1996: On the way to other places

The salmon have dwindled to near-endangered status, and the lumber trade has long disappeared from this island town in the Penobscot River. The paper mill across the river provides the bulk of Verona's employment. The "excellent bridge of stone and timber" connecting Verona with Bucksport was replaced by a modern highway bridge many years ago. The high Waldo-Hancock suspension bridge connects Verona with Prospect as well.

Small businesses, such as building contractors and Doane's building foundation company, are based here. There is no manufacturing and no commercial agriculture. Auto traffic entering Verona along U.S. Route 1 from the north or south typically passes through town without stopping. There are no tourism attractions, no lodging facilities or restaurants, no commercial fishermen. Verona is not a retirement community, although there are a few summer residents.

VERONA

Incorporated in 1861

Population in 1990: 515; 87.3 percent born in Maine
1940: 391
1880: 356

Cultural institutions

- Admiral Perry's ship ROOSEVELT was built here.

Important natural features

- Penobscot River, Eastern Channel

Chapter 10:
Island Towns

Opposite: One of Islesboro's "cottages" (Christopher Ayres)

Islands east and south of Islesboro and adjacent to the Muscle Ridge that do not fall within town boundaries are under the jurisdiction of the Maine Land Use Regulation Commission (LURC), as is Matinicus Island Plantation.

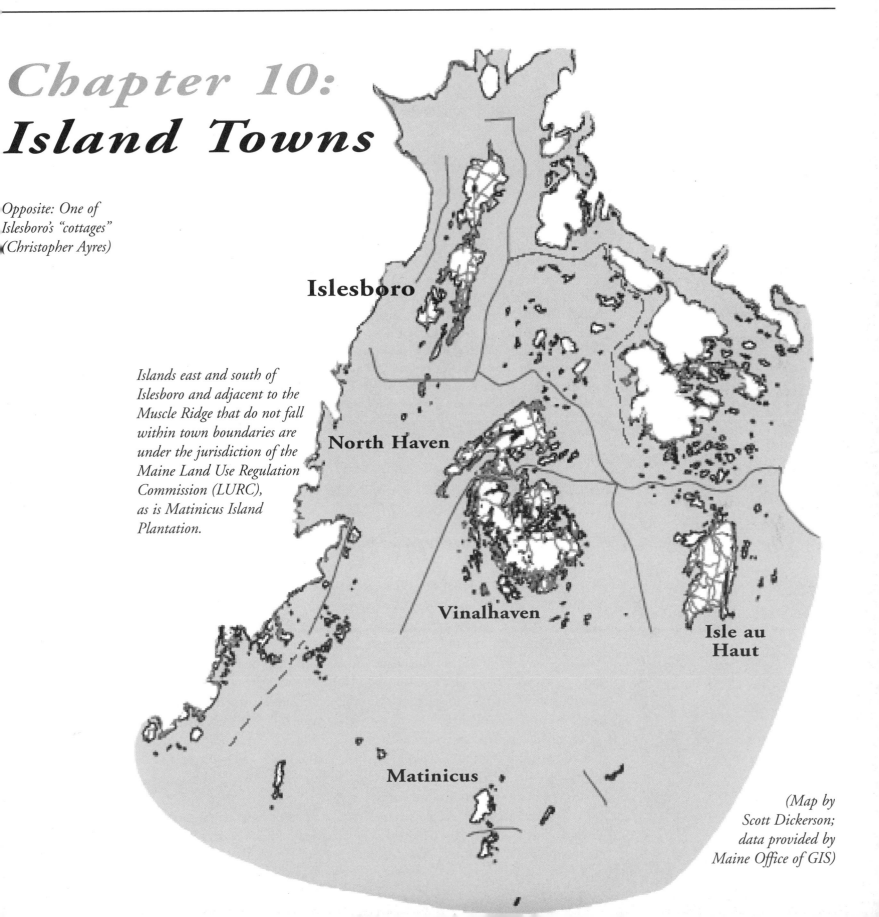

Islesboro

North Haven

Vinalhaven

Isle au Haut

Matinicus

(Map by Scott Dickerson; data provided by Maine Office of GIS)

ISLESBORO
1882: *"The inhabitants are hardy, industrious and intelligent"*

Islesborough consists of one long island and several small ones in Penobscot Bay, Waldo County. The largest of these, formerly known as "Long Island," is 11 miles in length, and three miles in width in the widest part, but scarcely more than three rods in the narrowest, which is at the middle. The other islands are Seven-hundred-acre Island, Warren's, Spruce, Ensign, Hob's Lime, Lasell's, Mark, Saddle, Mouse, and several others smaller. The entire land area is about 6,000 acres. The harbors are Sabbath Day Harbor and Bounty Cove, on the eastern side; Seal Harbor, Crow Cove, on the western side; and Gilkey's Harbor on the south-western side. The soil is fair, and, with the abundant dressing from shore and stable, yields well in hay and potatoes, which are the crops chiefly cultivated. Spruce and fir make up the bulk of the scanty forests. The inhabitants are hardy, industrious and intelligent. Fishing and navigation are the principal occupations of the inhabitants. In 1855, 153 vessels sailed from Islesborough, many of which were owned in the town,—where, also, most of the masters resided.

Islesborough has eight public schoolhouses; and the school property is values at $3,500. The population in 1870 was 1,230.

(A Gazetteer of the State of Maine, with Names and Illustrations, 1882)

1996: *The caretaking economy returns to lobstering*

With over 50 miles of shoreline for only 14 square miles of island, Islesboro enjoys an intimate relationship with Penobscot Bay. When steamship traffic was the primary transportation link in the region, Islesboro had close ties to surrounding communities in the upper bay. The distance to the mainland communities of Northport and Lincolnville to the west, Castine and Cape Rosier to the east and Searsport to the north is barely three miles, and Belfast, once the city center for the upper bay, lies only six miles northwest of the island.

"Islesboro always had relations with the mainland," said Ralph Gray, a long-time resident who came over from Cape Rosier when he was five years old. "The bay used to be more connected when steamers and packets ran service to Belfast, Castine and Northport. People used to go over to Belfast, which is the county seat, to do their banking or see the doctor, or over to Northport or Castine to find sweethearts." Gray recalled taking the steamship to his dentist in Belfast, and notes that he "had two sons born in the hospital there."

With the decline of steamship traffic on Penobscot Bay, the importance of proximity to these ports declined as well. This heralded a big change for Islesboro and Penobscot Bay. Traffic patterns that had for over a century flowed east and west over water began moving north and south, connecting communities on the mainland by road. When ferry service to Lincolnville took over as the island's only access to the mainland, Islesboro's focus shifted to Camden. Islanders took their bank accounts there and conducted all their other mainland commerce on the west shore of Penobscot Bay, as they still do today. "Camden was the up-and-coming town then," recalled Gray, "about the same time as Belfast was beginning to decline."

Today, Islesboro is an island community unto itself. Like Stonington and Bangor, it has experienced major transitions, except that Islesboro has come to accept and depend on its relationship with longtime summer residents. Locals and summer people have settled into an enduring partnership that safeguards a mutual vision of the way life on Islesboro should be.

Perhaps because of its easy access by boat, Islesboro evolved from its early roots as a fishing and agricultural community into the home of globe-spanning merchant sea captains. Before the turn of the century, Islesboro had five villages scattered along its length, making convenient landings for mail and supply boats steaming from all points of Penobscot Bay.

Even bigger changes occurred on Islesboro in the 1890s, when the island became a summer haven to wealthy families from Bangor, Boston, New York and Philadelphia. They constructed summer cottages of grand proportions, and to serve them, many in Islesboro's year-round community took on a caretaking role. Islesboro families began tending to the leviathan homes and grounds that required lawn mowing, landscaping and the services of woodworkers, painters and plumbers. Summers brought a demand for domestics, boatmen and gardeners. So began a relationship between Islesboro residents and summer families that has varied little in 100 years.

Many people ask why Islesboro's summer homes are called "cottages" instead of a term more consistent with their size. "Because, to the people who built them, that's what they were," said Gray, who has retired from a life of caretaking Dark Harbor cottages.

Tending to Islesboro's summer colony is scarcely what anyone would dare call a "tourist" economy, since many of the same families have been coming to Islesboro for generations, and have developed loyalties to the people who work on the island. More accurately, it is a relationship ingrained in tradition on Islesboro, fully supported by all parties.

Islesboro's town dock, near the ferry slip at Grindle's Point (Christopher Ayres)

Islesboro became a magnet for East Coast society in the late 1800s. The U.S. economy was booming, and life in the Gay Nineties would have been drab for wealthy families if they had had to spend the summer in cities choked with foul air and water.

"What they lacked at home, they found here," said Steve Miller, Islesboro resident and director of the local land preservation group, the Islesboro Islands Trust. "They found a pristine, healthy playground where their families could enjoy clambakes, breathe clean air, learn to sail and swim and return home after Labor Day with ruddy cheeks." Miller surmises that they may have chosen Islesboro over other surrounding communities not simply because it is an attractive setting, but because the island population was probably somewhat literate, having benefited from the worldly lifestyles of its peripatetic sea captains.

Islesboro's year-round population of 579 is self-sustaining: 93 percent of the island work force stays on the island to work. But the fact that only eight islanders commute off Islesboro for work every day belies the nature of the island economy: far from being a bustling commercial center, workers are largely self-employed caretakers, domestics and tradesmen. On the first ferry from Lincolnville to Islesboro on a bright December morning, nearly every vehicle was a tradesman's pickup: construction, painting, electrician services. Clearly, there is work enough to go around; maintaining the summer homes on Islesboro provides reliable employment.

One of several general stores on Islesboro before the turn of the century (Islesboro Historical Society)

In an employment survey of the island work force that the town of Islesboro conducted in 1992, island boatyards provided the highest employment on Islesboro. After that, in descending importance, came employment as domestics or caretakers, at the school, as builders/contractors and painters, and finally, in fishing. Fishing accounted for half as many jobs as domestics.

The recent boom times for lobstering haven't skipped the upper bay, however, and lobstering is luring Islesboro residents out of caretaking. Ralph Gray expressed skepticism that the fishing will remain as lucrative as it had been, and questioned why the young men of Islesboro have been so willing to make the heavy investment in boats and gear. "They're going along on this big bubble, buying $10,000 to $30,000 boats," he worried. "Lobsters have always gone in cycles." Gray agreed with the popular explanation around Penobscot Bay that the decrease in groundfish, and the corresponding decrease in their predation on lobster juveniles, was responsible for the boom in lobstering.

"Lobsters are back like the old-timers say they were three generations ago," said Ace Rolerson, who has a plumbing business. Rolerson recalls local legends of times when lobsters were so plentiful that dogs would retrieve them from under the seaweed at low tide. He agreed that lobster fishing is the biggest change he has seen in Islesboro employment in recent memory. Business was brisk enough in 1994 that a Lincolnville buyer came over to Islesboro to buy the local catch and provide bait. That saved island fishermen the headache of waiting hours in the hot summer sun for the ferry to bring their catch to the mainland, as well as the trip to Rockland to purchase bait.

Gray remains unconvinced that tradesmen are making a wise choice laying down their tools and getting into lobstering. His long experience on Islesboro, he said, tells him where dependable work resides. "Most of the island is dependent on summer people. Without them, we would have no stores, no work . . . I don't know what the hell people would do. If you were a carpenter or a painter, you counted on the summer people to keep employed. Lobsters have changed all that."

At the coffee stand in the Island Market, morning traffic flows freely, as do opinions. Rolerson and others opine that another big change on Islesboro in the last decade was the growth in the town's expenditures on infrastructure. Islanders recall the days when the Islesboro fire truck was a relic that needed to be shoveled out of the snow if the time came to use it; now the town has a reliable machine with a roof over it to keep the weather out. Another town expense is the 114-student island school: per-pupil costs have increased 36 percent in six years. While the services are appreciated, the high costs are of increasing concern to Islesboro residents. This is especially true for the very high proportion of retirees over 65 years of age, living on fixed incomes, who account for 21 percent of the island's population, compared to 13 percent for the state.

When the land rush in the 1980s came to Islesboro, the effect was to anneal the island community, both summer and year-round, into a united effort to chart a course for the island. "Subdivisions happened for the first time, and it was unheard of," said Devens Hamlen, a third-generation Islesboro summer resident. "Over hundreds of years, Islesboro took care of itself." Suddenly, the balance was tipped by outsiders threatening to develop the island.

So Islesboro took control of its destiny, by undertaking a massive planning effort to steer growth on the island rather than let it fall prey to random subdivision. "The townspeople took action," says Hamlen. A detailed questionnaire went to 600 seasonal and year-round households, and received an unheard-of 80 percent response. "The uniform reaction between summer and winter residents favored some growth, but said that ecological values of Islesboro are paramount," said Hamlen. "They had to create a planning board, find building codes officers and people to look after things as they developed, and undertake subdivision and zoning ordinances for the first time. It was a big event." Hamlen and others formed the Islesboro Islands Trust, with the conscientious inclusion of equal numbers of summer and year-round residents on the board.

Hamlen alludes to support for school, affordable housing and land trust activities as proof of the longstanding trust between year-round and summer residents. Islesboro's blend of active retirees, summer people and year-round residents may seem an unlikely partnership, but one that works. As if to secure it for the future, Islesboro's present character is etched in the town's comprehensive plan, which states: "Islesboro is a small community of low-density single-family homes on individually shaped lots along the town's narrow roads."

— **By Bob Moore**

NORTH HAVEN

1882: "Four small villages and one post office"

North Haven, in Knox County, is situated at the entrance of Penobscot Bay, 12 miles east of Rockland. It consists of an island about 8 miles long and from 4 to 5 wide. The town was formerly a part of Vinalhaven, from which it is separated by a strait, or thoroughfare, about 1 mile in width. It is the north Fox Island, and was incorporated by the name of Fox Island in 1846. The name was changed to the present one in 1847.

Thomas Pond, the only considerable sheet of fresh water, is 1 mile long and 1 1/2 miles wide. There is one saw mill carried by tide power. The surface of the town is not greatly varied in elevation. The soil is gravelly. The bed rock is of a black color. Fishing and farming are the principal occupations. There are four small villages and one post office. The Baptists have the only church edifice on the island. The town has a library of 200 volumes. The number of public schools is 6, and the school property is valued at $2,500. The population in 1870 was 806.

(Maine Gazetteer)

1996: Not a tourist island

There is an important distinction to be drawn between "tourists" and "summer residents." The latter own or sometimes rent island homes for the summer season. Tourists come to sightsee and shop for a day, and then leave on the ferry. North Haven residents want it known that theirs is not a tourist island. The summer population of North Haven swells to four or five times the year-round population. The summer residents have homes that, in many cases, have been in their families for several generations.

The North Haven economy is based on its two most abundant resources: the sea and summer homes. Fisheries include scalloping in winter and lobstering in summer, as well as a small number of urchin harvesters. Many North Haven workers are self-employed. Building trades keep many working year-round, in part caretaking the many island summer homes.

Scalloping is the dominant fishery during the winter months, lobsters and urchins in the summer. There are two boat yards on North Haven: the Y-Knot and Brown's. The island has two grocery stores. Its two restaurants are open in summer.

NORTH HAVEN

Incorporated 1846; the Fox Islands were one community that eventually split into Vinalhaven and North Haven

Population in 1990: 332; 71.5 percent born in Maine
1940: 460
1880: 755

Cultural institutions

• Goose Rock Lighthouse
• North Haven Library
• North Haven Historical Society

Important natural features

• Fox Islands Thorofare
• Pulpit Harbor, Pulpit Rock
• Scout Island
• Freshwater Pond (referred to in the *Gazetteer* as "Thomas Pond")

Launching, North Haven (Peter Ralston)

VINALHAVEN
1882: "Noted for their humanity and benevolence to strangers"

Vinalhaven, in Knox County, lies at the entrance of Penobscot Bay. With North Haven formerly included, the area of the town was 16,527 acres. It was what was known in the early history of New England as South Fox Island, taking its name from a number of silver-gray foxes seen there. On account of its safe and convenient harbors it was a place of much resort for the early voyagers. There was, however, no permanent settlement until 1765.

Vinalhaven has a bold shore; yet running in between projecting bluffs, are good harbors on every side. One of the best of these is Carver's Harbor, in the southern extremity of the island, where also is the principal village. The surface is very broken, so that not more than one-third of the area is suitable for cultivation. The crops are principally grain and potatoes. There are several excellent tide-powers on the island, which have, at one time or another, been improved. The manufactures are meal, flour, lumber, canned lobsters, horse-nets, harnesses, boots and shoes. Large quantities of granite are quarried here, and the Bodwell Granite Company has a polishing-mill for this material. The rock of the island is chiefly a blue and gray granite.

The Fox Islanders, it is said, were early "noted for their humanity and benevolence to strangers."

The number of public schoolhouses in the town is twelve. The value of the school property is estimated at $7,500. The population in 1870 was 1,851.

(Maine Gazetteer)

1996: A working harbor

Situated 16 miles east of Rockland (80 minutes by ferry), much of Vinalhaven's culture and economy revolve around "The Boat" — the ferry service operated by the Maine Department of Transportation. The island's economic base is predominantly fishing. Vinalhaven's is a working harbor with one of the largest working fishing fleets in Maine. Lobster, shrimp, urchins and scallop make up most of the landings. There are four lobster dealers in town, and one seasonal processor, Claw Island Foods (frozen lobster). Some finfish, such as halibut, is still landed. Vinalhaven fishermen land their catch in their own community: in 1994, five to seven million pounds of lobsters rode the ferry over to Rockland.

Other employment on the island includes municipal, school and retail jobs. Tourism consists primarily of day-trippers who come over on foot or on bikes for the day. Lack of lodging limits overnight stays; aside from a couple of bed-and-breakfast establishments, there is only one motel. Boatbuilding and repair comprise most of the island's manufacturing. Hopkins Boatyard is the largest, but there are other small boatbuilding operations.

VINALHAVEN

Incorporated 1789

Population in 1990:
1,072; 78 percent
born in Maine
1940: 1,629
1880: 2,855

Cultural institutions
- Vinalhaven Historical Society Museum
- Vinalhaven Public Library
- Vinalhaven Land Trust
- Brown's Head Lighthouse
- Goose Rocks Lighthouse
- Heron Neck Lighthouse

Important natural features
- Lanes Island Preserve
- The Basin
- Carvers Harbor
- Lawson's and Booth's quarries (swimming holes)
- Geary's Beach

ISLE AU HAUT

Incorporated in 1874, separated from Deer Isle

Population in 1990: 46; 50 percent born in Maine
1940: 97
1880: 274

Cultural institutions

- Robinson Point Lighthouse (now a private inn)
- Revere Memorial Hall (turn-of-century stone building that serves as an auditorium, theater, library and town offices)
- The tall, white steeple of the Union Congregational Church (1850s) is a local aid to navigation.

Important natural features

- Samuel de Champlain named Isle au Haut for its high cliffs on the north side. Mt. Champlain (550 feet) is the highest point. A 300-foot-high ridge runs the length of the island.
- Long Pond
- Four bald eagle nesting sites on Isle au Haut and its surrounding islands
- Wetlands/bogs: Moore's Harbor swale; Great Meadows

ISLE AU HAUT
1882: "The occupation of the inhabitants is wholly related to the sea"

Isle au Haut, the most south-westerly portion of Hancock County, is situated at the eastern entrance of Penobscot Bay, and one league directly south of Deer Isle. It is composed of the Isle au Haut, the two Spoon Islands, York's, Fogg's, Burnt, Merchant's, Kimball's, and all other islands south of Merchant's Row. The aggregate area is about 3,000 acres. The first settlement is said to have been made by Anthony Merchant, in 1772, on the island which has since borne his name.

The occupation of the inhabitants is wholly related to the sea. There is in town an establishment for canning lobsters and a boatbuilder's shop.

The town has a church edifice, occupied as a union house. There are two public schoolhouses, which with their appurtenances, are valued at $200.

(Maine Gazetteer)

1996: Visitors by quota

Though incorporated in 1874, Isle au Haut was first settled in 1792. According to the town office, the town's populaton is cyclical, and has grown since 1990 to an estimated 80 year-round residents. Most of the Isle au Haut labor force is self-employed. The economic base is still dominated by fisheries: approximately a dozen vessels leave Isle au Haut for lobster, urchins and scallops. The catch is taken to Stonington. The island's only lobster pound is kept full from October to March. Building trades make up the rest of the employment in town, along with a handful of workers at the local store, town office and Acadia National Park.

Isle au Haut has an agreement with the park allowing limited visitor use of the island. A daily quota of visitors get dropped off at the park campground, not in the town. Residents say they don't want a tourism economy, and other than a small number of campsites run by the park, there are no tourism facilities, bathrooms or restaurants on Isle au Haut.

Land ownership on Isle au Haut is roughly broken down to 50 percent national park, 20 percent town land, and the rest private. Private land ownership is concentrated among a few (five) families, much of which is in Tree Growth and assessed at a reduced rate. With 70 percent of the town's area not producing property taxes, the island's budget is limited. The park donates $2,000 a year to the town.

While residents are aware that a large lot could be sold for development, planning is not favored in Isle au Haut. Every year a few new summer homes are constructed, a trend selectmen say is slowly changing the town's character.

MATINICUS
1882: Weekly communication by packet

Matinicus Isle Plantation, in Knox County, is situated off Penobscot Bay, directly south of Vinalhaven. It is 20 miles S.S.E. from Rockland, with which it has weekly communication by packet. The plantation includes seven islands, viz.: Matinicus Isle, containing about 800 acres; Ragged Island, about 350 acres; Matinicus Rock, about 10 acres. The latter has a light station and a steam whistle. The next largest islands are Wooden Ball, Seal Rock and No Man's Land. On Matinicus Island are Old Wharf and Black Duck ponds, each containing about two acres. The forest trees are spruce and fir. The rock is chiefly granitic, and the soil is a sandy loam. Potatoes form the largest crop. The people are employed principally in the fisheries. The plantation was organized in 1840. It sent 11 of its citizens, beside substitutes, to the aid of the Union in the war of the Rebellion.

The principal entertainments are those of the Sunday-school. There are two public schoolhouses, and the school property is valued at $600. The population in 1870 was 277.

(Maine Gazetteer)

1996: Transportation by air

Changing technology has made remote island locations less important to the fishing industry than they once were. Today's fleet is capable of making trips offshore in much less time than the vessels of a century ago, and many fishing families that once lived on islands have moved to the mainland or left the business to others. On Matinicus, the exception to this rule is lobstering, which today supports a sizable island-based fleet. Ferries to Matinicus are infrequent, and most residents depend on other boats or air service for their needs.

The year-round community on Matinicus struggles to maintain the critical mass to keep the school, power company and post office alive. No other town in the Penobscot Bay other than Isle au Haut has experienced such a profound population reduction.

MATINICUS

Originated as a plantation in 1840

Population in 1990: 67; 62.3 percent born in Maine
1940: 112
1880: 243

Cultural institutions

- Community Church
- Library
- Museum
- Wreck of the tug D.T. Sheridan
- Monhegan Island Light
- Manna Island Fog Signal Station
- "The Square House"
- Fish Beach Breakwater
- Maine Historic Preservation Commission lists four pre-historic sites on Monhegan
- Matinicus Rock Lighthouse

Important natural features

- The Meadow
- Cathedral Woods
- The Ice Pond
- Swim Beach
- Duck Islands
- Seabird nesting colonies on Matinicus Rock, five miles south of Matinicus, and on other surrounding islands including Wooden Ball, Ragged (Criehaven), Seal, and Ten Pound Islands
- Sand Beach

ISLANDS UNDER STATE CONTROL

More than 100 islands in Penobscot Bay are outside the boundaries of organized towns and fall under the jurisdiction of the state Land Use Regulation Commission (LURC). A few of these islands were once self-governing or part of mainland towns and reverted to state control as their year-round residents departed early in this century. (At one time more than 300 of Maine's islands had year-round populations; today, statewide, only 14 fall into that category.)

LURC acts as a planning board for most of the territory under its jurisdiction, which includes vast stretches of Maine's North Woods. It regulates land use under a comprehensive plan, and issues permits for subdivisions, construction, mining, development in the shoreland zone, road building and other activities.

Penobscot Bay islands in LURC territory include groups east and south of Islesboro, along the western shore of Deer Isle and along the Muscle Ridge on the western side of the bay.

Some islands under LURC jurisdiction — Monhegan and Matinicus, for example — are organized as "plantations" and enjoy limited self-government.

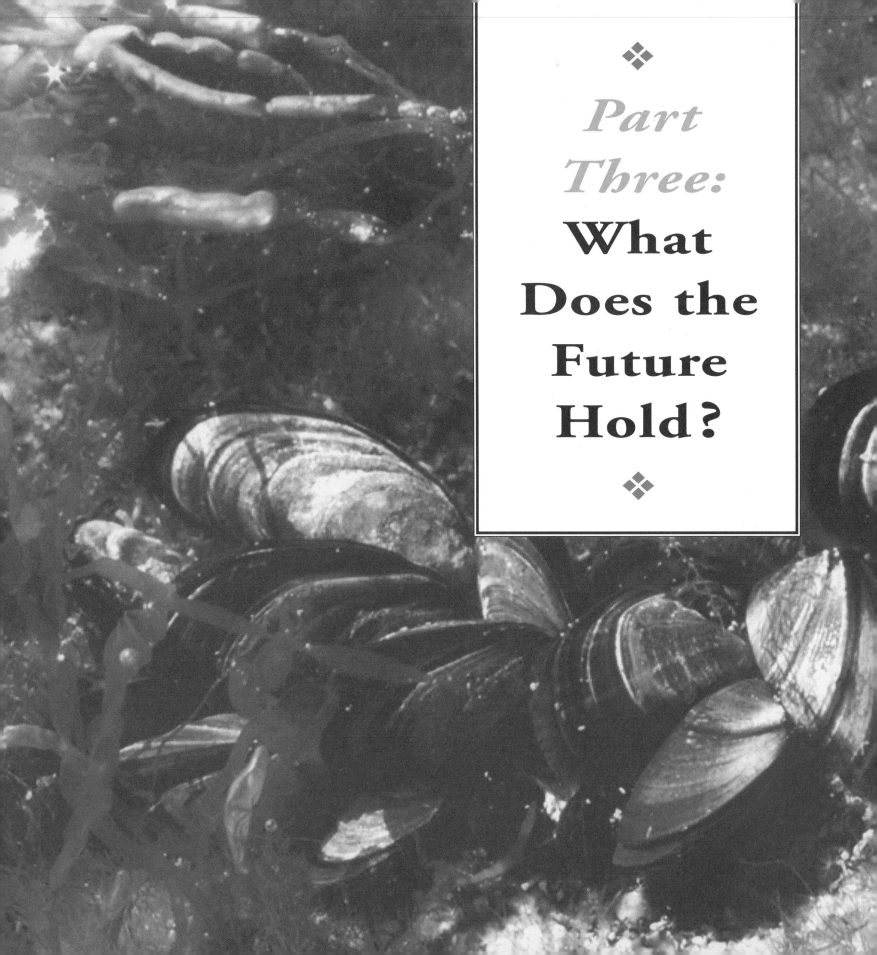

Part Three:

What Does the Future Hold?

Chapter 11: A Region at Risk

By Michael Herz and Bob Moore

Part I: Threats to the water

As the first two parts of this book have shown, the Penobscot region is the product of three centuries of settlement, two centuries of shifting industrial development and a century of tourism that today draws two million visitors a year. The legacy of all this human activity is reflected in the water quality of the river, estuary and bay, and in the economic life of every resident.

A variety of water quality problems compromise the health of the bay and its resources. Some pollution sources are legacies from decades-old practices (toxic hot spots left over from mining, shipyards, lumber mills and military bases) and contribute to elevated levels of heavy metals in sediment and shellfish. Others are more recent — large and small oil spills contributing to high levels of poly aromatic hydrocarbons (PAHs) in sediments throughout the head of the bay; bacterial contamination from sewage plants, overboard discharges and surface runoff resulting in nearly 50 percent of the bay's 23,445 acres of shellfish beds being closed to harvest; paper mills and other sources of dioxin leading the state to issue health advisories recommending no consumption of lobster tomalley by pregnant women, nursing mothers and women of childbearing age.

Sources of pollution

One of the region's many sources of pollution is the Penobscot River itself, which, with its tributaries, drains more than 8,592 square miles of upland and contributes its runoff to the bay. Nearly 50 communities with 30 wastewater treatment plants, 58 industrial dischargers, seven power plants, plus approximately 300 household overboard discharges and 13 combined sewage overflows (discharge pipes that carry both sewage and storm water and overflow with sewage and other wastes during storms). These sources empty into the river and bay, annually discharging billions of gallons of wastewater containing hundreds of thousands of pounds of inorganic and organic chemicals and biological pollutants including bacteria and viruses. These sources represent only part of the toxic load received by the river and the bay — they do not include an equal amount that is estimated to come from "non-point" sources such as farm fields, parking lots, septic systems, fertilized lawns and storm water runoff. Compared to point sources, such as identifiable discharge pipes, non-point source pollution is "a whole category of pollution we're just beginning to understand," said Bill Ferdinand of the State Planning Office. "We're in the same position now with non-point source pollution as we were in the 1970s with point sources."

Sewage

Despite a rigorous federal permit process, no one is charged with measuring (or even estimating) of the total volume of wastewater or the quantities of toxic pollutants discharged. In addition,

Opposite: Mussels filter water and accumulate pollutants, making them an indicator of environmental health. (A. Gingert)

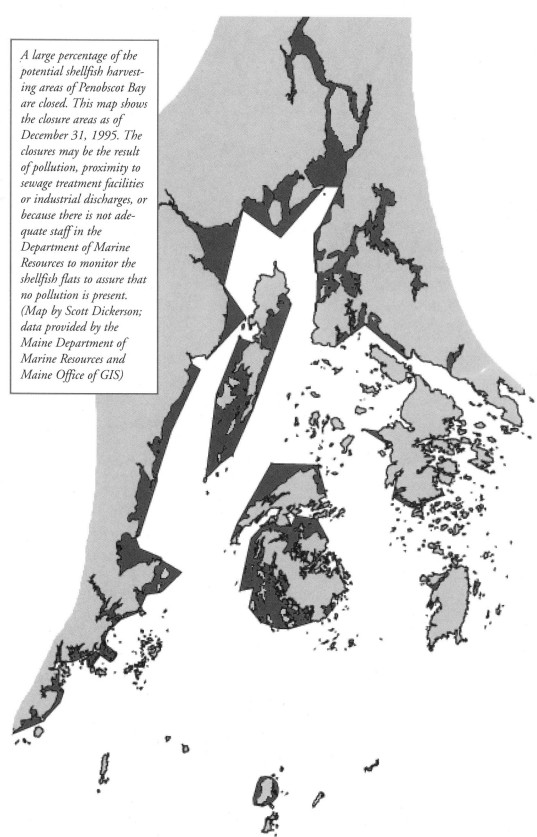

A large percentage of the potential shellfish harvesting areas of Penobscot Bay are closed. This map shows the closure areas as of December 31, 1995. The closures may be the result of pollution, proximity to sewage treatment facilities or industrial discharges, or because there is not adequate staff in the Department of Marine Resources to monitor the shellfish flats to assure that no pollution is present. (Map by Scott Dickerson; data provided by the Maine Department of Marine Resources and Maine Office of GIS)

the lack of any regular sampling of receiving water, sediment or animal tissues for concentration of toxics of concern makes it extremely difficult to monitor trends, leaving us uninformed regarding potential health consequences of exposure to water, fish or shellfish. State and federal regulations have, however, established "safe" levels of coliform bacteria for swimming and for growing shellfish. The state Department of Marine Resources (DMR) monitors 398 stations in Penobscot Bay to determine whether water quality is adequate for shellfish harvesting. Current data indicate that 47 percent of the 23,445 acres of beds in the bay are closed to harvesting. The DMR also performs tests to detect dinoflagellates ("red tide") that can cause paralytic shellfish poisoning.

Petroleum products

One of the byproducts of virtually all the oil and gas we consume is polynuclear aromatic hydrocarbons (PAHs). They are of major concern because of their ability to cause cancer, change the genetic material of cells and cause birth defects. A good deal of evidence exists that documents their ability to accumulate in shellfish tissue and to affect feeding, respiration, growth, reproduction and population structure. In addition, liver tumors, reproductive failures, reduced immune responses, higher disease susceptibility and population declines have been observed in several species of fish inhabiting areas with elevated levels of PAHs in bottom sediments.

The human impact of eating PAHs-contaminated fish and shellfish is not well understood. There has been little investigation of the human health effects of hydrocarbon exposure. Major sources of PAHs are engine oil and street runoff discharged to storm sewers, large and small oil spills, leaking underground tanks, bilge water, wastewater treatment plants, leaking landfills and creosote leaching from wharves and pilings.

In the most systematic investigation of

Penobscot Bay sediments, researchers from the Bigelow Laboratory for Ocean Sciences sampled 49 stations located throughout the bay in 1983. They found the highest total PAHs concentrations at the head of the bay, with decreasing amounts further seaward. Similar gradients were observed in the mouth of the Penobscot River and in the harbors of Searsport, Belfast, Rockland and Camden: the highest concentrations at the innermost stations, decreasing as the distance from the river mouth and harbors increased. Concentrations at the 11 stations nearest the head of the bay exceeded levels that have been observed to produce toxicity in bivalve larvae.

A significant portion of Penobscot Bay is contaminated with PAHs to levels that are comparable to far more industrialized areas such as the New York Bight, Buzzards Bay, Massachusetts Bay and the Baltic Sea. In fact, among 23 Gulf of Maine sites, mean sediment PAHs levels at Sears Island rank third, with only Boston and Salem harbors being higher. In a similar, region-wide comparison, Penobscot Bay PAHs were the fifth highest among marine sediments throughout the entire northeast. New sampling for hydrocarbons is needed to determine whether current levels of PAHs are as high as those detected over a decade ago.

Whether PAHs have contributed to Penobscot Bay shellfish reproductive failures and population decreases remains to be determined, but sediment samples collected at Sears and Pickering islands by the National Oceanic and Atmospheric Administration (NOAA) in 1986 and 1987 exceeded PAHs levels associated with bivalve larvae toxicity.

Inorganic chemicals and heavy metals

Heavy metals are trace elements that can appear in estuarine waters, sediments and animal tissues as a result of human activities as well as from their occurrence in local geological formations. Arsenic, cadmium, chromium, copper, lead, mercury, nickel, silver and zinc can be found in both municipal sewage and industrial discharges, in street, road, parking lot, boat and shipyard runoff and in mine drainage. The metals accumulate in bottom sediments where they can become biologically available to shellfish, where, in turn, the metals "bioaccumulate" to levels thousands of times higher than their concentration in water.

Heavy metals can be highly toxic to both finfish and shellfish, waterfowl and shorebirds, marine mammals and humans. A number of these elements have been demonstrated to be carcinogenic, mutagenic or teratogenic.

The Bigelow Laboratory investigators also investigated trace metal concentrations in bottom sediments at the 49 stations they sampled for PAHs. As was the case with PAHs, there was a significant correlation between metal concentration and distance from the mouth of the bay, with the highest levels near the river mouth and the lowest at the seaward end of the bay, again suggesting outflow from the Penobscot as a major source. The highest concentrations for most of the metals were observed in the Belfast Bay-Searsport Harbor area that is adjacent to some of the most significant industrial activity on the bay. Concentrations of nickel in the Belfast Bay area, off Camden, and at several stations south of Searsport were the only metal values that exceeded NOAA thresholds for shellfish larvae toxicity.

NOAA sediment sampling in the Bay in 1985 and 1986 revealed higher levels of chromium, lead, mercury and zinc at Sears Island, Pickering Island and even at reference sites near the center of the Bay than Larsen and Johnson had found in 1983. Most of these values exceeded NOAA thresholds for toxicity in shellfish larvae. With the exception of cadmium, all of the metals analyzed were present in levels well above pre-industrial levels. Concentrations of chromium, copper and lead were comparable to those currently found in other New England sites considered to be highly industrialized.

Mussel Watch

In response to growing concerns about the levels of contaminants in U.S. coastal waters and their implications for environmental and human health, the Environmental Protection Agency in 1976 began a program called Mussel Watch using bivalve mollusks that filter water and particles (containing pollutants) as biological monitors of water and sediment quality (Goldberg et al, 1983).

This program was shifted to the National Oceanic and Atmospheric Administration (NOAA) in 1986. Two Maine sampling stations, Sears and Pickering Islands, have been included in the national program. This monitoring has been extremely useful for tracking changes in heavy metal, petroleum hydrocarbon and pesticide concentrations. Unfortunately, there are no guidelines concerning the public health effects of consuming shellfish containing high levels of petroleum hydrocarbons.

In more recent Mussel Watch sampling by the Maine Department of Environmental Protection, none of the tissue concentrations, including some from samples taken at Sears Island, exceeded FDA limits, suggesting that although contamination may be entering sediments, it is not accumulating in filter feeders such as mussels.

DDT, dioxin and other synthetic organic chemicals

These stable compounds have been made by humans and are highly persistent in sediments and fatty tissues, resistant to decomposition and extremely toxic to living organisms.

DDT is a pesticide that is associated with the thinning of eggshells and is thought to be responsible for serious population declines of bald eagles, ospreys and other bird species. Its use was banned in the U.S. in 1972 and eagle populations have since rebounded in Maine, but it continues to be detected in birds, fish, shellfish and agricultural products here and elsewhere in the world. DDT is a probable human carcinogen and animal studies indicate that it is also mutagenic and teratogenic.

Over 100,000 pounds of more than 50 other insecticides, fungicides and herbicides (such as chlordane and dieldrin) are used in the Penobscot River watershed each year, but little sampling has been done to determine their concentrations in water, sediment or animals.

In Maine, dioxin is often a byproduct of the kraft paper manufacturing process that bleaches wood pulp with chlorine, but it can also be an artifact of herbicide manufacture and can be formed during the incineration of organic wastes that contain chlorine. Dioxin produces a variety of cancer types in animals as well as birth deformities and fetal death, and has been implicated in soft tissue sarcoma in humans.

In 1988, the Maine Legislature established a dioxin monitoring program "... to determine the nature of dioxin contamination in the waters and fisheries of the state." Under this program the state Department of Environmental Protection is required to sample fish once a year below bleached pulp mills and municipal wastewater treatment plants suspected to be dioxin sources. For the Penobscot watershed, this has meant analyzing bass and suckers taken at a number of freshwater river stations, and lobsters collected at Stockton Springs, near Verona Island. There has been a gradual decrease in dioxin in freshwater fish since 1988, when the first samples were collected, but 1994 tissue levels in fish, suckers and lobster tomalley were still above the Bureau of Health's maximum acceptable concentrations. On the whole, the trends seem to suggest slowly improving conditions.

Nevertheless, these results led state officials to issue once again a health advisory against the eating "...of tomalley by pregnant women, nursing mothers and women of childbearing age. This recommendation is based on the principle that developing children are considered to be at highest risk for possible injury resulting from exposure to dioxin. Others should limit their consumption of tomalley, as dioxin found in tomalley will contribute to the overall intake of this chemical and to cancer risk generally."

PCBs were long considered not to be a problem in Maine sediments, and none were found in a comprehensive 1980 survey of Portland Harbor and other Casco Bay sediments. On the other hand, in an apparently much less industrial area, trace amounts of PCBs were detected at every station sampled in Penobscot Bay. Sampling also detected PCBs, but at levels approaching those that produce shellfish larval toxicity in NOAA tests. Data from the mid to late 1980s Mussel Watch also revealed significant tissue levels of PCBs at both Sears and Pickering Islands.

The Maine Department of Inland Fisheries and Wildlife has conducted three years of study of toxic bioaccumulation in bald eagles, finding that coastal birds carried the highest concentrations of PCBs of eagles in the state. While biologists are not able to pinpoint the sources, the contaminants have impaired the eagles' ability to produce young. Other regions in similar stages of eagle recovery are producing an average 1.2 fledglings per nesting attempt. Maine averages .65 to .8 per nest attempt.

Testing the waters

Protection of human health and the maintenance of ecosystems that sustain healthy, growing populations of fish, shellfish and other wildlife require periodic monitoring of the environment. Unfortunately, the little we already know about the state of Penobscot Bay's health is based, for the most part, on dated, often one-time sampling of a series of different bay sites. As a result of the high cost of conducting research on the quality of water, sediment and seafood, there has been almost no regular, repeated sampling of the same sites — the sort of monitoring needed to detect trends (increases or decreases) or sources of pollutants. For example, the price to analyze a single sediment sample to determine concentrations of heavy metals, dioxin, pesticides and hydrocarbons may be as much as $2,000. On the other hand, the U.S. Food and Drug Administration requires regular testing of shellfish for bacterial contamination (to protect consumers). But since the cost for these tests is relatively low ($10 to $20 per sample), the Maine Department of Marine Resources regularly tests numerous sites in Penobscot Bay.

The results of investigations of PAHs levels in sediment and shellfish tissue are sufficient to warrant concern regarding the health of molluscan and other crustacean populations. From this information, it is evident that Penobscot Bay has not escaped the byproducts of human civilization that are commonplace in bays and coastal waters adjacent to major industrialized metropolitan areas.

II: Risks on shore

Threats to wildlife

At the turn of the century a coastwide inventory found only three pairs of nesting eiders and only a handful of nesting herring gulls. All other seabirds had been extirpated as nesting species by the depredations of hunters, egg collectors and the agents of milliners who collected nesting birds for the manufacture of ladies' hats. One of the great conservation stories of this century has been the protection of seabird rookeries and their corresponding rebound.

Today the coast and islands of Penobscot Bay face increased recreational use as people rediscover solitude and natural beauty. "Increased coastal recreation has affected seals, seabird colonies and other sensitive wildlife areas," said Alan Hutchinson of the Maine Department of Inland Fisheries and Wildlife (IFW). "The trend is of concern but it's difficult to quantify. We have lively discussions on how to manage that."

The Maine Island Trail Association (MITA) exemplifies the growing conflict between escalating recreation in the region (particularly the islands in Penobscot Bay) and the natural environment. The organization finds itself in the dual role of stewardship (as a conservation organization concerned about human use of islands) and as a promoter of recreational island use along a string of public and private islands between Casco and Machias bays. Many of MITA's 3,000 members volunteer their services in island stewardship and monitoring island use. "We study patterns of island use," said Lucy Birkett, a MITA program coordinator. Volunteers track Maine Island Trail islands and report changes to state and private island owners. MITA educates its members in the responsible use of the islands along the trail and provides its guidebook only to members. Yet even with its corps of educated island stewards, MITA acknowledges that the sheer increase in the number of people visiting islands is placing stress on island trails, flora and fauna.

Osprey (Christopher Ayres)

Like tourism and recreation, increased development in Penobscot Bay, especially housing, is a tangible result of the lure of the region's many resources. "There has been an associated increase in the last 20 years of population, leisure time and disposable income," said Stewart Fefer of the U.S. Fish and Wildlife Service office in Portland. "People want homes on the islands." Fefer cited Metinic Island in western Penobscot Bay, which was subdivided in the mid-1980s by people desiring summer homes on the island, as an example. "Such encroaching development on the coast has the potential to be a major impact on wildlife," he said.

Ideal sites for fish-rearing pens tend to have abundant natural food, making them attractive to wildlife. "It's no coincidence the growers are picking high wildlife value areas," said Brad Allen of the IFW. It is costly to identify and establish an aquaculture site, often involving two years of planning and testing. If IFW says it has problems with a site after that extensive process is finished, acknowledges Allen, "that's hard for them. We aren't going stop them [aquaculture is exempt from permit review under the state Natural Resource Protection Act]. We try to get information to them early so they avoid significant wildlife areas. If we can start a dialogue with landowners, that's the best protection."

Direct and indirect human impacts on wildlife are difficult to measure. The Fish and Wildlife Service's Stewart Fefer, writing to Congress in a 1995 status report on seabirds, shorebirds, wading birds, waterfowl, bald eagles and ospreys, said these species are directly threatened by "human disturbance in feeding, roosting, and nesting areas, and damage from recreational use and development." Human activities with both direct and indirect impacts on wildlife include commercial dragging for marine species in intertidal and subtidal areas; contamination of habitats, feeding areas and wildlife by oil spills; and aquaculture operations adjacent to nesting colonies.

Contaminants from discharges, land-based runoff, sewage disposal and marine debris cause both direct and indirect impacts on wildlife. Indirect impacts on wildlife from human activities include competition for prey (such as fishing for capelin and sand lance). Artificially high gull populations can be an indirect threat to wildlife as well.

Gull and cormorants (Christopher Ayres)

Wildlife populations wax and wane naturally, depending on factors such as availability of food or prey, breeding and nesting habitat, climate fluctuations and losses due to predation. Historically, these influences on wildlife populations have been amplified or muted by human activity, and they can ripple through complex animal and plant communities with unforeseeable results. For example, when gull populations are artificially elevated because of the birds' affinity for human dumps, the result can be disastrous for other nesting seabirds, because of gull predation.

Some of these same forces are also threatening seal populations, according to Jim Gilbert, a longtime researcher at the University of Maine. Animals become entangled in drift and gill nets. Harassment by humans, including urchin divers and recreational boaters seeking a closer look, can be a problem during the seals' pupping season in early summer. "Seals are only lactating for 14 days in late May or early June," said Gilbert. "Missing even one of those 28 feedings would be detrimental to the young pups." The federal Marine Mammal Protection Act protects seals from such disturbances, but it is difficult to enforce.

The U.S. Biological Survey's Wildlife Cooperative Unit has been comparing wildlife species distributions to the distribution of conservation lands to determine if there are gaps in conservation strategies (areas with high biodiversity and no protection, for example). With the expanded goal of protecting biodiversity, more work is being put into preserving entire assemblages of plant and animal species that represent functioning ecosystems. This includes not only the 300 to 400 species of birds, mammals, reptiles and amphibians that inhabit the region; it also includes some 3,000 to 4,000 plant species that occupy the same area, and uncounted terrestrial invertebrate species —

Tourists aboard a Penobscot Bay ferry (Christopher Ayres)

insects and shellfish that inhabit the terrestrial and aquatic habitats of Penobscot Bay.

Tourism

Though hardly new, tourism is today a dominant industry in the Penobscot region. It is almost certain to grow as an economic force, testing the adaptability and resilience of communities, and its future development presents both opportunities and risks. Considered environmentally friendly, good for the economy and offering a range of employment for all income levels, tourism nonetheless bears costs, real and perceived, that have tarnished its reputation.

Tourism jobs carry a stigma -- the reputation that they are all low wage and entry level, and that they last only from June through August, thus limiting job market access to students and retirees.

Like many perceptions, those involving tourism aren't all true. Jim Ash, general manager of the Samoset Resort in Rockland, pointed out that the Samoset employs 265 throughout the year, expanding to about 365 during the summer season, and that 70 percent of them are full-time, year-round jobs — not low-pay or entry-level at all.

For the region as a whole to benefit, there must be a "critical mass" of tourism options for off-season tourists to choose from. "Tourism industry people will have to realize that they have to stay open year-round," believes Jim Thompson, former director of the Maine Publicity Bureau, a private, non-profit tourism information office that leverages private sector money and state funds to promote Maine as a destination.

Shaking the perception that tourism jobs mean three-month, entry-level employment won't be easy. Steep seasonal fluctuations are a way of life for tourism businesses in the Penobscot region, many of which close promptly after Labor Day. Lodging statistics for Maine in 1994 show the period from June through September generates by far the highest sales.

Tourist visitation can exceed a region's ability to absorb the impacts. This is especially true in areas that have fragile ecosystems, such as islands. Conflict can also arise with over-development of tourist amenities, resulting in degradation of the very environment designed to attract visitors. "We have to be careful we don't destroy the fabric that makes midcoast Maine the special place it is," said Ash.

Communities seeking more daily visitors need only look at Bar Harbor and Camden to realize that there are practical limits to their ability to handle high volumes of tourists.

Cruise ships are cited as one case where caution should prevail. "On one hand, cruise ships are good, because more people are coming to visit," said one state tourism official. "On the other hand, if you get a significant influx of people all at once, in places where there is already saturation, it's a serious problem — lining up big ships would change the character of Penobscot Bay." He added that cruise ships may appear to be a panacea to one harbor, a source of headaches to another.

The one-month or two-week family vacation is a fading pattern on the Maine coast. Modern American families more often have two working parents or single parents, and time and finances limit where and how much vacation they take. The vacation trend is toward "getaways" — shorter, more frequent escapes from home and work. The average length of stay in Maine has diminished, while the number of visits has increased over the last 15 years. Research shows the average stay in Maine has gone from six days to just over three.

As a rule, short-stay visitors do not fly in from far away. Most are native to New England, and a surprising number of those visiting the Penobscot region come from other parts of Maine. For the Samoset, 65 percent of all business is from Maine, even in summer.

The demise of the long vacation has other ramifications. The trips are often last-minute. The Samoset frequently gets reservations on Wednesday for weekend visits. Because the decision to get away on weekends is often impulsive, the resort advertises on television more than in the past. Ash likens short, getaway vacations to stopgap measures families use while saving up for less frequent, longer-distance travel: "We have become the filler in between years when people take themselves on vacations to Florida or Europe."

Communities that retain an integrated economy and their traditional character and values are most attractive to visitors, whereas towns that try too hard to cater to them can end up losing their soul. A feeling of authenticity in a place is often far more valuable than over-developing lodging and restaurants to accommodate more people. The Maine Publicity Bureau sees a need for a better understanding in the tourism industry that "you can't foul the nest" by ruining the attractive settings and pristine environment.

"Over-development is the greatest risk of tourist development," said Marjie Wright, tourism analyst at the Maine Office of Tourism. "In the rush for revenue, people get so excited, and they overbuild. Communities have to decide before getting into tourism, 'Who are we, what kind of growth is acceptable, what do we want to look like?'" Reluctance on the part of towns to implement comprehensive plans for the sake of individual independence can mean surrendering to the vagaries of haphazard development. "There are a lot of people in these local communities that are resistant to change," said one businessman. "But change is happening whether they want it or not. Outside is coming in and buying storefronts, waterfronts, wherever opportunities arise."

For years to come, Penobscot Bay communities will face the challenge of balancing traditional industries and tourism. Recalling the fable of the golden egg, there is much to lose if tourism is over-exploited at the expense of an integrated, diverse economy. A one-industry town is a risky place to live. Planning, its proponents argue, is the strongest form of home rule and community independence. Especially in smaller coastal communities where tourism has had a minimal impact, the message is: develop a sense of place, preserve what you have, sustain your authenticity.

Kayakers (Christopher Ayres)

Chapter 12: Stewardship Initiatives

By Annette Naegel and Bob Moore

Properly understood and managed, a region's natural resources can sustain its people for centuries, perhaps indefinitely. The Penobscot region's history since the arrival of the first Europeans reflects evolving attitudes toward its fisheries, timber, minerals and other resources — from a "boom and bust" mentality that has left parts of the region scarred and depleted from heavy cutting of timber and pulp, over-fishing and mining for granite to the beginning of a new era and a longer-term view embodying the idea of stewardship. Today dozens of stewardship projects are in place in the Penobscot region, including many local efforts aimed at increasing watershed awareness, ensuring the protection of watersheds and monitoring for water quality. The proliferation of stewardship efforts is a welcome sign that residents of the Penobscot region have grown to appreciate the magnificent resources that have been left to them, and that the condition of their children's resource inheritance is up to the present generation.

Partnerships for long-term protection

Penobscot Bay Network

Since 1992, a dozen different organizations committed to the long-term health of the region have been working to promote a regional identity. The organizations represent a broad spectrum of interests including the University of Maine, state agencies and the non-profit sector. They have formed an active network, promoting solutions to regional problems and educating the public.

In 1992, following the first conference of the Penobscot Bay Network, entitled "The Land, the Bay and the People," the Network developed the following statement of purpose:

- *Recognizing the integral and interdependent nature of the Penobscot Bay region, the interwoven connections between the sea, the river, the air, earth and islands, and all those species of plants and animals, including humans, who dwell therein; recognizing that fishing, farming, tourism and hundreds of other human ventures in the Penobscot Bay region are directly dependent on the health, integrity, and vitality of the whole Penobscot Bay region watershed; recognizing that the consequences of numerous common daily practices pose frequent threats to the purity and integrity of the Penobscot Bay region; therefore we have resolved to conduct a State of the Bay Conference for the following purposes:*
- *Improve communication and cooperation among all those interested in the Penobscot Bay region;*
- *Provide support and inspiration for all working to conserve, protect and restore the health and integrity of the Penobscot Bay region watershed;*
- *Assist current, planned, and future efforts to promote sustainable development and a high quality of life for all people in the Penobscot Bay region;*

Opposite: Red-winged blackbird (Christopher Ayres)

- *Identify and catalog Penobscot Bay region research -- its extent and authorship as well as its deficiencies, inadequacies and omissions.*

In 1993 the Network organized a second conference, entitled "Sustainable Economic and Environmental Indicators for the Region." This book, *Penobscot,* grew out of the Second Penobscot Bay Conference.

Through these conferences and several subsequent gatherings concerned with topics such as fishermen and oil spills, the Sears Island Cargo Port and the status of marine science, the Network has provided an opportunity for business interests, citizens, non profit organizations and elected officials to address regional problems.

With the Network's help, a marine docents program was established in the region to test the training of volunteers for stewardship and educational services in the Penobscot Bay area, funded by the State Planning Office.

Recently the Network has sponsored a statewide effort to redirect management of Maine's badly depleted clam fishery. An advisory committee representing a cross section of interests has focused on improving regulations, directed the distribution of funds to help the clam industry, and provided guidance to municipalities developing local ordinances.

Current members of the Network include:
- the Hancock County and Knox-Lincoln Cooperative Extension offices
- the Maine Coastal Program of the State Planning Office
- the Department of Marine Resources
- the Eastern Maine Development Cooperative
- the Maine Aquaculture Innovation Center
- the Penobscot Marine Museum
- the Island Institute
- the Maine/New Hampshire Sea Grant
- the Penobscot Land Trust Alliance
- the Penobscot Riverkeepers.

Organizations interested in dipping their oars into the efforts of the Network should contact Island Institute or the Hancock County Cooperative Extension Office.

Land trusts

Since 1989, a loose coalition of land trusts which conserve lands in the Penobscot Bay region has been meeting to share information and develop cooperative projects. Each of these land trusts identify lands in their communities with ecological, scenic or historic value and use conservation easements as their principal protection tool. Ten local land trusts rim the bay, and three coastwide organizations participate in the alliance.

In May of 1992, the Penobscot Bay Land Trust Alliance (PBLTA) accepted two statements of goals and purpose:
- *PBLTA will support all member conservation land trusts and their objectives to preserve and protect environmental/ecological/historical values and lands of significance and to build community awareness about environmental issues while increasing the constituency base for land protection.*
- *PBLTA will provide a regional Penobscot Bay perspective regarding preservation of environmental/ ecological/historical values and lands, building community awareness of environmental issues, and increasing the constituency base for land protection.*

PBLTA provides advice, support and expertise to member organizations, such as sponsoring property tax seminars.

Local land trusts continue to advance land protection projects and community-based educational programs about conservation and stewardship in the Penobscot Bay region. Many work with their local schools, produce local newsletters, assist local planning boards, cooperate with local conservation commissions and other community organizations, and create appropriate community economic development partnerships.

The Penobscot Nation

Penobscot Indians have lived on the river for thousands of years, and the Penobscot Nation may be one of the region's best examples of stewardship as a way of life. The lives of the Penobscots are linked to the river, which has provided food and a spiritual connection. In the words of a former tribal governor, James Sappier, "The Penobscots have always reaped a bountiful sustenance from the Penobscot waters and islands. The Great Spirit has been good to us, and in turn we have deep respect for the river, the animals, the fish, the birds and the plants for which we continuously give thanks. The river is the life-blood of our tribal existence."

Embodied in the Penobscots' relationship with the river is a strong commitment to stewardship, an understanding that activities that disrupt the natural balance of the river threaten the health of their community. "Any project that disrupts the spiritual and natural balance of the river and the people of the Penobscot Nation is considered an attempt to harm the people of the Penobscot Nation," stated the tribal governor.

Since the damming of the West Branch of the Penobscot in the 19th century, the Penobscot Indians have witnessed a dramatic reduction in the river's productivity and, in turn, its ability to support them. They have found mercury contamination in the fish they eat. Contamination along the river's banks has found its way into sediments and fish. In 1983, an oil spill prompted their insistence that federal and state leaders show more responsibility toward the river.

For the people of the Nation who believe the Penobscot yields and sustains life in all forms, these experiences have been devastating.

Through its Water Resources Program, the Penobscot Nation collects water samples at 37 sites along the main stem of the river and at 25 sites along its tributaries. It tests for 10 different parameters along the main stem, including temperature, dissolved oxygen, conductivity, biological oxygen demand, e. coli bacteria, color, total suspended solids, turbidity, foam and Secchi disc visibility (a system for checking the clarity of water). The information collected exceeds the standards for the state's water quality monitoring program, and the Indians are sharing this data with Maine officials. In addition, the Nation monitors ambient toxins, algae blooms during the summer months, daily water temperatures and sediment characteristics.

The water quality monitoring program is one project of the Nation's Natural Resources Department, which also focuses on fisheries management, forest management, wildlife conservation, fish and game law enforcement, wetlands protection and review of hydropower projects. "All the programs are integrated to reflect the inner-connectedness of all things in the natural world," commented department director John Banks. "The culturally driven stewardship responsibility provides the foundation for all thze goals and objectives of the programs." For the Penobscots, these efforts grow out of a stewardship ethic that is culturally based.

Clean Water/Partners in Monitoring Program

The Clean Water Project at the University of Maine Cooperative Extension and the Shore Stewards Program of the State Planning Office work jointly to alert citizens to water quality issues in their own backyards. The Deer Isle/Stonington Partners in Monitoring group, part of the Shore Stewards Program, seeks "accurate knowledge of the condition of coastal waters and an awareness of any activities that might impact water quality are essential to protecting and restoring water quality." The latter group is a network for relaying information and will study water quality, fisheries resource and land use in area watersheds. As a result of their monitoring, local clam flats closed because of pollution have been re-opened.

On Islesboro, closed clam flats and concern about the quality of the surrounding marine waters prompted citizens to launch a local water quality monitoring program. In its first season of activity, the Water Quality Club attracted 14 adult volunteers and several students to collect water samples, measure dissolved oxygen and the presence of fecal coliform bacteria. The group is building a database that will allow it to track bacterial contamination, and has motivated citizens in the community to watch for oil slicks, water discoloration, foul odors and illegal overboard discharges.

Through Clean Water/Partners in Monitoring, shellfish committees, watershed associations, conservation commissions and land trusts participate with schools in several Penobscot Bay communities to monitor their coastal waters, conduct watershed surveys and educate their communities about water quality. Money is available for equipment, public education efforts and other projects. Cooperative Extension offers classroom and field-based training, including follow-up with volunteers. Grants are made to local conservation groups to establish marine water quality monitoring programs that include local high schools.

As a result of these efforts, not only have clam flats been reopened, but towns in various watersheds have begun to work together and a much broader cross section of citizens has become active in conservation efforts. In Penobscot Bay, the participating groups include:

- Bagaduce Water Watch (Maine Maritime Academy and Castine Conservation Commission)
- Camden Partners in Monitoring (Camden-Rockport High School and Coastal Mountain Land Trust)
- Deer Isle/Stonington Partners in Monitoring (Deer Isle-Stonington High School and Deer Isle Conservation Commission)
- Georges River Tidewater Watch (Georges Valley High School and Georges River Tidewater Association
- Islesboro Water Quality Club (Islesboro Central School and Islesboro Islands Trust).

Groups interested in getting started should contact the Shore Stewards/Partners in Monitoring Program at the Maine State Planning Office in Augusta or the Clean Water Program at the University of Maine Cooperative Extension, Knox-Lincoln County Office.

Watershed projects

Clam Restoration Projects

Town-by-town clam management has been an option in Maine for a hundred years, but it has not always yielded a sustainable harvest. Today clam harvests are at historic lows, and local committees are often overwhelmed with the work needed to satisfy water quality mandates and to control harvester effort.

The Georges River clam restoration project is a model for the region. It encourages local clammers, municipalities and residents of five towns to manage their clam resource on a sustainable basis. Members have established a regional shellfish committee, the most sophisticated interlocal clam management agreement in Maine, and a regional shellfish management ordinance.

Organizers believe that any process must engage the individual clammer, who must be given the chance to "invest" in developing the governance structure for the fishery. Management may include stock enhancement efforts, monitoring, seeding and conservation closures.

The effort in the St. George parallels a statewide effort to address the long-term management of the clam resource in Maine.

Assisting the Georges River Clam Restoration Project are advisers from the University of Maine Cooperative Extension, the state Department of Environmental Protection, the National Marine Fisheries Service Fishing Retraining Program and the Island Institute, as well as local biologists, clam harvesters and wholesale shellfish distributors. For more information about the project, contact the Knox-Lincoln Cooperative Extension Office.

The Ducktrap River Project

Draining into Penobscot Bay, the Ducktrap River provides spawning and rearing habitat for one of seven river-specific populations of Atlantic salmon (*Salmo salar*). The Ducktrap salmon population's gene pool has been less affected by artificial stocking of fish than that of Maine's other rivers. Also, the Ducktrap salmon have maintained a relatively stable population level, in comparison to the drastic declines experienced by most river populations in downeast Maine. Still, the Ducktrap River has not received the attention necessary to understand the watershed and determine what management measures will be most effective.

Fifteen groups interested in the Ducktrap Watershed and its Atlantic salmon population began meeting in 1994 to discuss conservation objectives. Members include the Lincolnville municipal government, five state agencies, the U. S. Fish and Wildlife Service, and seven local and state conservation groups. Their mission is to promote the voluntary protection of the natural features of the Ducktrap River and Watershed. Coastal Mountains Land Trust is the program coordinator.

The coalition is developing a geographical information system database through the cooperative efforts of the Maine Atlantic Salmon Federation, the U. S. Fish and Wildlife Service and the Island Institute. This database will enable delineation of a buffer zone to protect water quality, and help set priorities for management. In addition, the coalition has been encouraging educational projects (such as salmon aquaria in the schools, newsletters and informational forums), and discussions with landowners in the watershed.

Protecting biodiversity

A patchwork of state and federal regulations are in place to protect some of the Penobscot region's important habitat for abundant and diverse plant and animal species. Sometimes these efforts overlap; other times there are gaps.

The federal Endangered Species Act provides protection to species on the brink of losing their ability to maintain natural populations in the wild. The federal Marine Mammal Protection Act makes it illegal to take seals, whales and porpoises in harvests or hunts or alter their behavior in the wild, and forbids disturbance of seal pupping and haulout areas.

Other state and local laws govern development siting, shoreland zoning, and construction in wetlands, permitting construction in areas where the least amount of habitat will be disturbed.

The Maine Natural Resource Protection Act (NRPA) protects fresh and saltwater wetlands, fragile mountain areas and significant wildlife habitat. "Significant wildlife habitat" is defined as deer yards, high- and moderate-value waterfowl and wading bird habitat, critical spawning and nursery areas for Atlantic salmon, shorebird nesting, feeding and staging areas; seabird nesting islands and vernal pools.

Mapping sensitive areas

Habitats of species sensitive to oil spills on the Maine coast are being entered into a comprehensive oil spill data set designed for oil spill response. The statewide natural resource agencies are tracking seabird nesting areas and coastal wildlife concentration areas, shorebird and wading bird data to support this project. The information will be entered onto a GIS, in which map overlays of seasonal species occurrences, weather conditions and sensitive habitats can be viewed simultaneously. This information and accessibility are especially valuable in deploying response teams in the event of an oil spill.

Island biodiversity

Some of the most fragile and productive areas within the region's natural system are islands. With the increase in outdoor recreation and boating, these areas are seeing additional and, in some instances, detrimental use.

Wildlife managers hope to mitigate increased recreational use of islands by minimizing human impact in sensitive areas. The state has produced videos on proper island use and educational public service announcements for broadcast, and has placed signs on important wildlife islands. The U.S. Fish and Wildlife Service has distributed over 20,000 copies of a brochure, "Island Ethics," advising the public about proper stewardship of islands throughout the year.

Educational outreach/volunteer service

Penobscot Riverkeepers 2000

This group is organized to teach people about the history and resources of the Penobscot and encourage watershed awareness and monitoring efforts.

Each spring for the last four years, an expedition has been organized along the river from its headwaters, down some of its tributaries and the main stem to the bay. The expedition brings together educators, students and citizens who live within the watershed of the river to learn about its history, people and resources. The expedition generates education and stewardship projects in dozens of schools throughout the watershed, involving hundreds of volunteers and teachers.

Penobscot Bay Marine Volunteer Program

In exchange for a commitment of community service, this program trains volunteers in ecology, history and current issues. Twenty volunteers are selected through a competitive application process. They do not need to have a science or marine-related background. The training covers such topics as oceanography, marine ecology, shoreline processes, maritime history, fisheries and aquaculture, current issues and eco-tourism. Sessions are led by local experts, university professors and representatives of state agencies and non-profit groups, and include field trips to sites of interest.

"Our goal is to provide volunteers with the knowledge and resources to inform their fellow citizens about the importance of coastal resources and to make an impact in their communities," said Evan Reichert, director of the State Planning Office, the agency that staffs the program. Volunteers design their own community service projects with the support and assistance of area organizations.

Citizens interested in the program should contact the Maine State Planning Office in Augusta.

Maine Island Trail Association

The Maine Island Trail Association (MITA) maintains a waterway trail that extends along the coast of Maine. The trail includes small state-owned islands considered appropriate for day visits or overnight camping, as well as selected privately owned islands. Members of the association are granted access to the trail islands, but with the understanding that they will abide by a low-impact ethic. In return, the association provides stewardship services to the island owners, monitors recreational use, keeps shores and campsites clean and conducts special projects.

The goal of the association is to establish a model of thoughtful use and volunteer stewardship for the Maine islands that will assure their conservation in a natural state, while seeing that a recreational asset is cared for by the people who use it. Members pay a fee to support the stewardship work of the organization.

The offices of the Maine Island Trail Association are located in Rockland and Portland.

An integrated conservation strategy

Educating people about the sensitivity of Penobscot Bay's rich biodiversity and diverse habitats is an important step, but education alone cannot prevent the destruction of important wildlife areas. Regulations often fall short. Conservation easements and outright purchases can help, and an array of federal, state and local government and private organizations are cooperating to preserve significant habitats. But it is important to begin to appreciate the Penobscot region as a whole — greater than the sum of the towns and counties that lie within its borders. By any objective measure, the assemblage of ecological resources — fish or fowl, fresh or salt, forest or field, mountain or island — are the Penobscot region's greatest assets. Cataloguing them, monitoring trends in the quality of the environment, appreciating the unknown elements of biodiversity for their inherent value, and acting as a voice for a unique region is what developing a stewardship ethic for the Penobscot region means.

LAND

ROCKLAND

Brewster Pt.

Brewster S.I.

Jameson's Pt.

Crocketts Pt.

South Ledge

ROCKLAND HARBOR

Breakwater

LIGHT Fl g. W. (TRUMPET)

Atlantic Pt.

S.3

WRECK Seal Ledge

Lowell Ledge

Spear's Rock

Broad Cove

Cove BEACON

Owl

LIGHT

SPINDLE

OWL'S HEAD BAY

Munroe

Chapter 13: Toward a Regional Identity

By David D. Platt and Philip W. Conkling

In 1880, the U.S. Coast and Geodetic Survey published its Chart No. 104, entitled "Penobscot Bay, Maine." With soundings in fathoms, a list of lights, information about storm warnings, buoys and other navigational aids, Chart No. 104 represented the government's best effort to inform the schooner captains and fishermen who plied Penobscot Bay about the risks they faced.

Topography, soundings and other data on the chart had been collected since the 1850s by a series of surveyors and hydrographers employed by the federal government, and considering that the surveyors had no access to aerial photography, fathometers, sonar or digital data from satellites, the chart was remarkably accurate and complete.

It had to be, of course. In 1880, Penobscot Bay and the "Bangor River" to its north were very busy places, and uncharted or poorly mapped hazards meant catastrophe. Much of the United States' post–Civil War prosperity was based on manufacturing, access to plentiful resources and transportation by water, and the U.S. Department of Commerce and Labor — the governmental parent of the agency that published Chart No. 104 — had the job of keeping products moving safely through the country's coastal waters.

Hundreds of navigational charts produced since the mid 19th century attest to the fact that mariners, at least, have regarded the Penobscot region as a distinct entity for a long time. Like its modern-day counterpart (No. 13302, "Penobscot Bay and Approaches"), the 1880 chart covers an area roughly from St. George on the west to Stonington on the east, running down as far as Matinicus and up to Fort Point at the mouth of the Penobscot River. Except for the section of navigable river to Bangor (which is usually depicted separately), Chart No. 104's picture of what we define as the Penobscot region is complete.

Geography makes it unlikely we would define this region any other way. Neatly situated at the juncture of navigable water and the timber-rich North Woods, Bangor inevitably became the region's principal city — and as long as the timber lasted, was its major port — while the Penobscot became this region's chief commercial artery. The water route between Bangor, the river towns, the coastal settlements and the island communities of Penobscot Bay was a strong regional bond; mail packets and steamers provided transportation for a century and a quarter that was faster, more reliable and much more comfortable than roads, wagons or stagecoaches.

The development of groundwood papermaking technology late in the 19th century had a great influence on the whole Penobscot region. The river inland, already developed for log driving to

Opposite: U.S. Coast & Geodetic Survey chart No. 104, 1880 (detail)

supply sawmills, was re-engineered to produce hydroelectric power for new paper mills at Millinocket and East Millinocket. The results: fewer logs and less sawdust in the water below Medway, new mill-related toxins and pollutants entering the water upstream of Bangor, an increase in municipal sewage, year-round river flows instead of the former flood-and-dry-out regime, and still poorly understood effects on the estuary and spawning grounds at the mouth of Penobscot Bay.

The watershed's ability to transport pollutants, products and people from the North Woods to Penobscot Bay is the clearest evidence we have that the entire region is closely tied together.

Geography is not the only linkage, however. Overall, the different parts of this region benefit (and suffer) from the same things: a national shift away from manufacturing; "homogenization" of retailing and other businesses as franchises and chains replace local firms; the rise of the service economy; the decline of farming; the lack of job opportunities in rural areas; the shifting strengths and weaknesses of the transportation system; the growing number of retirees in the population; the coast-wide explosion in recreation and tourism. Obvious differences continue to separate the suburban river towns from the islands, east bay from west, but on the whole, the region's communities continue to become more alike.

As noted in Chapter 11, the region faces a variety of water quality problems, some of which compromise the health of the bay and its resources. Taken together, these problems, including old toxic hot spots and newer pollution sources such as oil spills, bacteria associated with sewage, overboard discharges and non-point runoff from dozens of different sources, represent a shared risk of major proportions. They suggest once again that very little separates one community from another in this part of Maine. The effects of a malfunctioning septic system in Veazie or even the treated discharge from Bangor's waste water facility may be minuscule and indirect as far as the rest of the watershed is concerned, but on a specific clam flat or mussel bed, they can be very real.

Nor is the region's wildlife immune. Coastal bald eagles, including those that nest on Penobscot Bay islands, carry the highest concentrations of PCBs of eagles in the state, and the contaminants have impaired their ability to produce young. Increased coastal recreation all over the region has affected seals, seabird colonies and other sensitive wildlife areas, all the way from Bangor (well known for its roosting bald eagles) to the 50 fathom line south of Matinicus.

Other factors — the burgeoning tourism business is one example — can exceed a region's ability to absorb them. Fragile ecosystems on islands and in other places can be compromised, and over-development of tourist amenities results in the degradation of the very environment that brings visitors here in the first place. While some parts of the Penobscot region are more vulnerable to tourism's negative aspects than others, all communities are affected, albeit indirectly, over time.

As described in Chapter 3, fresh water, salt water, tides, temperatures and ocean currents all interact in a single system that helps define the region. Current gyres and persistent eddies enhance mixing at various points in Penobscot Bay and keep nutrients stirred in the water column, enriching marine life. The mixing of waters at the head of the bay sets up unique ecological conditions. An increase in the Penobscot River's flow each spring, the result of melting snow far up the river, reduces salinity and transports a fresh load of sediment out into the bay. Nutrients adhere to sediments, fertilizing plankton "blooms" that, in turn, affect the ability of fish and other species to spawn. Again, everything is connected to everything else.

Transportation routes and technology are further reminders that residents of the river, bay and island towns should regard their region as a single entity. When transportation was by water and routes ran up and down the bay and river, all communities benefited because they were "on the main highway." When the Interstate 95 corridor became Maine's growth area, all towns suffered as the Penobscot region was left on its outskirts. Waldo County, once a ship-owning center, became Maine's poorest county.

Still, there are bright spots in the region's transportation picture: roads and bridges have been improved, particularly on the western side of the bay, to handle a growing volume of traffic. Ferry service to the islands has improved, and vessels and terminals have been upgraded. The Bangor International Airport's traffic volume exceeds Portland's, at least in part because of the improvement of containers for shipping live lobsters overseas. Until environmental and cost considerations stopped the project, Sears Island was slated for significant cargo port improvements. For better or worse, the development of new cargo facilities in Penobscot Bay would have effects throughout the region. And finally, the "information age" has made the Penobscot region more attractive to businesses such as financial services that make location and quality of life as important a consideration as telephone and transportation networks.

The Penobscot region is subject to trends such as age that no one can control. The percentage of people age 85 and over in Knox County is projected to grow 24 percent between 1990 and 1997, for example, and the first of the people born during the Great Depression turned 65 in 1995. Combined with high in-migration by retirees (building facilities for the elderly is a booming business in a number of the Penobscot region's communities), these numbers suggest that the population of the region as a whole will be "grayer" than many parts of the state.

Identifying trends

Like the writings of George S. Wasson, Coast and Geodetic Survey Chart No. 104, the archival photographs included in this book and various other historic "snapshots," *Penobscot* considers a region of Maine at a particular point in time. The principal usefulness of this volume in the future, we believe, will be as a baseline for understanding trends affecting the region.

Identifiable changes — the decline of shipping and public transportation and the growth of highway transportation, for example — have transformed this region during this century. Many of these changes are significant enough to be considered trends, indicating the likelihood of further change, and as such they should be watched in the years to come.

Natural resources

Fish and forest products provide more than economic returns to the citizens of the Penobscot region; they form the basis of our view of ourselves and underlie the region's distinctive culture. Perhaps the most important marine resource indicators to monitor are the trends of fish and shell-fish landings, the number of marine species harvested and the number of species considered to be over-exploited, as well as those species that are newly utilized — or, for one reason or another, no longer exploited. An equally valuable indicator of ecosystem health in this region is the number of acres of clam flats that have been closed because of pollution or lack of information about their condition. Will as many acres be closed five years from now as are closed today?

Timber

Each decade, the U.S. Forest Service inventories standing timber in Maine, documenting the condition of the forests on which the state depends so heavily for its economic well-being. The forests of the Penobscot watershed form a major portion of the North Maine Woods that drew Thoreau here for his wilderness trips. This woods is today an "industrial forest" on which depend thousands of jobs. The inventory of standing timber in the watershed and the ecological health of the stands of trees that comprise the inventory will continue to be the focus of major public concern and debate, as demonstrated by the current conflict over clear cutting. Interestingly, the Penobscot study area, consisting of 39 towns in the southern part of the watershed, is far more heavily forested today than it was a century ago, when land was largely cleared within 50 miles of the coast, suggesting that these rural forests can contribute significantly to the supply of timber to local mills.

Wildlife and biodiversity

The explosion of this region's seal population was documented by researchers in the 1980s, and population/reproduction data for these animals should continue to be collected in the future. The population of seals is an indicator of the available food supply, which in turn provides information about the condition of the region's marine resources. The same could be said of the region's populations of ospreys, which appear to have recovered well from the effects of pesticides in the 1960s. But bald eagle populations, which continue to have low reproductive rates on the coast, are indicators of the lingering and long-lasting effects of toxins in the marine food web. Trends in nesting seabird populations and migratory shorebird populations are indicators of environmental health as well.

We have learned a great deal over the past two decades about terrestrial biodiversity. We have set aside thousands of acres of habitat on the mainland in protected areas — refugia for the land's store of biodiversity — and these efforts have paid off handsomely. But we have not even begun to catalog the significantly greater biodiversity of the marine ecosystem, let alone develop strategies to ensure that this diversity is available to future generations. The fact that Penobscot Bay alone is habitat to over 1,000 species of invertebrates underscores the importance of cataloging the region's marine health and wealth. Penobscot Bay supports a fantastic array of subtidal forests, grasslands, coves, canyons and plains – even an erupting underwater methane field that has no terrestrial analog.

Developing a strategy to protect the region's marine biodiversity is one of the most important tasks to focus on in the months and years ahead. The first step is to begin mapping the diversity of subtidal habitats of Penobscot Bay, from Verona Island to the 50 fathom line, and to develop appropriate fish and shellfish harvesting policies and regulations that are specific to different habitats. This is a daunting task and not likely to be successful without the support and participation of fishermen whose livelihoods depend on understanding the necessary limits to harvests of fish and shellfish. Easy or not, such an undertaking is vitally important, since among the ecosystem services that Penobscot Bay provides are functions on which all human life depends. The bay is a source of food, an untapped medicine chest, a storm surge protector, a regulator of weather and climate.

The Maine Natural Areas Biological Conservation Database only includes rare animal, plant and insect species and is not a measure of the region's true biodiversity, but it should be updated and consulted regularly as an indicator of regional trends. Although measuring marine biodiversity is a task new to science, we must begin to develop indices including measures of this important source of biodiversity in local and regional planning efforts.

Water quality

Water quality in the Penobscot River and Penobscot Bay is better than it was 20 years ago, when municipalities and industries were still dumping raw effluent into both. It is clear, however, that critical work remains to be done. Fifty-eight industrial discharges, seven power plants, plus approximately 300 household overboard discharges and 13 combined sewage overflows were still adding effluent to the Penobscot River in 1995; nearly 50 percent of the bay's 23,445 acres of shellfish beds were closed to harvest because of bacterial contamination; the presence of dioxin has necessitated a state warning to pregnant women not to eat lobster tomalley; mussels at various points in Penobscot Bay show elevated levels of heavy metals. Will these substances continue to show up in samples five years from now? At what levels? What pollutants have disappeared from the water; what new ones are showing up?

Human Patterns

Population, income

A glance at the entries from the 1882 *Gazetteer of the State of Maine* and subsequent census data suggest that the countryside has emptied out, while the larger towns have grown. But these sets of numbers mask a larger story, which is the role that both retirement and in- and out-migration are playing in the Penobscot region. Is the region becoming the retirement destination it appears to be? Will the population of the Penobscot region continue to age? In 1990, the 65-plus age group was only 12.7 percent of the Penobscot region's population, but the U. S. Bureau of the Census is projecting a rise to nearly 22 percent by the year 2030 because of the high number of people currently aged 45–64, suggesting the "mailbox economy" (see Chapter 6) will continue to play a major role in the region.

The median annual household income in Penobscot Bay is $24,949, which is well below the state median of $27, 854. The region has pockets of poverty today and will continue to have them. Where they occur in the future will be a function of transportation, education, the age and qualifications of the workforce and the nature of the new jobs that become available in the years to come.

A generation ago the pattern here, as in the rest of the country, was one of largely centralized workplaces, many of which were small manufacturing operations. Two generations ago, most residents of the region who weren't full-time fishermen worked on farms. Changes in the workplace, including the rise in the number of persons who are able to work at home using new technology, are significant indicators of regional economic conditions.

Housing

The cost of housing, particularly on islands and in coastal towns, has risen dramatically during the past 20 years, making it increasingly likely that some young people and long-time residents won't be able to remain in their communities. This trend has serious implications for communities, which must have a mix of income levels to remain something more than suburbs or summer settlements. Trends in housing prices should be monitored.

Education

The percentage of college graduates is much greater in the region than it was a century ago, as it is all over the country. The Penobscot region, in fact, confounds typical urban–rural patterns of educational attainment: compared to statewide averages, all four groups of towns in the region have markedly higher educational attainment. One question to be asking is whether these graduates are as well trained, or consider themselves as well qualified for the current job market as their educations would suggest.

"Quality of life" as a resource

The appearance of a major national credit card company which has built large offices in three towns and brought between 800 and 1,000 jobs to the region during the past five years underscores a new trend. "Quality of life" — the physical environment, a sense of community, a qualified workforce — did as much to induce MBNA to locate here as traditional factors like transportation links or access to natural resources. In an era of increasingly mobile capital, the factors which brought MBNA to the Penobscot region need to be considered in planning for a viable future. New communication technology that makes it possible for a major white-collar employer to locate itself in small towns up the Penobscot River and along the western shore of Penobscot Bay will continue to transform this region. The very qualities that kept the Penobscot region rural and relatively "unspoiled" have now become its newest resource. Where the cities, towns and hamlets of the region find themselves in the decades to come will depend as much on how this "resource" is understood and managed as it will on the way we manage other, more traditional resources.

During the past few years, thousands of citizens of this unique region have contributed tens of thousands of hours of volunteer time to monitoring its vital signs. Among all the other conflicting trends which indicate the region's health, none is more important than the rising number of people who have decided to get involved in the dialogue over the Penobscot region's future. We hope that in some small way this volume will contribute to this important new trend — inspiring more people to view the region *as a region;* to understand the connections among forest, river and bay; and then to act individually and collectively in hundreds of thousands of small ways to bequeath to future generations a region in better health than we found it.

Appendix:

Bibliography of Penobscot Bay Scientific Research

The Penobscot region hosts some of Maine's most significant coastal wildlife habitat; its rich, productive waters support a diverse and longstanding fishing industry; and its highly configured shoreline and vast number of islands are destination points for many people.

In spite of these riches, the scientific data and literature available about the overall health of the region are minimal. Even without the information, the evidence is clear that the bay has problems with toxic and water pollution, increased residential and recreational development and threatened fisheries.

Two regional conferences were held in 1993 and 1994, hosted by the Penobscot Bay Network, to gather existing information, resources and people interested in the bay. The goals were to establish what is known about the bay, develop better communication among all players and identify whether there is a need to create a regional identity and agenda to promote the long term health of the bay.

A clear directive from the conferences was the need to develop a state of the bay report and a scientific bibliography. Participants identified the need to develop more research on the bay. Without enough baseline information and baseline data about this region, how can informed decisions be made about its future?

As one of the Penobscot Bay Network members, the Island Institute offered to research, write and publish **Penobscot** and the scientific bibliography. What follows is the result of the second effort.

This scientific bibliography compiles the known, scientific, published research conducted over the past 20 years in the Penobscot region. This collection includes works conducted in the fields of archaeology, marine resources, wildlife, botany, water quality, forestry and geology, to name a few. Once the information was collected, it was reviewed by a scientific advisory group to ensure that citations were not omitted and that the collection repesented high-quality and reputable research.

Reviewers were Paul Anderson, Director, Shellfish Sanitation Program, Department of Marine Resources (DMR); John G. T. Anderson, College of the Atlantic; John Barlow, Maine Maritime Academy (MMA); Dan Belknap, Dept. of Geological Sciences, Univerity of Maine (UM); Joceline Boucher, Chemistry Dept., Colby College; Don Card, DMR; Dr. A. Jim Chacko, Division of Environmental

Programs, Unity College; Cynthia B. Erickson, Co-Director, Gaia Crossroads Project, Bigelow Laboratory for Ocean Sciences; Stewart I. Fefer, Gulf of Maine Project, U.S. Fish and Wildlife Service; Dr. Steven R. Fegley, MMA; Mary K. Foley, National Park Service; Nick Houtman, Dept. of Public Affairs, UM; Mac Hunter, UM; Richard W. Langton, DMR; Dr. Peter Larsen, Bigelow Laboratory for Ocean Sciences; James McCleave, Dept. of Oceanography, UM; Carter Newell, Great Eastern Mussel; John Sowles, Marine Program, Department of Environmental Protection; Dr. Robert S. Steneck, Darling Marine Center, UM; David Townsend, Dept. of Oceanography, UM; Hank Tyler, Marine Natural Areas Program; Barbara Vickery, The Nature Conservancy; and Dr. Gail Wippelhauser, Dept. of Conservation, Maine Natural Areas Program.

Our thanks to Steve Miller who undertook the responsibility of collecting the research, soliciting the input from the researchers and preparing the initial draft of this document.

The bibliography includes over 140 citations and is presented by author and subject headings.

Hard copies of these documents will be available at the Penobscot Marine Museum in Searsport, in their reference library.

This is a project of the Penobscot Bay Network, with research, design and production provided by the Island Institute. Members of the Network assisted in printing costs. The Network includes the following organizations: Eastern Maine Development Corporation, the Island Institute, Maine Maritime Academy, Maine Aquaculture Association, Maine Coastal Program/State Planning Office, Maine/New Hampshire Sea Grant, Maine Department of Marine Resources, Penobscot Bay Land Trust Alliance, Penobscot River and Bay Institute, Penobscot Marine Museum and University of Maine Cooperative Extension.

Alphabetical Listings

Aho, R.A. 1984. *Marine Resources Atlas: Spruce Head to Isle Au Haut, Maine* DEP. 134 pp. [A companion document to Oil Pollution Research, Card. 1984.]

Ayer, W.C. 1971. *Some Aspects of Amphipod Distribution in the Penobscot River (Maine) estuary.* Zoology.

Barry, M. and Yevich, P.P. 1975. *The Ecological, Chemical and Histopathological Evaluation of an Oil Spill Site, Part III.* Marine Pollution Bulletin, Histopathological Studies. 6:171 - 173.

Beck, F.M. 1970. *Marine Challenges Encountered by a Small Mine on the Maine Coast.* 1970. Offshore Technology Conference, Houston, Texas. OTC 1256.

Bertrand, D.E. 1977. *Seasonal Succession of the Plankton of Penobscot Bay.* U. of Rhode Island, Kingston, R.I.

Bickel, C.E. 1971. *Bedrock Geology of the Belfast Quadrangle, Maine.* Harvard University, Cambridge, MA. 322 pp.

Birge, R.P. 1978. *Water Mass Flow Measurements from Drogue Observations in an Area West of Sears Island, Maine.* Central Maine Power Co. Environmental Studies Dept., SI-78-1. 13 pp.

Bobalek, E.G. 1969. *Phase II - Study of a River System as a Chemical Reactor.* Land & Water Resources Center. U of M, Orono,ME. 21 pp.

Bobalek, E.G., Mumme, K. and Lewis, R.A. 1967. *Chemical Reactor Theory Applied to Modeling the Dynamics of a Control System for Water Quality of a River: Phase 1 - A Feasibility Study.* Land & Water Resources Center, U of M, Orono, ME. 39 pp.

Bouley, B.A. 1978. *Volcanic Stratigraphy, Stratabound Sulfide Deposits, and Relative Age Relationships in the East Penobscot Bay Area, Maine.* University of Western Ontario, London, Ontario, Canada. 168 pp.

Bowdoin College Marine Research Laboratory. 1981. *A Description of the Near Shore Oil Spill Control Project Proposed for Long Cove, earsport, ME*. Maine DEP, Augusta, ME. 17 pp.

Brewer, T., Genes, A.N., and Prescott, G.C., Jr. 1979. *Sand and Gravel Aquifers Map 18, Lincoln, Knox, Waldo, and Kennebec Counties, Maine*. Maine Geological Survey Open File Report 79-13. 6 pp.

Brookins, D.G. 1976. *Geochronologic Contributions to Stratigraphic Interpretation and Correlation in the Penobscot Bay Area, Eastern Maine*. In: L.R. Page, ed., *Contributions to the Stratigraphy of New England*. Geological Society of America Memoir 148:129-145.

Bryan, M. 1971. *The Effects of Heavy Metals Other Than Mercury on Marine and Estuarine Organisms*. Proc. Royal Society of London Bull. B. Biol. Sci. 177:289 - 410.

Burgund, H.R. 1995. *The Currents of Penobscot Bay, Maine: Observations and a Numerical Model*. Department of Geology and Geophysics, Yale University. 71 pp.

Burkholder, B.R. 1933. *A Study of the Phyto-Plankton of Frenchmans Bay and Penobscot Bay, Maine*. Intern. Rev. Ges. Hydrobiolo. Hydrogr. 28:262-284. [Note age, but still best source]

Card, D.J., Stockwell, L.T., and Gillfillan, E.S. 1984. *Oil Pollution Research*. Maine DEP. 456pp.

Caswell, W.B., Thompson, W.B., Cotton, J.E., and Prescott, G.C., Jr. 1981. *Sand and Gravel Aquifers Map 29, Penobscot and Waldo Counties, Maine*. Maine Geological Survey Open File Report 81-61. 6 pp.

Central Maine Power Company. 1978. *Scope and Description of Aquatic Studies, Upper Penobscot Bay, for Sears Island Coal Unit No. 1*. Central Maine Power Company, Augusta, ME. 35 pp.

Cheney, E.S. 1969. *Geology of the Blue Hill – Castine Mining District, Southwestern Hancock County, Maine*. Maine Geological Survey, Second Annual Report. 148 pp.

Cobb, W. 1979. *Socioeconomic Characterization of Coastal Knox and Waldo Counties*. N.E. Coastal Oceanographic Group. Cutler, ME.

Cotton, J.E., Welsh, M., and Prescott, G.C., Jr. 1981. *Sand and Gravel Aquifers Map 30, Somerset, Kennebec, Waldo, and Penobscot Counties, Maine*. Maine Geological Survey Open File Report 81-62. 6 pp.

Council on Environmental Quality. 1979. *Environmental Quality - 1979*. Washington, D.C.

Courtemanch, D.L. 1977. *Investigation of Copper Sediments of Silver Lake, Bucksport, Maine*. Maine DEP, Augusta, ME.

Dean, D. 1970. *Water Quality - Benthic Invertebrate Relationships in Estuaries*. Water Resources Center, U of M, Orono, ME. 9 pp.

Dow, G.M. 1965. *Petrology and Structure of North Haven Island and Vicinity, Maine*. University of Illinois, Urbana, IL. 146 pp.

Dow, R.L. 1975. *Reduced Growth and Survival of Clams Transplanted to an Oil Spill Site*. Marine Pollution Bull. 6:12 - 125.

Dow, R.L. 1978. *Size Selective Mortality of Clams in an Oil Spill Site*. Marine Pollution Bull. 9(2):45 - 48.

Dow, R.L., and Hurst, J.W., Jr. 1975. *The Ecological, Chemical, and Histopathological Evaluation of an Oil Spill Site, Part I*. Marine Pollution Bull. Ecological Studies 6:164 - 166.

Dow, Robert L., and Hurst, John W. Jr. 1972. *Renewable Resource Problems of Heavy Metal Mining in Coastal Maine*. Maine Dept. of Sea and Shore Fisheries, reprinted by *National Fisherman*. Research Bulletin #35.

Doyle, Robert G. 1970. *Penobscot Bay Physical Resources Report: Preliminary*. Maine Dept. of Economic Development.

Edwards, B.J., and Woodward, F.E. 1979. *A Simple Pollution Vulnerability Index for Preliminary Coastal Water Quality Management Planning*. Land & Water Resources Center, U of M, Orono, ME. Report # A-047-ME. 26 pp.

ERCo, et. al. 1977. *Systems Study of Oil Pollution Prevention, Abatement and Control for Penobscot Bay*. Maine Department of Environmental Protection.

Faulkner, A., and Faulkner, G.F. 1987. *The French at Pentagoet, 1635-1674*. Maine Historic Preservation Commission, Augusta, ME.

Fidler, R.B. 1979. *An Approach for Hydrodynamic Modeling of Maine's Estuaries*. U of M, Orono, ME. 74 pp.

Findlay, R.H., and Watling, L. 1994. *Toward a Process Level Model to Predict the Effects of Salmon Net-Pen Aquaculture on the Benthos*. Can. Tech. Report of Fish. and Aquatic Sci. 1949 xi + 125 pp. Sea Grant MSG-R-94-21.

Fink, L.K., Harris, A.B., and Schick, L.L. 1980. *Trace Metals in Suspended Particulates, Biota, and Sediments of the St. Croix, Narraguagus, and Union Estuaries and the Goose Cove Region of Penobscot*. Land & Water Resources Center, U of M, Orono, ME. Report A-041-ME & B-015-ME. 293 pp.

Fink, L.K., Jr. 1977. *Heavy Metals.* Darling Center, U. of M., Walpole, ME.

Fish and Wildlife Service, U.S. Dept. of the Interior. 1980. *An Ecological Characterization of Coastal Maine, Volumes 1-6.* Fish & Wildlife Service, Dept. of Interior, Washington, D.C.

Flagg, Lewis N. 1984. *Penobscot River Shad and Alewife Restoration Potential.* Maine Dept. of Marine Resources, Augusta, ME. 7 pp.

Flagg, Lewis N., and Squiers, Thomas S. 1978. *American Shad Restoration and Rainbow Smelt Population Dynamics.* Maine Dept. of Marine Resources, Augusta, ME. AFS-19-R. 25 pp.

Fontaine, R.A. 1981. *Drainage Areas of Surface Water Bodies of the Penobscot River Basin in Central Maine.* U.S. Geological Survey Open File Report 78-556F. 92 pp.

Fried, Stephen M., McCleave, James D., and LaBar, George W. 1978. *Seaward Migration of Hatchery-Reared Atlantic Salmon, Salmo salar, Smolts in the Penobscot River Estuary, Maine: Riverine Movements.* Journal of the Fisheries Research Board of Canada. 35 (1): 76-87.

Gilfillan, E.S., Hanson, S.A., Page, D.S., Mayo, D., Cooley, J., Chalfant, J., Archambeault, T., West, A., and Harshbarger, J.C. 1977. *Comprehensive Study of Petroleum Hydrocarbons in the Marine Environment at Long Cove, Searsport, ME.* Maine DEP, Augusta, ME. Contract # 906439.

Goldberg, E.D., Koide, M., Hodge, V., Flegal, A.R., and Martin, J. 1983. U.S. *Mussel Watch: 1977-1978 Results on Trace Metals and Radionuclides.* Estuar. Coast. Shelf Sci. 16: 69-93.

Graham, J.J. *Profiles of Temperature and Salinity: Inshore Waters of Central Maine.* Maine DMR, Fisheries Research Station. 7 pp.

Greene, C.W., Mittelhauser, G.H., Jacobs, J., and Gregory, L.L. 1992. *Historical Resource Inventory for Acadia National Park, Volume 1.* National Park Service, Boston. Technical Report NPS/NAROSS/NRTR-92/01. 623pp.

Gulf of Maine Council on the Marine Environment. 1994. *Evaluation of Gulfwatch 1992, Second Year of the Gulf of Maine Environmental Monitoring Plan.* 141 pp.

Haefner, P.A., Jr. 1967. *Hydrography of the Penobscot River (Maine) Estuary.* Journal of the Fisheries Research Board of Canada 24 (7):1553-1571.

Hansen, B.P. 1980. *Ground Water Availability in Acadia National Park and Vicinity, Hancock and Knox Counties, Maine.* U.S. Geological Survey Open File Report 80-1050. 8 pp.

Hartman, F.E. 1963. *Estuarine Wintering Habitat for Black Ducks.* The Journal of Wildlife Management 27:339-347. [Study area between Winterport and Sandy Point]

Hatch, R.W. 1971. *Temperature, Dissolved Oxygen and Salinity Data for the Penobscot River Estuary, 1966-1970.* Water Resources Center, U of M, Orono, ME. 18 pp.

Hidu, H. 1974. *Cooperative Oyster Mariculture.* In: *Maine Renewable Marine Resources Forum.* Maine Maritime Academy, Castine, ME.

Humphreys, A.C., III, and Pearce, B.R. 1981. *A Hydrodynamic Investigation of the Penobscot Bay Estuary.* Dept. of Civil Engineering, U of M, Orono, ME.

Humphreys, A.C., III, and Pearce, B.R. 1981. *"Currents in Penobscot Bay, Maine."* In: Oceans 81 - Conference record of The Ocean - An International Workplace. Boston. 805-809.

Hurst, J.W., Jr., and Dow, R.L. 1972. *Renewable Resource Problems of Heavy Metal Mining in Coastal Maine. National Fisherman* 52(10).

Hyland, H.B.N. 1970. *A Review of Oil Polluting Incidents In and Around New England.* Ecol. Res. Ser EPA. 600/3-77-064.

Imhoff, E.A., and Harvey, R.L. 1972. *Penobscot River Study.* Environmental Studies Center, U of M, Orono, ME. Tech Report # 1. 288 pp.

Jacobson, G.L., Jr. and Jacobson, H.A. 1989. *An Inventory of Settings Along the Maine Coast.* Maine Geol. Surv. Bull. "Crustal Warping Project". [See Jacobson (1987) comment]

Jacobson, H.A., and Jacobson, G.L., Jr. 1989. *Variability of Vegetation In Tidal Marshes of Maine, USA.* Canadian Journal of Botany 67:230-238. [See Jacobson (1987) comment]

Jacobson, H.A., Jacobson, G.L., Jr., and Kelley, J.T. 1987. *Distribution and Abundance of Tidal Marshes Along the Coast of Maine.* Estuaries 10:126-131. [Horseshoe Cove (Cape Rosier) salt marsh relative to all other marshes]

Johnson, A.C., Larsen, P.F., Gadbois, D.F., and Humason, A.W. 1985. *The Distribution of Polycyclic-Aromatic Hydrocarbons in the Surficial Sediments of Penobscot Bay in Relation to Possible Sources and to Other Sites Worldwide.* Marine Environmental Research,

Essex, England 15 (1):1 - 16.

Jury, S. H., Field, J. D., Stone, S. L., Nelson, D. M., and Monaco, M. E. 1994. *Distribution and Abundance of Fishes and Invertebrates in North Atlantic Estuaries.* NOAA/NOS Strategic Environmental Assessments Division, Silver Spring, MD. ELMR Report Number 13. 221 pp.

Keeley, D. 1979. *Socioeconomic Characterization of Coastal Hancock County.* New England Coastal Oceanographic Group, Cutler, ME.

Kelley, J.T., and Belknap, D.F. 1989. *Geomorphology and Sedimentary Framework of Penobscot Bay and Adjacent Inner Continental Shelf.* Maine Geological Survey, Report # 89-3. 35 pp.

Kelley, J.T., Belknap, D.F., Shipp, R.C., and Miller, S.B. 1989. *An Investigation of Neotectonic Activity in Coastal Maine by Seismic Reflection Methods,* In: *Neotectonics of Maine.* Maine Geological Survey Bulletin 40:23 - 34.

Kelley, J.T., Dickson, S.M., Belknap, D.F., Barnhardt, W.A., and Henderson, M. 1994. *Giant Sea-Bed Pockmarks: Evidence for Gas Escape from Belfast, Maine.* Geology 22:59 - 62.

Knebel, H.J. 1986. *Holocene Depositional History of a Large Glaciated Estuary, Penobscot Bay, Maine.* Marine Geology 73 (3-4):215 - 236.

Knebel, H.J., and Scanlon, K.M. 1985. *Sedimentary Framework of Penobscot Bay, Maine.* Marine Geology 65 (3-4):305 - 324.

Krouse, J.S. 1981. *Occurrence of Albino Rock Crabs, Cancer irroratussay (Decapoda, Brachyura) in Penobscot Bay, Maine, USA.* Crustaceana 40 (2):219 - 220.

LaBar, George W., McCleave, James D., and Fried, Stephen M. 1977. *Seaward Migration of Hatchery-Reared Atlantic Salmon (Salmo salar) Smolts in the Penobscot River Estuary, Maine.* Open Water Movements. J. Cons. int. Explor. Mer. 38 (2):257 - 269.

Larson, B.R., Vadas, R.L., and Keser, M. 1980. *Feeding and Nutritional Ecology of the Sea Urchin Stronglylocentrotu drobachiensis in Maine, USA.* Marine Biology 59:49-62. [Some urchins collected from Moose Point State Park for study]

Larsen, P.F. 1992. *Marine Environmental Quality in the Gulf of Maine: A Review.* Reviews in Aquatic Sciences 6(1): 67-87.

Larsen, P.F., Zdanowicz, V., and Johnson, A.C. 1983. *Trace Metal Distributions in the Surficial Sediments of Penobscot Bay, Maine.* Bull. Environ. Contam. Toxicol., New York 31:566 - 573.

Larsen, P.F, and Johnson, A.C. 1983. *Sediment Quality Studies in Casco Bay and Penobscot Bay, Maine.* Bigelow Laboratory for Ocean Sciences Technical Report #33. West Boothbay Harbor, ME. 56 pp.

Larsen, P.F., Gadbois, D.F., and Johnson, A.C. 1984. *Sediment PCB Distribution in the Penobscot Bay Region of the Gulf of Maine.* Marine Pollution Bull., Great Britain. 15(1):34 - 35.

Larsen, P.F., and Johnson, A.C. 1985. *The Macrobenthos of Penobscot Bay, Maine.* Bigelow Laboratory, Tech. Report #51.

Lauenstein, G.G., Robertson, A., and O'Connor, T.P. 1990. *Comparison of Trace Metal Data in Mussels and Oysters from a Mussel Watch Programme of the 1970s with Those from a 1980s Programme.* Mar. Pollut. Bull. (21): 440-447.

Maine DEP. 1976. *Penobscot River Basin Water Quality Management Plan.* Maine DEP. 136 pp.

Maine DEP. 1988. *State of Maine 1988 Water Quality Assessment.* Maine DEP. 74 pp.

Maine DEP. 1989. *State of Maine Nonpoint Source Pollution Assessment Report.* Maine DEP. 192 pp.

Maine DEP. 1992 & 1994. *State of Maine Water Quality Assessment: A Report to Congress Prepared Pursuant to Section 305(b) of the Federal Water Pollution Control Act as Amended.* Maine DEP.

Maine DMR. 1976. *Maine Landings: 1955 - 1976.* US Dept of Commerce, Washington, D.C.

Maine DOT. 1977. *Maine Port Development Study, Phase I.* DOT, Augusta, ME.

Maine Water Improvement Commission. 1964. *Penobscot River Classification Report.* Maine Dept. of Sea Shore Fish., Augusta, ME. 226 pp.

McCleave, James D., and Kleckner, Robert C. 1982. *Selective Tidal Stream Transport in the Estuarine Migration of Glass Eels of the American Eel (Anguilla rostrata).* J. Cons. int. Explor. Mer. 40:262 - 271.

McCleave, James D., and Wippelhauser, Gail S. 1987. *Behavioral Aspects of Selective Tidal Stream Transport in Juvenile American Eels.* American Fisheries Society Symposium 1:138 - 150.

McCleave, James D. 1978. *Rhythmic Aspects of Estuarine Migration of Hatchery-Reared Atlantic Salmon (Salmo salar) Smolts.* J. Fish Biol. 12:559 - 570.

Moroney, J.F. 1973. *A Study of the Macrophytes and Benthos in the Lower Penobscot River.* Wildlife Management.

Mower, B. 1995. *Dioxin monitoring program.* Maine DEP, Augusta, ME. 100 pp.

New England River Basins Commission. 1981. *Maine Central Coastal River Basins Overview.*

New England River Basins Commission. 1981. *Penobscot River Basin Overview.* 137 pp.

Newell, C.R. 1990. *The Effects of Mussel (Mytilus edulis, Linnaeus, 1758) Position In Seeded Bottom Patches on Growth at Subtidal Lease Sites in Maine. Journal of Shellfish Research* 9 (1):113 - 118.

Newell, C.R., Shumway, S.E., Cucci, T.L., and Selvin, R. 1989. *The Effects of Natural Seston Particle Size and Type on Feeding Rates, Feeding Selectivity and Food Resource Availability for the Mussel (Mytilus edulis, Linnaeus) at Bottom Culture Sites in Maine. Journal of Shellfish Research,* 8 (1): 187 - 196.

Newell, C.R., Hidu, H., McAlice, B.J., Podiesinski, G., Short, F,. and Kindblom, L. 1991. *Recruitment and Commercial Seed Procurement of the Blue Mussel Mytilus edulis in Maine.* Journal of the World Aquaculture Society 22 (2):134 - 152.

NOAA. 1988. *National Status and Trends Program for Marine Environmental Quality: Progress Report - A Summary of Selected Data on Chemical Contaminants in Sediments Collected During 1984, 1985, 1986 and 1987.* NOAA Tech. Memorandum NOS OMA 44. [Sears and Pickering Islands]

NOAA. 1989. *National Status and Trends Program for Marine Environmental Quality: Progress Report - A Summary of Data on Tissue Contamination from the First Three Years (1986-1988) of the Mussel Watch Project.* NOAA Tech. Memorandum NOS OMA 49. Rockville, MD.

NOAA. 1991. *National Status and Trends Program for Marine Environmental Quality: Progress Report - Second Summary of the Data on Chemical Contaminants in Sediments from the National Status and Trends Program.* NOAA. Rockville, MD.

NOAA. 1994. *Gulf of Maine Point Source Inventory: A summary by watershed for 1991.* NOAA. Silver Spring, MD.

Normandeau Associates Inc. 1974. Environmental Survey of Upper Penobscot Bay, Maine. In: *First Quarterly Report for Central Maine Power Company.* Central Maine Power Company 250 pp.

Normandeau Associates, Inc. 1975. *Environmental Survey of Upper Penobscot Bay, Maine. Second Quarterly Report for Central Maine Power Company.* 385 pp.

Normandeau Associates, Inc. 1982. *Hydrographic Characteristics of Upper Penobscot Bay, a Technical Summary In: Sears Island Marine Dry Cargo Terminal, Searsport, Maine, Technical Appendices.* Maine DOT, vol. 2, Technical Appendices. 38 pp.

Normandeau Associates, Inc. 1991. *Harriman Cove Environmental Studies, April 1990 - March 1991,* Data Report. 68 pp.

Noyes, G.S. 1970. *The Biology of Aglaophamus sp. (polychaete nephtyidae) from Maine.* U of M, Orono, ME. 70 pp.

Ostericher, C. 1965. *Bottom and Subbottom Investigations of Penobscot Bay, ME, 1959.* U.S. Naval Oceanographic Office Technical Report, TR-173. 177 pp.

Panchang, V., Guo, C., and Newell, C. 1993. *Application of Mathmatical Models in the Environmental Regulation of Net-Pen Aquaculture.* Sea Grant, U of M, Orono, ME. Sea Grant MSG-TR-93-1. 105 pp.

Parker, J.G., and Wilson, F. 1975. *Incidence of Polychlorinated Biphenyls in Clyde Seaweed. Bioscience* 46 - 47.

Penobscot River Study Team. 1972. *Penobscot River Study.* Environmental Studies Center, U of M, Orono, ME. Report # 1. 288 pp.

Prescott, G.C., Jr. 1981. *Sand and Gravel Aquifers Map 20, Hancock, Waldo, and Knox Counties, Maine.* Maine Geological Survey Open File Report 81-53. 6 pp.

Prescott, G.C., Jr. 1981. *Sand and Gravel Aquifers Map 21, Hancock County, Maine.* Maine Geological Survey Open File Report 81-54. 6 pp.

Prescott, G.C., Jr., Tepper, D.H., Caswell, W.B., and Thompson, W.B. 1981. *Sand and Gravel Aquifers Map 28, Hancock, Penobscot, and Waldo Counties, Maine.* Maine Geological Survey Open File Report 81-60. 6 pp.

Rabeni, C.F and Gibbs, K.E. 1977. *Benthic Invertebrates As Water Quality Indicators in the Penobscot River, Maine.* Land and Water Resources Institute, U of M, Orono, ME. Report A-028-ME. 75 pp.

Richards, T.L. 1969. *Physiological Ecology of Selected Polychaetous Annelids Exposed to Different Temperatures, Salinity and Dissolved Oxygen Combinations.* U of M, Orono, ME. 171 pp.

Rieser, A., and Vestal, B. 1991. *Commercial Fishing and the Marine Mammal Protection Act.* Sea Grant MSG-E-91-5, Guide #7. 4 pp.

Roberts, D.A., et al. 1994. *Biological Assessment of Shortnose Sturgeon (Acipenser brevirostrum) in the Lower Penobscot River, ME.* US EPA Region I. 101pp.

Scanlon, K., and Knebel, H.J. 1989. *Pockmarks in the Floor of Penobscot Bay, Maine.* Geo-Marine Letters 9:53 - 58.

Sheldon, M.R., and McCleave, J.D. 1985. *Abundance of Glass Eels of the American Eel, Anguilla Rostrata, In Mid-Channel and Near Shore During Estuarine Migration.* Naturaliste Can. (Rev. Ecol. Syst.) 112: 425 - 430.

Shorey, W.K. 1973. *Macrobenthis Ecology of a Sawdust-Bearing Substrate in the Penobscot River Estuary (Maine).* J. Fish. Res. Bd. Can. 30:493-497. [Based on another UMaine thesis in Wildlife.]

Sowles, J. 1993. *Maine Musselwatch Heavy Metal Baseline Survey in Blue Mussels: 1988-92.* Maine DEP.

Sowles, J. 1995. *Gulf of Maine 1993-94 Mussel Samples.* Maine DEP.

Sowles, J., Crawford, R., Machell, J., Atkinson, G., Hennigar, P., Jones, S., Pederson, J., and Coombs, K. 1992. *Evaluation of Gulfwatch, 1991 Pilot Project of the Gulf of Maine Marine Environmental Monitoring Plan.* The Gulf of Maine Council on the Marine Environment. 36 pp.

Sowles, J., Crawford, R., Machell, J., Hennigar, P., Jones, S., Pederson, J., Coombs, K., Atkinson, G., Mathews, S., Taylor, D., and Harding, G. 1994. *Evaluation of Gulfwatch 1992, Second Year of the Gulf of Maine Environmental Monitoring Plan.* The Gulf of Maine Council on the Marine Environment. 126 pp.

Spencer, H.E., Jr., and Hutchinson, A. 1974. *An Appraisal of the Fishery and Wildlife Resources of Eastern Penobscot Bay.* Planning Unit, Coastal Planning Group, State Planning Office, Augusta,ME. 27 pp.

Spiess, A., and Hedden, M. 1983. *Kidder Point and Sears Island in Prehistory.* Maine Historic Preservation Commission, Augusta, ME.

Stevenson, D.K., and Pierce, F. 1985. *Life History Characteristics of Pandalus montagui and Dichelopandalus leptocerus in Penobscot Bay, Maine.* Fishery Bulletin 83 (3):219 - 233.

The Center for Natural Areas, et al. 1978. *An Oil Pollution Prevention, Abatement and Management Study for Penobscot Bay, Maine.* Maine Department of Environmental Protection. 4 volumes.

Townsend, D.W., ed. 1985. *Temperature, Salinity and Dissolved Oxygen Data for the Penobscott River Estuary, Maine 1963-1977.* Bigelow Laboratory for Ocean Sciences. Technical Report No. 52.

Trainer, D.G. 1969. *Notes on the Biology of Pygospio elegans from Maine.* U of M, Orono, ME. 69 pp.

ten Brink, M.B., and Manheim, F.T. 1995. *Gulf of Maine Contaminated Sediment Workbook.* U.S. Geological Survey. Woods Hole, MA.

Turgeon, D.D., Bricker, S.B., and O'Connor, T.P. 1992. *National Status and Trends Program: Chemical and Biological Monitoring of U.S. Coastal Waters.* In: McKenzie, D.H., Hyatt, D.E., and McDonald, V.J., eds. *Ecological Indicators,* Vol. 1. Elsevier Applied Science, London.

U.S. Fish and Wildlife Service. 1980. *Atlantic Coast Ecological Inventory, Bangor.* U.S. Fish and Wildlife Service, Washington, D.C. [Map: shows location of birds, mammals, fish]

U.S. Govt. Printing Office. 1979. *The Nation's Water Resources 1975 - 2000, Volume 1.* U.S. Water Resources Council.

U.S. Dept. of the Interior. 1968. *Interim Report on Chemical and Biological Characterization of Water and Sediments from Cape Rosier, Maine.* Federal Water Polution Control Adm., Merrimack River Project - NE Region, Boston, MA.

U.S. Dept. of the Interior. 1967. *Conference on the Pollution of the Navigable Waters of the Penobscot River and Upper Penobscot Bay and Their Tributaries, Belfast, ME.* Federal Water Pollution Control Adm. 394 pp.

U.S. Dept. of the Interior. 1967. *Report on Pollution - Navigable Waters of the Penobscot River and Upper Penobscot Bay in Maine.* Federal Water Polution Control Adm., Merrimack River Project - NE Region, Boston, MA. 94 pp.

U.S. Dept. of the Interior. 1970. *Effects of Strip-Mine Discharges on the Marine Environment, Cape Rosier, Maine.* Federal Water Polution Control Adm., Merrimack River Project - NE Region, Needham Heights, MA.

U.S. Dept. of the Interior. 1975. *Penobscot Wild and Scenic River Study.* Bureau of Outdoor Recreation, New England Regional Office. 95 pp.

White, G.C. 1972. *Establishing a Quantitative Biological Base in the Penobscot Estuary Using Benthic Macroinvertebrates.* U of M, Orono, ME. 102 pp.

Wingard, P.S. 1958. *Geology of the Castine – Blue Hill Area, Maine.* University of Illinois, Urbana, IL. 138 pp.

Wippelhauser, Gail S. and McCleave, James D. 1988. *Rhythmic Activity of Migrating Juvenile American Eels Anguilla Rostrata.* F. Mar. Biol. Ass. U.K. 68:81 - 91.

Wippelhauser, Gail S., and McCleave, James D. 1987. *Precision of Behavior of Migrating Juvenile American Eels (Anguilla rostrata) Utilizing Selective Tidal Stream Transport.* J. Cons. Int Explor. Mer. 44:80 - 89.

Wong, K.C. 1994. *Spatial Variation of Tidal and Residual Currents in East and West Penobscot Bay.* University of Delaware, Graduate College of Marine Studies, Newark, Delaware. [abstract + research proposal]

Woodward, F.E., Sylvester, H.C., and Foster, J.A. 1974. *Development of a Water Quality Management Program for the Lower Penobscot River and Estuary, Final Report, Phase I.* Environmental Studies Center, U of M, Orono, ME. Report # 3-74 105 pp.

Woodward, S., Hutchinson, A., and McCollough, M. 1986. *The Penobscot Bay Conservation Plan.* Maine Dept. of Inland Fisheries and Wildlife, Augusta, ME. 105 pp.

Listings by Subject

Acadia National Park

Greene, C.W., Mittelhauser, G.H., Jacobs, J., and Gregory, L.L. 1992. *Historical Resource Inventory for Acadia National Park, Volume 1.* National Park Service, Boston. Technical Report NPS/NAROSS/NRTR-92/01. 623pp.

Aquaculture

Findlay, R.H., and Watling, L. 1994. *Towards a Process Level Model to Predict the Effects of Salmon Net-Pen Aquaculture on the Benthos.* Can. Tech. Report of Fish. and Aquatic Sci. 1949 xi + 125 pp. Sea Grant MSG-R-94-21

Fried, Stephen M., McCleave, James D., and LaBar, George W. 1978. *Seaward Migration of Hatchery-Reared Atlantic Salmon, Salmo salar, Smolts in the Penobscot River Estuary, Maine: Riverine Movements.* Journal of the Fisheries Research Board of Canada. 35 (1): 76 - 87.

Hidu, H. 1974. *Cooperative Oyster Mariculture. In: Maine Renewable Marine Resources Forum.* Maine Maritime Academy, Castine, ME

LaBar, George W., McCleave, James D., and Fried, Stephen M. 1977. *Seaward Migration of Hatchery-Reared Atlantic Salmon (Salmo salar) Smolts in the Penobscot River Estuary, Maine: Open Water Movements.* J. Cons. Int. Explor. Mer. 38 (2):257-269.

McCleave, James D. 1978. *Rhythmic Aspects of Estuarine Migration of Hatchery-Reared Atlantic Salmon (Salmo salar) Smolts.* J. Fish Biol. 12:559-570.

Newell, C.R. 1990. *The Effects of Mussel (Mytilus edulis, Linnaeus, 1758) Position In Seeded Bottom Patches on Growth at Subtidal Lease Sites in Maine.* Journal of Shellfish Research 9 (1):113-118.

Newell, C.R., Shumway, S.E., Cucci, T.L. and Selvin, R. 1989. *The Effects of Natural Seston Particle Size and Type on Feeding Rates, Feeding Selectivity and Food Resource Availability for the Mussel (Mytilus edulis, Linnaeus) at Bottom Culture Sites in Maine.* Journal of Shellfish Research, 8 (1):187-196.

Newell, C.R., Hidu, H., McAlice, B.J., Podiesinski, G., Short, F. and Kindblom, L. 1991. *Recruitment and Commercial Seed Procurement of the Blue Mussel Mytilus edulis in Maine.* Journal of the World Aquaculture Society 22 (2):134-152.

Panchang, V., Guo, C., and Newell, C. 1993. *Application of Mathmatical Models in the Environmental Regulation of Net-Pen Aquaculture.* Sea Grant, U of M, Orono, ME. Sea Grant MSG-TR-93-1. 105 pp.

Aquifers

Brewer, T., Genes, A.N., and Prescott, G.C., Jr. 1979. *Sand and Gravel Aquifers Map 18, Lincoln, Knox, Waldo, and Kennebec Counties, Maine.* Maine Geological Survey Open File Report 79-13. 6 pp.

Caswell, W.B., Thompson, W.B., Cotton, J.E., and Prescott, G.C., Jr. 1981. *Sand and Gravel Aquifers Map 29, Penobscot and Waldo Counties, Maine.* Maine Geological Survey Open File Report 81-61. 6 pp.

Cotton, J.E., Welsh, M., and Prescott, G.C., Jr. 1981. *Sand and Gravel Aquifers Map 30, Somerset, Kennebec, Waldo, and Penobscot Counties, Maine.* Maine Geological Survey Open File Report 81-62. 6 pp.

Hansen, B.P. 1980. *Ground Water Availability in Acadia National Park and Vicinity, Hancock and Knox Counties, Maine.* U.S. Geological Survey Open File Report 80-1050. 8 pp.

Prescott, G.C., Jr. 1981. *Sand and Gravel Aquifers Map 20, Hancock, Waldo, and Knox Counties, Maine.* Maine Geological Survey Open File Report 81-53. 6 pp.

Prescott, G.C., Jr. 1981. *Sand and Gravel Aquifers Map 21, Hancock County, Maine.* Maine Geological Survey Open File Report 81-54. 6 pp.

Prescott, G.C., Jr., Tepper, D.H., Caswell, W.B., and Thompson, W.B. 1981. *Sand and Gravel Aquifers Map 28, Hancock, Penobscot, and Waldo Counties, Maine.* Maine Gelogical Survey Open File Report 81-60. 6 pp.

Benthos

Dean, D. 1970. *Water Quality - Benthic Invertebrate Relationships in Estuaries.* Water Resources Center, U of M, Orono, ME. 9 pp.

Larsen, P.F. and Johnson, A.C. 1985. *The Macrobenthos of Penobscot Bay, Maine.* Bigelow Laboratory, Tech. Report #51.

Moroney, J.F. 1973. *A Study of the Macrophytes and Benthos in the Lower Penobscot River.* Wildlife Management.

Noyes, G.S. 1970. *The Biology of Aglaophamus sp. (polychaete nephtyidae) from Maine.* U of M, Orono, ME. 70 pp.

Rabeni, C.F and Gibbs, K.E. 1977. *Benthic Invertebrates As Water Quality Indicators in the Penobscot River, Maine. Land and Water Resources.* Institute, U of M, Orono, ME. Report A-028-ME. 75 pp

Richards, T.L. 1969. *Physiological Ecology of Selected Polychaetous Annelids Exposed to Different Temperatures, Salinity and Dissolved Oxygen Combinations.* U of M, Orono, ME. 171 pp.

Shorey, W.K. 1973. *Macrobenthis Ecology of a Sawdust-Bearing Substrate in the Penobscot River Estuary (Maine).* J. Fish. Res. Bd. Can. 30:493-497. [Based on another UMaine thesis in Wildlife.]

White, G.C. 1972. *Establishing a Quantitative Biological Base in the Penobscot Estuary Using Benthic Macroinvertebrates.* U of M, Orono, ME. 102 pp.

Circulation

Burgund, H.R. 1995. *The Currents of Penobscot Bay, Maine: Observations and a Numerical Model.* Department of Geology and Geophysics, Yale University. 71pp.

Fidler, R.B. 1979. *An Approach for Hydrodynamic Modeling of Maine's Estuaries.* U of M, Orono, ME. 74 pp.

Haefner, P.A., Jr. 1967. *Hydrography of the Penobscot River (Maine) Estuary.* Journal of the Fisheries Research Board of Canada 24 (7):1553 - 1571.

Humphreys, A.C., III, and Pearce, B.R. 1981. *A Hydrodynamic Investigation of the Penobscot Bay Estuary.* Dept. of Civil Engineering, U of M, Orono, ME.

Humphreys, A.C.,III, and Pearce, B.R. 1981. *"Currents in Penobscot Bay, Maine."* In: Oceans 81 - Conference record of The Ocean - An International Workplace. Boston. 805-809.

Wong, K.C. 1994. *Spatial Variation of Tidal and Residual Currents in East and West Penobscot Bay.* University of Delaware, Graduate College of Marine Studies, Newark, Delaware. [abstract + research proposal]

Coastal Ecology

U.S. Fish and Wildlife Service. 1980. *Atlantic Coast Ecological Inventory, Bangor.* U.S. Fish and Wildlife Service, Washington, D.C. [map - shows location of birds, mammals + fish]

Crustacea

Ayer, W.C. 1971. *Some Aspects of Amphipod Distribution in the Penobscot River (Maine) estuary.* Zoology.

Krouse, J.S. 1981. *Occurrence of Albino Rock Crabs, Cancer irroratussay (Decapoda, Brachyura) in Penobscot Bay, Maine, USA.* Crustaceana 40 (2):219 - 220.

Stevenson, D.K. and Pierce, F. 1985. *Life History Characteristics of Pandalus montagui and Dichelopandalus leptocerus in Penobscot Bay, Maine.* Fishery Bulletin 83 (3):219 - 233.

Ecology

Fish and Wildlife Service, U.S. Dept. of the Interior. 1980. *An Ecological Characterization of Coastal Maine, Volumes 1 - 6.* Fish & Wildlife Service, Dept. of Interior, Washington, D.C.

Greene, C.W., Mittelhauser, G.H., Jacobs, J., and Gregory, L.L. 1992. *Historical Resource Inventory For Acadia National Park, Volume 1.* National Park Service, Boston. Technical Report NPS/NAROSS/NRTR-92/01. 623pp.

Jury, S. H., Field, J. D., Stone, S. L., Nelson, D. M., and Monaco, M. E. 1994. *Distribution and Abundance of Fishes and Invertebrates in North Atlantic Estuaries.* NOAA/NOS Strategic Environmental Assessments Division, Silver Spring, MD. ELMR Report Number 13. 221 pp.

Rabeni, C.F., and Gibbs, K.E. 1977. *Benthic Invertebrates As Water Quality Indicators in the Penobscot River, Maine.* Land and Water Resources Institute, U of M, Orono, ME. Report A-028-ME. 75 pp

Stevenson, D.K., and Pierce, F. 1985. *Life History Characteristics of Pandalus montagui and Dichelopandalus leptocerus in Penobscot Bay, Maine.* Fishery Bulletin 83 (3):219 - 233.

Trainer, D.G. 1969. *Notes on the Biology of Pygospio elegans from Maine.* U of M, Orono, ME. 69 pp.

White, G.C. 1972. *Establishing a Quantitative Biological Base in the Penobscot Estuary Using Benthic Macroinvertebrates.* U of M, Orono, ME. 102 pp.

Economics – Sociological Aspects

Cobb, W. 1979. *Socioeconomic Characterization of Coastal Knox and Waldo Counties.* N.E. Coastal Oceanographic Group. Cutler, ME.

Keeley, D. 1979. *Socioeconomic Characterization of Coastal Hancock County.* N.E. Coastal Oceanographic Group, Cutler, ME

Environmental Monitoring

Doyle, Robert G. 1970. *Penobscot Bay Physical Resources Report: Preliminary.* Maine Dept. of Economic Development.

Larsen, P.F. 1992. *Marine environmental quality in the Gulf of Maine: A Review.* Reviews in Aquatic Sciences 6(1): 67-87.

Normandeau Associates, Inc. 1974. *Environmental Survey of Upper Penobscot Bay, Maine, In: First Quarterly Report for Central Maine Power Company.* Central Maine Power Co. 250 pp.

Normandeau Associates, Inc. 1975. *Environmental Survey of Upper Penobscot Bay, Maine. Second Quarterly Report for Central Maine Power Company.* 385 pp.

Normandeau Associates, Inc. 1991. *Harriman Cove Environmental Studies, April 1990 - March 1991.* Data Report. 68 pp.

Turgeon, D.D., Bricker, S.B. and O'Connor, T.P. 1992. *National Status and Trends Program: Chemical and Biological Monitoring of U.S. Coastal Waters.* In: McKenzie, D.H., Hyatt, D.E., and McDonald, V.J., eds. Ecological Indicators Vol. 1. Elsevier Applied Science, London.

Environmental Protection

Council on Environmental Quality. 1979. *Environmental Quality - 1979.* Washington, D.C.

Fisheries

Flagg, Lewis N. 1984. *Penobscot River Shad and Alewife Restoration Potential.* Maine Dept. of Marine Resources, Augusta, ME. 7 pp.

Flagg, Lewis N., and Squiers, Thomas S. 1978. *American Shad Restoration and Rainbow Smelt Population Dynamics.* Maine Dept. of Marine Resources, Augusta, ME. AFS - 19 - R. 25 pp.

Jury, S. H., Field, J. D., Stone, S. L., Nelson, D. M., and Monaco, M. E. 1994. *Distribution and Abundance of Fishes and Invertebrates in North Atlantic Estuaries.* NOAA/NOS Strategic Environmental Assessments Division, Silver Spring, MD. ELMR Report Number 13. 221 pp.

Maine DMR. 1976. *Maine Landings: 1955 - 1976.* US Dept of Commerce, Washington, D.C.

McCleave, James D., and Kleckner, Robert C. 1982. *Selective Tidal Stream Transport in the Estuarine Migration of Glass Eels of the American Eel (Anguilla rostrata).* J. Cons. int. Explor. Mer. 40:262 - 271.

McCleave, James D., and Wippelhauser, Gail S. 1987. *Behavioral Aspects of Selective Tidal Stream Transport in Juvenile American Eels.* American Fisheries Society Symposium 1:138 - 150.

Roberts, D.A. et. al. 1994. *Biological Assessment of Shortnose Sturgeon (Acipenser brevirostrum) in the Lower Penobscot River, ME.* US EPA Region I. 101pp.

Sheldon, M.R., and McCleave, J.D. 1985. *Abundance of Glass Eels of the American Eel, Anguilla Rostrata, In Mid-Channel and Near Shore During Estuarine Migration.* Naturaliste Can. (Rev. Ecol. Syst.) 112: 425 - 430.

Spencer, H.E., Jr., and Hutchinson, A. 1974. *An Appraisal of the Fishery and Wildlife Resources of Eastern Penobscot Bay.* Planning Unit. Coastal Planning Group, State Planning Office, Augusta, ME. 27 pp.

Wippelhauser, Gail S., and McCleave, James D. 1988. *Rhythmic Activity of Migrating Juvenile American Eels Anguilla Rostrata.* F. Mar. Biol. Ass. U.K. 68:81 - 91.

Wippelhauser, Gail S., and McCleave, James D. 1987. *Precision of Behavior of Migrating Juvenile American Eels (Anguilla rostrata) Utilizing Selective Tidal Stream Transport.* J. Cons. Int Explor. Mer. 44:80 - 89.

Fishes – Migration

Fried, Stephen M., McCleave, James D., and LaBar, George W. 1978. *Seaward Migration of Hatchery-Reared Atlantic Salmon, Salmo salar, Smolts in the Penobscot River Estuary, Maine: Riverine Movements.* Journal of the Fisheries Research Board of Canada. 35 (1): 76 - 87.

LaBar, George W., McCleave, James D., and Fried, Stephen M. 1977. *Seaward Migration of Hatchery-Reared Atlantic Salmon (Salmo salar) Smolts in the Penobscot River Estuary, Maine: Open Water Movements.* J. Cons. Int. Explor. Mer. 38 (2):257-269.

McCleave, James D. 1978. *Rhythmic Aspects of Estuarine Migration of Hatchery-Reared Atlantic Salmon (Salmo salar) Smolts.* J. Fish Biol. 12:559-570.

McCleave, James D., and Kleckner, Robert C. 1982. *Selective Tidal Stream Transport in the Estuarine Migration of Glass Eels of the American Eel (Anguilla rostrata)*. J. Cons. int. Explor. Mer. 40:262 - 271.

McCleave, James D., and Wippelhauser, Gail S. 1987. *Behavioral Aspects of Selective Tidal Stream Transport in Juvenile American Eels.* American Fisheries Society Symposium 1:138 - 150.

Sheldon, M.R., and McCleave, J.D. 1985. *Abundance of Glass Eels of the American Eel, Anguilla Rostrata, In Mid-Channel and Near Shore During Estuarine Migration.* Naturaliste Can. (Rev. Ecol. Syst.) 112: 425 - 430.

Wippelhauser, Gail S., and McCleave, James D. 1988. *Rhythmic Activity of Migrating Juvenile American Eels Anguilla Rostrata.* F. Mar. Biol. Ass. U.K. 68:81 - 91.

Wippelhauser, Gail S., and McCleave, James D. 1987. *Recision of Behavior of Migrating Juvenile American Eels (Anguilla rostrata) Utilizing Selective Tidal Stream Transport.* J. Cons. Int Explor. Mer. 44:80 - 89.

French – American – Maine – History

Faulkner, A., and Faulkner, G.F. 1987. *The French at Pentagoet, 1635-1674.* Maine Historic Preservation Commission, Augusta, ME.

Geology

Bickel, C.E. 1971. *Bedrock Geology of the Belfast Quadrangle, Maine.* Harvard University, Cambridge, MA. 322 pp.

Bouley, B.A. 1978. *Volcanic Stratigraphy, Stratabound Sulfide Deposits, and Relative Age Relationships in the East Penobscot Bay Area, Maine.* University of Western Ontario, London, Ontario. 168 pp.

Brewer, T., Genes, A.N., and Prescott, G.C., Jr. 1979. *Sand and Gravel Aquifers Map 18, Lincoln, Knox, Waldo, and Kennebec Counties, Maine.* Maine Geological Survey Open File Report 79-13. 6 pp.

Brookins, D.G. 1976. *Geochronologic Contributions to Stratigraphic Iinterpretation and Correlation in the Penobscot Bay Area, Eastern Maine.* In: L.R. Page, ed., *Contributions to the Stratigraphy of New England.* Geological Society of America Memoir 148:129-145.

Caswell, W.B., Thompson, W.B., Cotton, J.E., and Prescott, G.C., Jr. 1981. *Sand and Gravel Aquifers Map 29, Penobscot and Waldo Counties, Maine.* Maine Geological Survey Open File Report 81-61. 6 pp.

Cheney, E.S. 1969. *Geology of the Blue Hill – Castine Mining District, Southwestern Hancock County, Maine.* Maine Geological Survey, Second Annual Report. 148 pp.

Dow, G.M. 1965. *Petrology and Structure of North Haven Island and Vicinity, Maine.* University of Illinois, Urbana, IL. 146 pp.

Prescott, G.C., Jr. 1981. *Sand and Gravel Aquifers Map 20, Hancock, Waldo, and Knox Counties, Maine.* Maine Geological Survey Open File Report 81-53. 6 pp.

Prescott, G.C., Jr. 1981. *Sand and Gravel Aquifers Map 21, Hancock County, Maine.* Maine Geological Survey Open File Report 81-54. 6 pp.

Prescott, G.C., Jr., Tepper, D.H., Caswell, W.B., and Thompson, W.B. 1981. *Sand and Gravel Aquifers Map 28, Hancock, Penobscot, and Waldo Counties, Maine.* Maine Gelogical Survey Open File Report 81-60. 6 pp.

Wingard, P.S. 1958. *Geology of the Castine – Blue Hill Area, Maine.* University of Illinois, Urbana, IL. 138 pp.

Gulfwatch 1991

Sowles, J., Crawford, R., Machell, J., Atkinson, G., Hennigar, P., Jones, S., Pederson, J., and Coombs, K. 1992. *Evaluation of Gulfwatch, 1991 Pilot Project of the Gulf of Maine Marine Environmental Monitoring Plan.* The Gulf of Maine Council on the Marine Environment. 36 pp.

Gulfwatch 1992

Gulf of Maine Council on the Marine Environment. 1994. *Evaluation of Gulfwatch 1992, Second year of the Gulf of Maine Environmental Monitoring Plan.* 141 pp.

Sowles, J., Crawford, R., Machell, J., Hennigar, P., Jones, S., Pederson, J., Coombs, K., Atkinson, G., Mathews, S., Taylor, D., and Harding, G. 1994. *Evaluation of Gulfwatch 1992, Second Year of the Gulf of Maine Environmental Monitoring Plan.* The Gulf of Maine Council on the Marine Environment. 126 pp.

Heavy Metals

Bryan, M. 1971. *The Effects of Heavy Metals Other Than Mercury on Marine and Estuarine Organisms.* Proc. Royal Society of London Bull. B. Biol. Sci. 177:289 - 410.

Courtemanch, D.L. 1977. *Investigation of Copper Sediments of Silver Lake, Bucksport, Maine.* Maine DEP, Augusta, ME.

Dow, Robert L., and Hurst, John W. Jr. 1972. *Renewable Resource Problems of Heavy Metal Mining in Coastal Maine.* Maine Dept. of Sea and Shore Fisheries, reprinted by National Fisherman.Research Bulletin #35.

Fink, L.K., Harris, A.B., and Schick, L.L. 1980. *Trace Metals in Suspended Particulates, Biota, and Sediments of the St. Croix,*

Narraguagus, and Union Estuaries and the Goose Cove Region of Penobscot. Land & Water Resources Center, U of M, Orono, ME. Report A-041-ME & B-015-ME. 293 pp.

Fink, L.K., Jr. 1977. *Heavy Metals.* Darling Center, U. of M., Walpole, ME.

Hidu, H. 1974. *Cooperative Oyster Mariculture.* In: *Maine Renewable Marine Resources Forum.* Maine Maritime Academy, Castine, ME

Hurst, J.W., Jr., and Dow, R.L. 1972. *Renewable Resource Problems of Heavy Metal Mining in Coastal Maine.* National Fisherman 52(10).

Sowles, J. 1993. *Maine Musselwatch Heavy Metal Baseline Survey in Blue Mussels: 1988-92.* Maine DEP.

Hydrography

Normandeau Associates, Inc. 1982. *Hydrographic Characteristics of Upper Penobscot Bay, a Technical Summary In: Sears Island Marine Dry Cargo Terminal, Searsport, Maine.* Technical Appendices. Maine DOT, vol. 2, Technical Appendices. 38 pp.

Marine Geology

Kelley, J. T., and Belknap, D. F. 1989. *Geomorphology and Sedimentary Framework of Penobscot Bay and Adjacent Inner Continental Shelf.* Maine Geological Survey, Report # 89-3. 35 pp.

Kelley, J.T., Belknap, D.F., Shipp, R.C., and Miller, S.B. 1989. *An Investigation of Neotectonic Activity In Coastal Maine by Seismic Reflection Methods.* In: *Neotectonics of Maine.* Maine Geological Survey Bulletin 40:23 - 34.

Kelley, J.T., Dickson, S.M., Belknap, D.F., Barnhardt, W.A., and Henderson, M. 1994. *Giant Sea-Bed Pockmarks: Evidence for Gas Escape from Belfast, Maine.* Geology 22:59 - 62.

Knebel, H.J. 1986. *Holocene Depositional History of a Large Glaciated Estuary, Penobscot Bay, Maine.* Marine Geology 73 (3-4):215 - 236.

Knebel, H.J. and Scanlon, K.M. 1985. *Sedimentary Framework of Penobscot Bay, Maine.* Marine Geology 65 (3-4):305 - 324.

Ostericher, C. 1965. *Bottom and Subbottom Investigations of Penobscot Bay, ME, 1959.* U.S. Naval Oceanographic Office Technical Report, TR-173. 177 pp.

Scanlon, K. and Knebel, H.J. 1989. *Pockmarks in the Floor of Penobscot Bay, Maine.* Geo-Marine Letters 9:53 - 58.

Marine Pollution

Beck, F.M. 1970. *Marine Challenges Encountered by a Small Mine on the Maine Coast.* 1970. Offshore Technology Conference, Houston, Texas. OTC 1256.

Larsen, P.F. 1992. *Marine Environmental Quality in the Gulf of Maine: A Review.* Reviews in Aquatic Sciences 6(1): 67-87.

Larsen, P.F., Gadbois, D.F., and Johnson, A.C. 1984. *Sediment PCB Distribution in the Penobscot Bay Region of the Gulf of Maine.* Marine Pollution Bull., Great Britian. 15(1):34 - 35.

Larsen, P.F., Zdanowicz, V., and Johnson, A.C. 1983. *Trace Metal Distributions in the Surficial Sediments of Penobscot Bay, Maine.* Bull. Environ. Contam. Toxicol., New York 31:566 - 573.

Larsen, P.F., and Johnson, A.C. 1983. *Sediment Quality Studies in Casco Bay and Penobscot Bay, Maine.* Bigelow Laboratory for Ocean Sciences Technical Report #33. West Boothbay Harbor, ME. 56 pp.

Lauenstein, G.G., Robertson, A., and O'Connor, T.P. 1990. *Comparison of Trace Metal Data in Mussels and Oysters from a Mussel Watch Programme of the 1970s with Those from a 1980s Programme.* Mar. Pollut. Bul. (21): 440-447.

Mower, B. 1995. *Dioxin Monitoring Program.* Maine DEP, Augusta, ME. 100 pp.

NOAA. 1988. *National Status and Trends Program for Marine Environmental Quality: Progress Report - A Summary of Selected Data on Chemical Contaminants in Sediments Collected During 1984, 1985, 1986 and 1987.* NOAA Tech Memorandum NOS OMA 44. [Sears and Pickering Islands.]

NOAA. 1989. *National Status and Trends Program for Marine Environmental Quality: Progress Report - A Summary of Data on Tissue Contamination from the First Three Years (1986-1988) of the Mussel Watch Project.* NOAA Tech. Memorandum NOS OMA 49. Rockville, MD.

NOAA. 1991. *National Status and Trends Program for Marine Environmental Quality: Progress Report - Second Summary of the Data on Chemical Contaminants in Sediments from the National Status and Trends Program.* NOAA. Rockville, MD.

Parker, J.G., and Wilson, F. 1975. *Incidence of Polychlorinated Biphenyls in Clyde Seaweed.* Bioscience 46 - 47.

ten Brink, M.B., and Manheim, F.T. 1995. *Gulf of Maine Contaminated Sediment Workbook.* U.S. Geological Survey. Woods Hole, MA.

Turgeon, D.D., Bricker, S.B., and O'Connor, T.P. 1992. *National Status and Trends Program: Chemical and Biological Monitoring of U.S. Coastal Waters.* In: McKenzie, D.H., Hyatt, D.E., and McDonald, V.J., eds. Ecological Indicators Vol. 1. Elsevier Applied Science, London.

U.S. Dept. of the Interior. 1968. *Interim Report on Chemical and Biological Characterization of Water and Sediments from Cape Rosier, Maine.* Federal Water Polution Control Adm., Merrimack River Project - NE Region, Boston, MA.

U.S. Dept. of the Interior. 1970. *Effects of Strip-Mine Discharges on the Marine Environment, Cape Rosier, Maine.* Federal Water Polution Control Adm., Merrimack River Project - NE Region, Needham Heights, MA.

Marine Resources – Maps

Aho, R.A. 1984. *Marine Resources Atlas: Spruce Head to Isle Au Haut, Maine.* DEP. 134 pp. [A companion document to Oil Pollution Research, Card. 1984.]

Marine Sediments

Larsen, P.F., Zdanowicz, V., and Johnson, A.C. 1983. *Trace Metal Distributions in the Surficial Sediments of Penobscot Bay, Maine.* Bull. Environ. Contam. Toxicol., New York 31:566 - 573.

Larsen, P.F., Gadbois, D.F., and Johnson, A.C. 1984. *Sediment PCB Distribution in the Penobscot Bay Region of the Gulf of Maine.* Marine Pollution Bull., Great Britian. 15(1):34 - 35.

Larsen, P.F,. and Johnson, A.C. 1983. *Sediment Quality Studies in Casco Bay and Penobscot Bay, Maine.* Bigelow Laboratory for Ocean Sciences Technical Report #33. West Boothbay Harbor, ME. 56 pp.

NOAA. 1988. *National Status and Trends Program for Marine Environmental Quality: Progress Report - A Summary of Selected Data on Chemical Contaminants in Sediments Collected During 1984, 1985, 1986 and 1987.* NOAA Tech Memorandum NOS OMA 44. [Sears and Pickering islands.]

NOAA. 1991. *National Status and Trends Program for Marine Environmental Quality: Progress Report - Second Summary of the Data on Chemical Contaminants in Sediments from the National Status and Trends Program.* NOAA. Rockville, MD.

ten Brink, M.B., and Manheim, F.T. 1995. *Gulf of Maine Contaminated Sediment Workbook.* U.S. Geological Survey. Woods Hole, MA.

U.S. Dept of the Interior. 1968. *Interim Report on Chemical and Biological Characterization of Water and Sediments from Cape Rosier, Maine.* Federal Water Polution Control Adm., Merrimack River Project - NE Region, Boston, MA.

Marshes, Tide

Jacobson, G.L., Jr,. and Jacobson, H.A. 1989. *An Inventory of Settings Along the Maine Coast.* Maine Geol. Surv. Bull. "Crustal Warping Project".[see Jacobson (1987) comment]

Jacobson, H.A., and Jacobson, G.L., Jr. 1989. *Variability of Vegetation In Tidal Marshes of Maine, USA.* Canadian Journal of Botany 67:230-238. [see Jacobson (1987) comment]

Jacobson, H.A., Jacobson, G.L., Jr., and Kelley, J.T. 1987. *Distribution and Abundance of Tidal Marshes Along the Coast of Maine.* Estuaries 10:126-131. [Horseshoe Cove (Cape Rosier) salt marsh relative to all other marshes]

Mollusks

Dow, R.L. 1975. *Reduced Growth and Survival of Clams Transplanted to an Oil Spill Site.* Marine Pollution Bull. 6:12 - 125.

Dow, R.L. 1978. *Size Selective Mortality of Clams in an Oil Spill Site.* Marine Pollution Bull. 9(2):45 - 48.

Goldberg, E.D., Koide, M., Hodge, V., Flegal, A.R., and Martin, J. 1983. U.S. *Mussel Watch: 1977 - 1978 Results on Trace Metals and Radionuclides.* Estuar. Coast. Shelf Sci. 16: 69-93.

Hidu, H. 1974. *Cooperative Oyster Mariculture. In: Maine Renewable Marine Resources Forum.* Maine Maritime Academy, Castine, ME

Lauenstein, G.G., Robertson, A., and O'Connor, T.P. 1990. *Comparison of Trace Metal Data in Mussels and Oysters from a Mussel Watch Programme of the 1970s with Those from a 1980s Programme.* Mar. Pollut. Bul. (21): 440-447.

Newell, C.R. 1990. *The Effects of Mussel (Mytilus edulis, Linnaeus, 1758) Position In Seeded Bottom Patches on Growth at Subtidal Lease Sites in Maine.* Journal of Shellfish Research 9 (1):113-118.

Newell, C.R., Shumway, S.E., Cucci, T.L., and Selvin, R. 1989. *The Effects of Natural Seston Particle Size and Type on Feeding Rates, Feeding Selectivity and Food Resource Availability for the Mussel (Mytilus edulis, Linnaeus) at Bottom Culture Sites in Maine.* Journal of Shellfish Research, 8 (1):187-196.

Newell, C.R., Hidu, H., McAlice, B.J., Podiesinski, G., Short, F., and Kindblom, L. 1991. *Recruitment and Commercial Seed Procurement of the Blue Mussel Mytilus edulis in Maine.* Journal of the World Aquaculture Society 22 (2):134-152.

NOAA. 1989. *National Status and Trends Program for Marine Environmental Quality: Progress Report - A Summary of Data on Tissue Contamination from the First Three Years (1986-1988) of the Mussel Watch Project.* NOAA Tech. Memorandum NOS OMA 49. Rockville, MD.

Sowles, J. 1993. *Maine Musselwatch Heavy Metal Baseline Survey in Blue Mussels: 1988-92.* Maine DEP.

Sowles, J. 1995. *Gulf of Maine 93/94 Mussel Samples.* Maine DEP.

Ocean Currents

Birge, R.P. 1978. *Water Mass Flow Measurements from Drogue Observations in an Area West of Sears Island, Maine.* Central Maine Power Co. Environmental Studies Dept., SI-78-1. 13 pp.

Oil Pollution

Barry, M., and Yevich, P.P. 1975. *The Ecological, Chemical and Histopathological Evaluation of an Oil spill Site, Part III.* Marine Pollution Bulletin, Histopathological Studies. 6:171 - 173.

Bowdoin College Marine Research Laboratory. 1981. *A Description of the Near Shore Oil Spill Control Project Proposed for Long Cove, Searsport, ME.* Maine DEP, Augusta, ME. 17 pp.

Card, D.J., Stockwell, L.T., and Gillfillan, E.S. 1984. *Oil Pollution Research.* Maine DEP. 456pp.

The Center for Natural Areas, et al. 1978. *An Oil Pollution Prevention, Abatement and Management Study for Penobscot Bay, Maine.* Maine Department of Environmental Protection. 4 volumes.

Dow, R.L. 1975. *Reduced Growth and Survival of Clams Transplanted to an Oil Spill Site.* Marine Pollution Bull. 6:12 - 125.

Dow, R.L. 1978. *Size Selective Mortality of Clams in an Oil Spill Site.* Marine Pollution Bull. 9(2):45 - 48.

Dow, R.L., and Hurst, J.W., Jr. 1975. *The Ecological, Chemical, and Histopathological Evaluation of an Oil Spill Site, Part I.* Marine Pollution Bull. Ecological Studies 6:164 - 166.

ERCo, et. al. 1977. *Systems Study of Oil Pollution Prevention, Abatement and Control for Penobscot Bay.* Maine Department of Environmental Protection.

Gilfillan, E.S., Hanson, S.A., Page, D.S., Mayo, D., Cooley, J., Chalfant, J., Archambeault, T., West, A., and Harshbarger, J.C. 1977. *Comprehensive Study of Petroleum Hydrocarbons in the Marine Environment at Long Cove, Searsport, ME.* Maine DEP, Augusta, ME. Contract # 906439.

Hyland, H.B.N. 1970. *A Review of Oil Polluting Incidents In and Around New England.* Ecol. Res. Ser EPA. 600 / 3-77-064.

Johnson, A.C., Larsen, P.F., Gadbois, D.F., and Humason, A.W. 1985. *The Distribution of Polycyclic-Aromatic Hydrocarbons in the Surficial Sediments of Penobscot Bay in Relation to Possible Sources and to other Sites Worldwide.* Marine Environmental Research, Essex, England 15 (1):1 - 16.

Penobscot River

Haefner, P.A., Jr. 1967. *Hydrography of the Penobscot River (Maine) Estuary.* Journal of the Fisheries Research Board of Canada 24 (7):1553 - 1571.

Imhoff, E.A., and Harvey, R.L. 1972. *Penobscot River Study.* Environmental Studies Center, U of M, Orono, ME. Tech Report # 1. 288 pp.

Maine Water Improvement Commission. 1964. *Penobscot River Classification Report.* Maine Dept. of Sea Shore Fish., Augusta, ME. 226 pp.

Penobscot River Study Team. 1972. *Penobscot River Study.* Environmental Studies Center, U of M, Orono, ME. Report # 1. 288 pp.

U.S. Dept. of the Interior. 1975. *Penobscot Wild and Scenic River Study.* Bureau of Outdoor Recreation, New England Regional Office. 95 pp.

Plankton

Bertrand, D.E. 1977. *Seasonal Succession of the Plankton of Penobscot Bay.* U. of Rhode Island, Kingston, R.I.

Burkholder, B.R. 1933. *A Study of the Phyto-Plankton of Frenchmans Bay and Penobscot Bay, Maine.* Intern. Rev. Ges. Hydrobiolo. Hydrogr. 28:262-284. [note age: but best source]

Polychaetes

Noyes, G.S. 1970. *The Biology of Aglaophamus sp. (polychaete nephtyidae) from Maine.* U of M, Orono, ME. 70 pp.

Richards, T.L. 1969. *Physiological Ecology of Selected Polychaetous Annelids Exposed to Different Temperatures, Salinity and Dissolved Oxygen Combinations.* U of M, Orono, ME. 171 pp.

Ports

Maine DOT. 1977. *Maine Port Development Study, Phase I.* DOT, Augusta, ME.

Sea Urchins

Larson, B.R., Vadas, R.L., and Keser, M. 1980. *Feeding and Nutritional Ecology of the Sea Urchin Stronglylocentrotu drobachiensis in Maine, USA.* Marine Biology 59:49-62. [Some urchins collected from Moose Point State Park for study]

Sears Island – Archaeology

Spiess, A. and Hedden, M. 1983. *Kidder Point and Sears Island in Prehistory.* Maine Historic Preservation Commission, Augusta, ME.

Trace Metals

Goldberg, E.D., Koide, M., Hodge, V., Flegal, A.R. and Martin, J. 1983. U.S. *Mussel Watch: 1977 - 1978 Results on Trace Metals and Radionuclides.* Estuar. Coast. Shelf Sci. 16: 69-93.

Larsen, P.F., Zdanowicz, V., and Johnson, A.C. 1983. *Trace Metal Distributions in the Surficial Sediments of Penobscot Bay, Maine.* Bull. Environ. Contam. Toxicol., New York 31:566 - 573.

Larsen, P.F., and Johnson, A.C. 1983. *Sediment Quality Studies in Casco Bay and Penobscot Bay, Maine.* Bigelow Laboratory for Ocean Sciences Technical Report #33. West Boothbay Harbor, ME. 56 pp.

Lauenstein, G.G., Robertson, A., and O'Connor, T.P. 1990. *Comparison of Trace Metal Data in Mussels and Oysters from a Mussel Watch Programme of the 1970s with Those from a 1980s Programme.* Mar. Pollut. Bul. (21): 440-447.

NOAA. 1988. *National Status and Trends Program for Marine Environmental Quality: Progress Report - A Summary of Selected Data on Chemical Contaminants in Sediments Collected During 1984, 1985, 1986 and 1987.* NOAA Tech Memorandum NOS OMA 44. [Sears and Pickering islands.]

NOAA. 1989. *National Status and Trends Program for Marine Environmental Quality: Progress Report - A Summary of Data on Tissue Contamination from the First Three Years (1986-1988) of the Mussel Watch Project.* NOAA Tech. Memorandum NOS OMA 49. Rockville, MD.

NOAA. 1991. *National Status and Trends Program for Marine Environmental Quality: Progress Report - Second Summary of the Data on Chemical Contaminants in Sediments from the National Status and Trends Program.* NOAA. Rockville, MD.

Sowles, J. 1995. *Gulf of Maine 1993-94 Mussel Samples.* Maine DEP.

ten Brink, M.B., and Manheim, F.T. 1995. *Gulf of Maine Contaminated Sediment Workbook.* U.S. Geological Survey. Woods Hole, MA.

U.S. Dept. of the Interior. 1970. *Effects of Strip-Mine Discharges on the Marine Environment, Cape Rosier, Maine.* Federal Water Polution Control Adm., Merrimack River Project - NE Region, Needham Heights, MA.

Water – Pollution

Bobalek, E.G. 1969. *Phase II - Study of a River System as a Chemical Reactor.* Land & Water Resources Center. U of M, Orono,ME. 21 pp.

Bobalek, E.G., Mumme, K., and Lewis, R.A. 1967. *Chemical Reactor Theory Applied to Modeling the Dynamics of a Control System for Water Quality of a River: Phase 1 - A Feasibility Study.* Land & Water Resources Center, U of M, Orono, ME. 39 pp.

Mower, B. 1995. *Dioxin Monitoring Program.* Maine DEP, Augusta, ME. 100 pp.

Maine DEP. 1989. *State of Maine Nonpoint Source Pollution Assessment Report.* Maine DEP. 192 pp.

NOAA. 1994. *Gulf of Maine Point Source Inventory: A Summary by Watershed for 1991.* NOAA. Silver Spring, MD.

Shorey, W.K. 1973. *Macrobenthis Ecology of a Sawdust-Bearing Substrate in the Penobscot River Estuary (Maine).* J. Fish. Res. Bd. Can. 30:493-497. [Based on another UMaine thesis in Wildlife.]

U.S. Dept. of the Interior. 1967. *Conference on the Pollution of the Navigable Waters of the Penobscot River and Upper Penobscot Bay and Their Tributaries, Belfast, ME.* Federal Water Pollution Control Adm. 394 pp.

U.S. Dept. of the Interior. 1967. *Report on Pollution - Navigable Waters of the Penobscot River and Upper Penobscot Bay in Maine.* Federal Water Polution Control Adm., Merrimack River Project - NE Region, Boston, MA. 94 pp.

Water Quality

Central Maine Power Company. 1978. *Scope and Description of Aquatic Studies, Upper Penobscot Bay, for Sears Island Coal Unit No. 1.* Central Maine Power Co., Augusta, ME. 35 pp.

Dean, D. 1970. *Water Quality - Benthic Invertebrate Relationships in Estuaries.* Water Resources Center, U of M, Orono, ME. 9 pp.

Edwards, B.J., and Woodward, F.E. 1979. *A Simple Pollution Vulnerability Index for Preliminary Coastal Water Quality Management Planning.* Land & Water Resources Center, U of M, Orono, ME. Report # A-047-ME. 26 pp.

Graham, J.J. *Profiles of Temperature and Salinity: Inshore Waters of Central Maine.* Maine DMR, Fisheries Research Station. 7 pp.

Haefner, P.A., Jr. 1967. *Hydrography of the Penobscot River (Maine) Estuary.* Journal of the Fisheries Research Board of Canada 24 (7):1553 - 1571.

Hatch, R.W. 1971. *Temperature, Dissolved Oxygen and Salinity Data for the Penobscot River Estuary, 1966-1970.* Water Resources Center, U of M, Orono, ME. 18 pp.

Maine DEP. 1976. *Penobscot River Basin Water Quality Management Plan.* Maine DEP. 136 pp.

Maine DEP. 1988. *State of Maine 1988 Water Quality Assessment.* Maine DEP. 74 pp.

Maine DEP. 1992 and 1994. *State of Maine Water Quality Assessment: A Report to Congress Prepared Pursuant to Section 305(b) of the Federal Water Pollution Control Act as Amended.* Maine DEP.

Maine Water Improvement Commission. 1964. *Penobscot River Classification Report.* Maine Dept. of Sea Shore Fish., Augusta, ME. 226 pp.

Rabeni, C.F., and Gibbs, K.E. 1977. *Benthic Invertebrates As Water Quality Indicators in the Penobscot River, Maine.* Land and Water Resources Institute, U of M, Orono, ME. Report A-028-ME. 75 pp

Townsend, D.W., ed. 1985. *Temperature, Salinity and Dissolved Oxygen Data for the Penobscot River Estuary, Maine 1963-1977.* Bigelow Laboratory of Ocean Sciences. Technical Report No. 52.

Woodward, F.E., Sylvester, H.C., and Foster, J.A. 1974. *Development of a Water Quality Management Program for the Lower Penobscot River and Estuary, Final Report, Phase I.* Environmental Studies Center, U of M, Orono, ME. Report # 3-74. 105 pp.

Water Resources

U.S. Govt. Printing Office. 1979. *The Nation's Water Resources 1975 - 2000, Volume 1.* US Water Resources Council.

Waterfowl

Hartman, F.E. 1963. *Estuarine Wintering Habitat for Black Ducks.* The Journal of Wildlife Management 27:339-347. [study area between Winterport and Sandy Point]

Watersheds

Fontaine, R.A. 1981. *Drainage Areas of Surface Water Bodies of the Penobscot River Basin in Central Maine.* U.S. Geological Survey Open File Report 78-556F. 92 pp.
New England River Basins Commission. 1981. *Maine Central Coastal River Basins Overview.*
New England River Basins Commission. 1981. *Penobscot River Basin Overview.* 137 pp.

Wildlife

Spencer, H.E., Jr., and Hutchinson, A. 1974. *An Appraisal of the Fishery and Wildlife Resources of Eastern Penobscot Bay.* Planning Unit. Coastal Planning Group, State Planning Office, Augusta,ME. 27 pp.
Woodward, S., Hutchinson, A., and McCollough, M. 1986. *The Penobscot Bay Conservation Plan.* Maine Dept. of Inland Fisheries and Wildlife, Augusta, ME. 105 pp.

Additional Resources

Information about the following subjects was obtained from the State Library in Augusta by Edward L. Hawes, Ph.D., for the Penobscot Marine Museum in Searsport, and is included here with permission.

Natural History
Maps
U.S. Fish and Wildlife Service, Atlantic Coast Ecological Inventory, Bangor, 1:15,000,000 scale. Washington. D.C., 1 sheet

Human History
Books, general
Bacon, George Fox. *Rockland, Belfast and Vicinity: Its Representative Business Men and Its Points of Interest.* Newark Glenwood, 1892. 176 pp.

Books concerning towns
Belfast:
White, William. *A History of Belfast.* Belfast: E. Fellowes, 1827, 119 pp.
Williamson, Joseph. *The History of the City of Belfast, Vol. 1.* Somersworth, N.H.; New England History Press, 1982. 956 pp.
Johnson, Alfred. *History of the City of Belfast, Vol. 2.* Somersworth: New England History Press, 1983. 695 pp.

Castine:
Bourne, Miriam Anne. *The Ladies of Castine: From the Minutes of the . . . Women's Club.* New York: Arbor, c. 1986. 148 pp.
Doudiet, Ellenore W. Majabigwaduc. *Castine, Penobscot, Brooksville, Castine.* Castine Scientific Society, 1978. 116 pp.
Parker, A. =P. *History of Pemaquid with Sketches of Monhegan, Popham and Castine.* Boston: MacDonald & Evans, 1925. 226 pp.
Wheeler, George Aug. *Castine: Past and Present; The Ancient Settlement of Pentagoet and the Modern Town.* Boston: Rockwell, [c. 1896]. 112 pp.
History of Castine, Penobscot and Brooksville. Bangor: Burr and Robinson, 1875. 401 pp.

Wheeler, George, and Wheeler-Bartlett, Louise. *History of Castine*. Cornwall, N.Y.: Cornwall Press, 1923. 444 pp.

Islesboro:

Cook, Joel A. *Islesboro Sketch*. Boston: Boston Photogravure, 1890. 35 pp.

Daniels, Caroline T. *Facts and Fancies and Repetitions about Dark Harbor*. Cambridge [Cosmos], 1935. 58 pp.

Farrow, John Pendleton. *History of Islesborough, Maine, 1764-1893*. Islesboro: Historical Society, 1984. 429 pp.

Islesboro Historical Society. *History of Islesboro, Maine, 1893-1983*. Islesboro: Historical Society, 1984. 429 pp.

Searsport:

Black, Frederick Fraser. *Searsport Sea Captains*. Searsport: Penobscot Marine Museum, 1960. 226 pp.

Eastman, Joel. *A History of Sears Island*. Searsport: Historical Society, 1976. 72 pp.

Stockton Springs:

Ellis, Alice V. *The Story of Stockton Springs, Maine*. Stockton Springs: Historical Committee, 1955. 223 pp.

Hitchborn, Faustina. *Historical Sketch of Stockton Springs*. Waterville: Central Maine Publishing, 1908. 133 pp.

Vinalhaven:

Calderwood, Ivan E. *Days of Uncle Tom's Fishhouse: Vinalhaven's Seafarers are Recalled*. Rockland: Courier Gazette, 1969. 274 pp.

[Lyons, O.P.] *A Brief Historical Sketch of the Town of Vinalhaven with Continuation to the Present*. Rockland: Starr, 1900. 84 pp.

Winslow, Signey. *Fish Scales and Stone Chips*. Portland: Machigonne Press, 1952. 256 pp.

Annual Reports, etc.
General:

Bureau of Labor Statistics. *16th Annual Report* (1902). Augusta: *Kennebec Journal*, 1903. 220 pp.

Town Annual Reports:

To find out the years for which the annual reports of any town in the region are available, check with one of the Reference Librarians at the State Library in Augusta who will consult the Shelf List. The Maine Historical Society apparently has some reports for one town only, Stockton Springs, and these are for 1882, 1884 and 1885. These are invaluable sources for a variety of topics such as the development of thinking and practice about school, economic development, public health and environmental issues.

School Reports:

Annual reports of school committees or superintendents of schools are sometimes included in town annual reports, and sometimes published separately. In the region, apparently only Belfast's School Committee issued its own report, and that was in the years 1894-98.

Directories:
Belfast:

Mitchell, H.E. et al, *The Belfast Register*. Brunswick, ME: Mitchell, 1907. 215 pp.

Sparrow, A.B. *The Belfast City Directory 1894-95*. Shirley Village, MA: Sparrow, 1894. 120 pp.

___. *The Belfast and Camden Directory*. Ayer, MA: Butterfield, 1890. 219 pp.

Castine:

Mitchell, H.E., et al. *The Town Register: Islesboro, Castine, Penobscot, Brooksville 1906*. Brunswick: H. E. Mitchell, 1906. 247 pp.

Islesboro:

Mitchell, H.E., et al. *The Town Register: Islesboro, Castine, Penobscot, Brooksville 1906*. Brunswick: H. E. Mitchell, 1906. 247 pp.

Searsport:

Mitchell, H.E., et al. *The Town Register: Searsport, Stockton Springs, Prospect*. 2 vols.; Brunswick: Mitchell, 1907. 103 + 126 pp.

Stockton Springs:

Mitchell, H.E., et al. *The Town Register: Searsport, Stockton Springs, Prospect*. 2 vols.; Brunswick: Mitchell, 1907. 103 + 126 pp.

Photographs, Photographic Books, etc.
Belfast:

Anon., *Illustrated Belfast*. Belfast, Maine: Belfast Publishing Company, c. 1910. 44 pp.

Archival Records (Penobscot Marine Museum)

The holdings of the museum library and archive are extremely well endowed in the environmental, social and community history of the region. There are many possibilities for developing sets of materials for school and special group programs drawing from these resources. Here is an overview of the records:

Family Papers:

There are approximately 37 archival boxes alphabetically arranged. There are two ways to approach the material. Names of people who are shipbuilders, mariners, merchants, etc., could be selected in the federal population censuses, then the researcher or interpretive planner could see if they left records now in the museum holdings. This could result in a meaningful sample and a social cross-section of a town. The other approach is to see what can be found by chance by going to the boxes directly, and this may be as useful in some cases. However, remember that this latter method does not yield data that really leads to well-founded conclusions about the history of the community networks.

Business Records, especially on Shipping:

The boxed "ships records" include official measurement papers, harbor entry papers and customs papers by ship and include both coastal and deep-sea vessels.

Sources of information about transportation and energy

Babcock, Robert H. 1979. Economic development in Portland (Maine) and St. John (New Brunswick) during the age of iron and steam, 1850-1914. *American Review of Canadian Studies* 9(1):3-37.

Barringer, Richard E. (ed.) 1990. *Changing Maine*. Portland: University of Southern Maine, Muskie Institute.

Commission on Comprehensive Energy Planning. May 1992 *Report*. Augusta: Maine Senate, State House.

Conkling, Philip W. 1981. *Islands in time*. Camden, Maine: Down East Books.

Duncan, Roger F. 1992. *Coastal Maine: A Maritime History*. New York: W. W. Norton.

Eastman, Joel W. 1976. *A History of Sears Island*. Searsport, Maine: Searsport Historical Society.

Federal Energy Regulatory Commission. 1994. Draft Environmental Impact Statement, Lower Penobscot River Basin, Maine. Washington, D.C.: Office of Hydro-power Licensing. FERC/DEIS-0082.

Governor's Advisory Council on International Trade. 1995. *Final report to Governor Angus S. King, Jr.* Augusta: State House.

Hugill, Peter J. 1993. *World trade since 1431, geography, technology, and capitalism*. Baltimore: Johns Hopkins University Press.

Irland, Lloyd C. 1989. Maine's Economic Heritage. Report to the commission on Maine's future. Augusta: Executive Department, State House.

Jewett, Sarah Orne. 1994 (1896). *The Country of the Pointed Firs*. New York: Dover Thrift Edition.

Judd, Richard W., Edwin A. Churchill, and Joel W. Eastman (eds.). 1995. *Maine: the Pine Tree State from Prehistory to the Present*. Orono, Maine: University of Maine Press.

Maine: A Guide Downeast. 1937. WPA Writers Project guidebook series. Boston: Houghton Mifflin.

Maine Department of Transportation. 1995. *Twenty-year Statewide Transportation Plan*. Augusta: Maine Department of Transportation.

New England Governors' Conference. 1995. *New England Transportation Initiative, Final Report*.

Rowe, William Hutchinson. 1948. *The Maritime History of Maine*. Gardiner, Maine: Harpswell Press.

Smith, D. C. 1972. *History of Lumbering in Maine 1860-1960* (Maine Studies, No. 93). Orono, Maine: University of Maine.

Thoreau, Henry David. (1987) 1864. *The Maine Woods*. New York: Harper & Row.

U.S. Army Corps of Engineers. 1989. *Waterborne Commerce of the United States. Part I, Atlantic Coast*. New Orleans: Water Resources Support Center.

U.S. Dept. of Commerce, Bureau of the Census. 1993. *Statistical Abstract of the United States*. Washington, D.C.: Government Printing Office.

U.S. Department of Transportation, Federal Highway Administration, and Maine Department of Transportation. 1995. Sears Island marine dry cargo terminal, Searsport. Draft Environmental Impact Statement, FHWA-ME-EIS-95-01-DS. Washington, D.C.: GPO.

Non-government organizations working in the Penobscot region

Bigelow Laboratory for Ocean Sciences

McKown Point, P.O. Box 475
West Boothbay Harbor, ME 04575
(207) 633-9600
Engages in basic research on the biological, chemical and physical processes that determine ocean productivity; contributes to studies of how the ocean atmosphere system relates to global climate and environmental changes; and provides information for developing rational means of conserving and managing living resources in coastal systems.

Chewonki Foundation

Box 1200
Wiscasset, ME 04578
(207) 882-7323
Originally a boys' camp, Chewonki provides environmental education programs for families, children and adults.

College of the Atlantic

105 Eden Street
Bar Harbor, ME 04609
(207) 288-5015
A degree-granting college that emphasizes environmental studies, including programs in marine and coastal studies, environmental education and policy. COA also houses Allied Whale (207) 288-5644.

Conservation Law Foundation

119 Tillson Avenue
Rockland, ME 04841
(207) 594-8107
Uses the law to further protection and wise management of all of New England's natural resources.

Eastern Maine Development Corporation

1 Cumberland Place, Suite 300
P.O. Box 2579
Bangor, ME 04402-2579
(207) 942-6389
Provides technical assistance, community development assistance and planning expertise to local governments and businesses, and assists in public infrastructure and business development programs.

Hurricane Island Outward Bound School

Box 429
Rockland, ME 04841
(207) 594-5548
Operates a variety of experiential education programs for teenagers and adults, based principally on Hurricane Island in Penobscot Bay.

Island Institute

410 Main Street
Rockland, ME 04841
(207) 594-9209
An advocate for Maine's coastal islands and the Gulf of Maine generally, the Island Institute works to maintain island communities and encourage the wise use of island resources.

Maine Aquaculture Innovation Center

141 North Main Street
Brewer, ME 04112
(207) 989-5310

Maine Island Trail Association

328 Main Street
Rockland, ME 04841
(207) 596-6456
Has established a model of thoughtful use and volunteer stewardship for the Maine islands that will assure their conservation in a natural state, while seeing that a recreational asset is cared for by the people who use it.

Maine Audubon Society

P.O. Box 6009
Falmouth, ME 04105-6009
(207) 781-2330
Environmental education and advocacy, with an emphasis on habitats at risk and the promotion of environmental literacy. Maine Audubon runs a wide variety of coastal field trips.

Maine Coast Heritage Trust

169 Park Row
Brunswick, ME 04011
(207) 729-7366
Works with landowners, local land trusts and public agencies to preserve land and open space through conservation easements, purchases and donations

The Nature Conservancy, Maine Chapter

Fort Andross
14 Maine Street, Suite 401
Brunswick, ME 04011
(207) 729-5181
The Conservancy works to protect outstanding natural areas and biological diversity. It maintains a series of preserves in Maine, many of them on coastal islands.

Natural Resources Council of Maine

271 State Street
Augusta, ME 04330
(207) 622-3101
A statewide advocacy organization focusing on environmental public policy.

Penobscot Marine Museum

P.O. Box 498
Searsport, ME 04974-0498
(207)-548-2529
Educates the people of Maine about their maritime heritage and the history of Searsport, a town which, a century ago, produced one-tenth of all deep-water shipmasters

Penobscot Riverkeepers 2000

33 Howard St.
Old Town, ME 04468
(207)-827-0369
Teaches people about the history and resources of the Penobscot River and encourages watershed awareness and monitoring efforts.

Sierra Club, Maine Chapter

192 State Street
Portland, ME 03101
(207) 761-5616
Works to protect the environment, promote awareness and protect wildlife and the wilderness.

University of Maine Cooperative Extension Hancock County Office

RFD 5 Box 508A
Ellsworth, ME 04605
(207) 667-8212
Helping local people learn new knowledge and skills, develop leadership abilities, and solve problems using local resources and research-based information from the land-grant/sea-grant university.

University of Maine Cooperative Extension Knox/Lincoln Counties Office

375 Main Street
Rockland, Me 04841
(207) 594-2104
See above. Tanglewood Learning Center and 4-H Camp is a program of the Knox/Lincoln Extension and provides environmental education programs for children and adults at a camp in Lincolnville.

University of Maine

Darling Marine Center
25 Clark's Cove Road
Walpole, ME 04573
(207) 563-3146
University of Maine's marine laboratory. The center is committed to marine research, teaching and interaction with public school science teachers.

Local Land Trusts

Belfast-Northport-Lincolnville Land Trust

P.O. Box 51
Belfast, ME 04915
(207)-789-5885

Blue Hill Heritage Trust

P.O. Box 222
Blue Hill, ME 04614
(207)-374-5118

Castine Conservation Trust

P.O. Box 421
Castine, ME 04421
(207)-3326-4166

Coastal Mountain Land Trust

P.O. Box 101
Rockport, ME 04856
(207)-594-5074

Georges River Land Trust

P.O. Box 133
South Thomaston, ME 04858
(207)-594-5166

Georges River Tidewater Association

P.O. Box 336
Thomaston, ME 04861
207-594-8806

Island Heritage Trust

P.O. Box 55
Sunset, ME 04683
(207)-367-5519

Islesboro Islands Trust

P.O. Box 182
Islesboro, ME 04848
(207) 734-6907

Monhegan Associates, Inc.

P.O. Box 84
Monhegan, Maine 04852
(207)- 594-2696

Vinalhaven Land Trust

P.O. Box 268
Vinalhaven, ME 04863
(207)-863-2543

Coalitions

The Ducktrap River Coalition

c/o Coastal Mountains Land Trust
Promotes the voluntary protection of the natural features of the Ducktrap River and Watershed.

Georges River Clam Restoration Project

c/o University of Maine Cooperative Extension
Knox/Lincoln Counties Office
375 Main Street
Rockland, Me 04841
(207) 594-2104
Encourages local clammers, municipalities and residents of five towns to manage their clam resource on a sustainable basis.

Penobscot Bay Land Trust Alliance

c/o Islesboro Islands Trust
P.O. Box 182
Islesboro, ME 04848
(207) 734-6907
Supports all member conservation land trusts, and provides a regional Penobscot Bay perspective regarding preservation of environmental/ecological/historical values and lands, building community awareness of environmental issues, and increasing the constituency base for land protection. Provides advice, support and expertise to member organizations.

Penobscot Bay Network

c/o University of Maine Cooperative Extension
Hancock County Office
RFD 5 Box 508A
Ellsworth, ME 04605
(207) 667-8212
Organizations committed to the long-term health of the Penobscot region and working to promote a regional identity.

Contributors

Ted Ames is Marine Resources Director of the Island Institute in Rockland, Maine.

John F. Battick is a professor at the University of Maine at Orono, specializing in the study of maritime history. His contributions to Chapter 1 were adapted with permission from *Penobscot Bay: The Historical Background,* an essay Professor Battick wrote for "Goodly Ships on Painted Seas: Ship Portraiture by Penobscot Bay Artists," published in 1988 by the Penobscot Maritime Museum and the William A. Farnsworth Library and Art Museum.

Philip W. Conkling is President of the Island Institute. He is editor of *From Cape Cod to the Bay of Fundy: An Environmental Atlas of the Gulf of Maine* (MIT Press).

Michael Herz, the former San Francisco BayKeeper, is a freelance researcher and writer who works in Alna, Maine.

Lloyd C. Irland is a consultant in Winthrop, Maine. He served in the Maine Department of Conservation and as State Economist.

Steve Miller is director of the Islesboro Islands Trust.

Bob Moore is a consultant and freelance writer who works in Freeport, Maine.

Annette S. Naegel is Science and Stewardship Director of the Island Institute.

David D. Platt is Publications Director of the Island Institute.

Renny Stackpole is director of the Penobscot Marine Museum in Searsport, Maine.

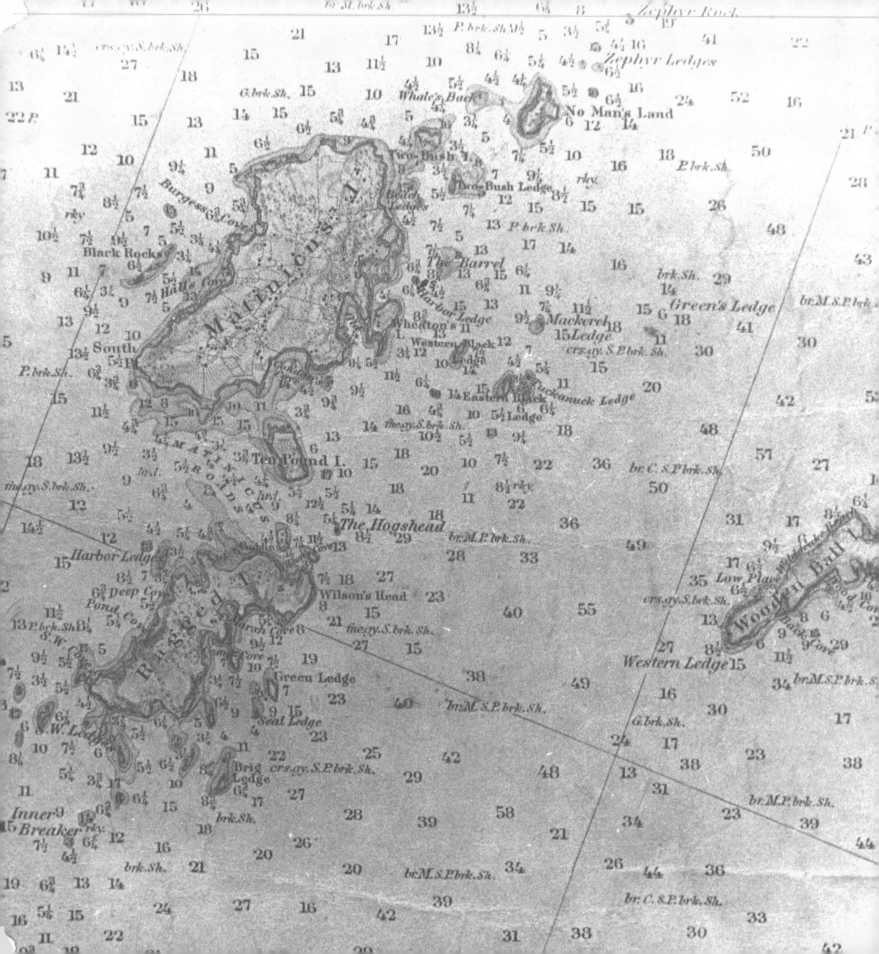